BARRYISMS

BARRYISMS

Adventures of a Person Who Marches to a Different Drummer

Barry McAlister

authorHOUSE®

AuthorHouse™
1663 Liberty Drive
Bloomington, IN 47403
www.authorhouse.com
Phone: 1-800-839-8640

Published by AuthorHouse 10/28/2014

ISBN: 978-1-4969-4985-1 (sc)
ISBN: 978-1-4969-4984-4 (e)

Library of Congress Control Number: 2014919311

FORWARD: The idea for this book arose from my cousin's actions to return sounds of wild America to people living in a big city, actually the Big Apple. Ned would come down to Florida, along the Wakulla River; record sounds of Frogs and Crickets then return to Manhattan to entertain friends who had never been: in a swamp; viewed the glowing red eyes of Alligators at nite; boated on wild rivers or lingered in woods at night with only the sounds of nature.

Whereas I've lived on the wild side of nature and in this book describe a few adventures: scuba diving in caves, alone; catching Alligators bare handed; solo sailed to Central America; being bitten by a Shark; encounter with a Wolverine; driven thru a hurricane; rappelled down a waterfall, at age 70; backpacked over high mountains; climbed among remote Mayan ruins; worked with Dolphins and Whales in Florida and Australia; endured a Mexican jail and visited some of the most beautiful places on this earth and on and on.

Narrator: Barry McAlister: born Michael Barrett McAlister on April 22, 1941 (Earth Day) in Lakeland Florida. In as few words as possible, Barry is an active person 'who from childhood has always trod to a different drummer.'

Barry has a degree in Marine Biology from Florida State University and served 4 years in the US Air Force.

Characters: Judy-first wife, born Elk Grove California, married 19 years; Michelle-daughter, born in St Augustine Florida; Linda-second wife (from Jacksonville Florida) married 12 years; Grandchildren: Justin and Lori and Great-grandchild-Orion; Brothers-David; Paul and Joe; Sisters: Patty and Mary Lou; Cousins: Richard; Jeff; Ned and Ronnie (Ron); Mother's parents: Barrett and Dad's parents-McAlister; Diana: a Secretary and more; Rip: longtime friend from Tallahassee; Lance: school friend from Ocala; Phil (Felipe): friend from Ft Collins Colorado who I met in Baja; Vice (Jimmy): a friend from school in High Springs; Brian and Catherine: good friends from Florida who moved to California; Joe: friend from Moab Utah; Bobby: High School friend from High Springs and Randy: long-time friend from Shell Point. Janice; SueAnn; Damijan; 2 Judys; Gail; Linda; Terry and Brenda are women who have joined me at times in my travels. **Vehicles**: Tonja I, 1986 Toyota pickup; Sammie, 1987 Suzuki Samurai; Tonja II, 2003 Toyota pickup and Tonja III, 2007 Toyota Tacoma pickup truck. **Vessels**:

My Sharona, 48 foot cabin cruiser; *The Rose*, 25' Hunter sailboat; *Rose Bud*, 10' rubber dinghy; *Al*, 14' aluminum skiff and **River Shanty**, 18' pontoon boat. **RVs: Maybellene**, 34' motorhome and **Big Bertha**, 37' motor home.

Many of these stories are taken from the Journals I created over the past 15 years of travel. Also, I didn't begin taking digital photos until 2005, so a few photos are from prints.

So this is an odyssey into the experiences of Barry who has always pursued exploration and adventure, unrestricted by the perils of risk.

VIA FERRATA

Only those who dare truly live. Ruth Freedman

Tuesday August 9th 2011 (at 70 young years) was one of the most frightening days of my life. A couple weeks ago I had seen an article in a magazine about a secret adventure, the Via Ferrata in the cliffs above Telluride Colorado. The term Via Ferrata is Italian for 'road with irons'.

I mentioned this article to Brent and Steve (the OHV crew in Silverton) discovering that they had also heard about the Via Ferrata. So we planned the climb, not knowing the exact location or what was involved. The weather was rainy for a couple weeks and now this was 'our day'. We drove up toward Bridal Veil Falls to where we thought the trail began. Fortunately a group of locals showed up to do the Via Ferrata and confirmed we were in the correct location. The 'trail head' was at the Meldrum mine; below a waterfall, along the Black Bear Road. First we had to scramble straight up the cliffs, then onto a narrow ledge several hundred feet above the mine. We hiked along the ledge for a ways not knowing what to expect. Sometimes the ledge was only a couple feet wide and the cliff face was hundreds of feet DOWN! Then we come to a sheer drop-off with metal bars spaced along the cliff wall and a thin cable above.

Brent had loaned me a harness and two safety straps with carbineers. Unfortunately my straps were too short. For maximum safety we tried to have at least two carbineers on the safety cable, but sometimes I could only get one on the cable.

That passage wasn't too frightening, nor the next, however soon we came to an area where footing was totally absent and we had to scramble around on vertical cliffs using only the <u>widely spaced</u> metal bars bolted into the cliff face. This is called the **Main Event**.

Barry on the Main Event

I tried not to look down since there was nothing below but a fall of hundreds of feet. To traverse from bar to bar I'd have to stretch way out in space to get my toe onto the next bar. When I was in my 50's I had become accustomed to rope work into caves and deep pits (sinkholes), one with a 310 foot drop, however I just did not feel secure here on a 400 foot wall standing on small pieces of iron some unknown person had installed, using gear unfamiliar to me. To say that I was now frightened would be an enormous understatement.

Well we made that OK and hiked some more on the narrow ledge, sometimes around bushes and trees. Brent and Steve were going much too fast for me to safely walk on the gravely trail, sometimes scrambling up narrow crevices. Sometimes the 'trail' was only a foot or so wide. [Keep in mind that these guys are in their 20's and I'm 70].

After a couple more frightening traverses, while hanging in space, I thought we had passed the most difficult situations, wrong again! We came to a place where you're climbing along the cliff face with no more than 4 inches of rock on which to place my feet. That accelerated my heartbeat a tad!

I had a couple of impulses to turn back, but really didn't relish retracing that experience at the Main Event.

We passed across another scary area evidently built by a guy with long legs. I had to bend the safety cable down to get just one carbineer on the line and sometimes just my toes reached the metal bars below. I would not look down; just concentrate on clipping in and getting my feet on a bar. I waited while they passed over so I could get a picture, now I felt obligated to hurry up and climbed down into a crevasse without hooking to the safety line. Now I came to an impossible place where I had to lean back at a perilous angle and stretch my legs far across a crevasse to rock; there were three places where the cable was bolted to the wall and I had to unclip while hanging over the cliff backwards. That again got my adrenaline pumping!

At this point I REALLY wanted this to end. However more traverses awaited us, fortunately nothing like the last one. Finally we passed the narrow ledges and cliffs with bars and onto a trail down. We were still hundreds of feet above the Pandora mine and I dreaded any more cliff crossings. To my relief we just hiked steeply down the mountainside, then came to a mine road that was so steep I don't see how vehicles could climb it. As we walked, one of my safety straps fell loose. The knot that Brent had tied had come undone. I hate to think about the times I was hanging off the cliff by this one 'safety' strap.

Before we arrived at the Via Ferrata I imagined a short traverse along the cliff face of a hundred or so yards, NOT! This took us almost 3 very intense hours of physical effort and fright. This certainly didn't take into consideration my Mother's constant advice to be safe.

So what did we do a few days later, we rappelled down a 125 foot waterfall!

THE NIGHT MARTIANS INVADED OCALA FLORIDA

The setting is a period of time in the 1950's when UFO paranoid was rampant. Looking from the Hickory Nut Tree (in front of our house) I also saw unidentified lights in the sky and it was reported that UFOs flew in formation over the airport. It was also a time that people perpetuated hoaxes such as burning grass circles saying they saw a UFO land there and shaving a Monkey claiming it was an Alien. Anyway, UFOs and Aliens were constantly in the news so a report of an Alien in Ocala wasn't too farfetched, this was believable.

We had some Yankees from Peoria Illinois move in next door and they had an unattractive, gangly daughter about my age. Her name was Toots and she needed to be frightened. Also, my cousin Ronnie was visiting and needed some excitement in his humdrum life. My parents had gone into town leaving me unsupervised, they should know better. So I dressed up in a long raincoat; a military gas mask (with the eyes mostly covered in aluminum foil) and a long hose dangling from the front and a Palmetto frond was attached above my head. We rang the doorbell, then waiting under the yellow bug lite and sure enough she came to the door shrieking out a blood curdling scream. However, what we didn't count on was that her father was at the door within seconds with his pistol. Ronnie and I literally ran for our lives.

In a short time we doubled back and crawled into the attic of my house, just as several police cars came screeching up, then we could hear all sorts of commotion in the front yard. We figured we were really in trouble so sneaked back into the woods, where we were camping. Unknown to us the radio had broadcast a warning that a 9 foot Martian had been seen in southeast Ocala. My parents heard this; justifiably assumed it was me, so rushed home. After a while a policeman with a megaphone called us from the woods and gave us a stern lecture about scaring people and possibly getting shot.

LANDING OF AN UFO

We were living in Ocala Florida, I was 12ish and one nite headed up to the Frog Pond to gig some Bull Frogs to eat (well, just the legs). Approaching the pond I could see a greenish glow through the vines and Palmettos. The closer I crept the more convinced I became that this must be an Alien spaceship and the longer I hesitated the more exaggerated my imagination became. Suddenly I had an uncontrollable impulse to sprint back down the hill for home. The trail was curvy, but the path I took was straight through thorny vines and Palmetto's; over the ditch, across the railroad tracks to home and safety. My parents weren't home so I went to the neighbor's (the Liggetts) to excitedly relay my story. This was in the 1950's when sighting 'Flying Saucers' was not uncommon. The neighbors were from up north and (from past experience) knew the father had a pistol, so he followed me back up to the Frog Pond. As we approached the glow he became nervous and wouldn't go closer. Finally I inched my way toward the 'Martians', ready to die from the flash from a particle beam. Moving closer I realize the glow came from a large tree stump. This was a new experience for me; the light came from a huge deposit of Foxfire. I hadn't previously seen this phenomenon, being 'cold light' that fuels Fireflies. In this stump was a deposit of bioluminescence from beetles or worms. Well I was relieved that it wasn't an invasion, but disappointed it wasn't something more exciting. Later we camped in that area; after a rain the tips of leaves and sticks glowed, so we could put them in a jar and have light in the tent.

PAYNES PRAIRIE FLORIDA

To dare is to sometimes to lose one's footing,
not to dare can lead to losing oneself.

In January 2014 I visited Paynes Prairie near Gainesville Florida. When William Bartram came thru here in 1774 this was an open prairie, however in the latter part of the 1800's the sinkhole (where excess water flowed down into the aquifer) became clogged, forming a lake that was plied by paddle wheelers until suddenly the 'drain' (Alachua Sink) reopened; the lake drained, reforming the prairie.

Native Americans used this area for thousands of years, when Bison; Red Wolves; Horses and certainly Mammoth roamed the prairie. In the 1600's a Spanish ranch was established on its northern bluffs where they brought in Horses; Cattle; Hogs and Citrus Trees. [I recently discovered that citrus trees originated in Southeast Asia and India.] Later French pirates attacked the ranch and made away with Cattle and a ransom. The pirates had sailed up the Suwannee River and hiked the 40 miles over to the ranch.

When Europeans first came to this continent Bison ranged from the Rockys to the East Coast. Spanish reported the killing (by Native Americans) of two Bison near Gainesville. For millions of years Horses in North America were plentiful especially in the prairies of what in now Florida. However they became extinct more than 8000 years ago and in the early 1500's Spanish explorers reintroduce Horses back into North America. [Current fossil evidence indicates that Horses originally evolved in North America; passed over the Bering Straits into Asia; became extinct in North America, then came full circle on Spanish ships.] In the past 20 years Spanish Horses (a variation called Marshtackie by the Seminoles); Cattle (the Andalusian from Southern Spain) and western Bison have been reintroduced into this prairie. This photo is a horse from the original Spanish stock, with a newly arrived Cattle Egret. [In tropical storms, Egrets blew over the Atlantic Ocean from Africa to South America and later migrated into Florida.]

HORSE AND CATTLE EGRET AT PAYNES PRAIRIE

While hiking on a narrow dike I came face to face with a Bison almost blocking my passage. As I walked past he charged me. I yelled "*Stop That!*" and he stopped about 2 feet away. [I knew you should never run from a wild animal because that stimulates the animal to chase you, so I had stood my ground.] The attached photo was **not** taken with a telephoto lens.

BISON 'UP CLOSE AND PERSONAL' AT PAYNES PRAIRIE

On my way out I saw a sign that said not to get closer than 100 feet from Bison. Oh, well.

While visiting **Yellowstone National Park** I saw the same warnings, not to approach wild Bison. A few years ago I was in Lamar Valley (where Wolves had been reintroduced) attempting to photograph a Bison when they wallow in the dust. After hiking for a couple miles I came to a large herd of Bison and while concentrating on finding a Bison thrashing around on the ground I realized that I was almost surrounded by the entire herd. What really got my attention were 3 young Bison staring at me. My immediate thought was: *'Here are 3 teenagers determined to make an impression and I was their target'*. Looking behind me I saw a huge male Bison approaching, following a female who was almost in heat. Steam was rising from the excited male; he was making huffing sounds and my thought switched to:

'Here is a horny male who had staked out this female and he definitely didn't take to competition from me'. I was in a very uncomfortable situation that called for slowly moving away from these formidable threats.

Later, on a foggy morning, while sneaking thru a forested area I heard a huffing noise then suddenly a steaming male and a female Bison emerged from the fog much closer than at first I realized. I remained still and they passed within 5 feet without incident. So, I again cheated death.

Another time I was hiking to Wolf Lake and after a few miles came to a creek with only one place to cross and there was a huge male Bison standing in my way or was it that I was violating his territory. For some time we stood apart from each other, in a way trying to stare down each other. Well that wasn't working so I cautious moved toward him and to my relief the Bison moved aside. However he remained just few feet away and I was not at all sure he didn't intend to charge at me. Obviously I also survived that encounter.

An Elk and I had an incident during a previous visit to Yellowstone. In the Fall the Bull Elk go into rut and become unpredictable and frequently dangerous. The Park introductory film shows Elk attacking vehicles and I was told that recently an Elk became so troublesome that Rangers cut off the ends of his antlers. I had backpacked into the Heart Lake area and was leaving early the next morning as I approached a huge Bull Elk beside the trail. I attempted to quietly pass, then he looked up at me, with what I thought resembled a twisted smile. Here, in an open meadow was an Elk raging with hormones with Barry as the only potential victim. He took a couple of steps toward me and evidently decided that I was not a female in heat, so resumed feeding. That allowed my beating heart to return to my chest.

Back at Paynes Prairie, this was a cold morning that brought out Gators to sun on the banks of the lake, I mean huge Gators, in one place 7 in a mass of prehistoric 'lizardness' looking just like a gaggle of Crocs in Africa.

That reminded me of trips to Salt Springs when I was in High School in Ocala. We would boat down the Run and camp on some Indian mounds near Lake George where we would catch snakes to sell at Ross Allen's Reptile Institute at Silver Springs. One nite Phil, Freddie and I decided we'd catch a Gator, so rigged up a pole with a rope noose on the end. Motoring up a narrow slough we came to a wide area and spied a Gator, I mean a really BIG Gator. Distance from eye to nose appeared to be 2 feet, so her length was much greater than our boat. Evidently we had entered a Gator wallow (or locally, a waller) and this was a female aggressively protecting her nest. As she approached our little boat we did a U turn and rapidly exited stage left.

We did catch a bunch of water snakes (locally called Moccasins, although most were Brown Water Snakes) however Ross Allen was overstocked with water snakes. This was the first year that Ocala High School occupied its new location on Ft King St.; there was a pond in the middle of the grounds, so I felt compelled to dump the snakes into the pond to the delight of many students and the consternation of the teachers.

Recently I heard a tale that I'd forgotten. Jimmy and I had taken some Water Snakes to school to show the class. While the teacher was distracted we agitated the Snakes and when the teacher grabbed, a normally docile Snake, he was bitten. I wonder if we passed that course.

[I diverge: I recall a time a few years ago when Bats could have resulted in my death. I doubt that they were getting me back for my dastardly act in High School, but stranger things have happened. In this tale I was exploring an abandoned mine east of Quartzsite Arizona when I encountered flocks of Bats. So I was walking deep into the mine taking video of the Bats flapping around me. After a while a little voice said: *You had better watch where you are stepping.* I stopped; turned on my light and just a few before me was a vertical shaft so deep that my light did not reach the bottom. Years ago I had used up my '9 lives' so maybe I'll not pass my 10th until I take my final 'dirt nap'.]

THE MAMMOTH IN BAJA MEXICO

In my adventure filled years of traveling around North America via RV I've boondocked (camped for free) in some of the loveliest locations in the world and this one in Baja was certainly one of those settings. In 2005, with other RVers (mostly Canadians) we pulled our rigs onto a picturesque sandy beach lined with Palm Trees, near Juncalito in Baja California Sur (southern Baja Mexico). Just to the west, about a mile away, lays a procession of craggy mountains, the Sierra la Giganta. From the beach a rock formation can be seen that resembles an Elephant or to some people, a Mammoth. I had heard that someone had climbed the mountain to reach that 'Elephant', so that became my most recent goal.

CAMPING AT JUNCALITO BAJA

Elephant Rock

MAYBELLENE AND SAMMIE

Trek number 1 began not far off the hiway; up a rocky wash lined with Cactus and the infamous Cats Claw Acacia. [This tree is aptly named because the limbs are covered with backward curved thorns that delight in ripping your flesh.] On the way up I came across a huge Tarantula, then trying to take video got some Teddy Bear Cactus spines in my ankle and butt. [This is another plant that plagues humans, like sandspurs and poison ivy. It is called Teddy Bear or Jumping Cactus because all you have to do is come near the spiny balls and they jump to your body; the spines are shaped like arrows and are extremely difficult to remove.]

Undaunted I hiked on to the base of the mountain and began climbing. These Giganta Mountains are geologically old and covered in crumbly granite rocks. In several places I'd be climbing almost vertically, grab a rock and have it break loose or just crumble in my hand. Numerous times I'd have to backtrack after coming to a vertical rockface. Finally I came within 20 feet of the summit, but just could not find a way to scramble thru the huge jumble of rocks, some as large as trucks. After 9 hours, feeling very disappointed, I returned to camp.

A couple days later I examined the mountain face with binoculars and found a route that appeared to be passable. This time, before beginning my climb, I drove to a location closer to the base of the mountain. After a ways I spied some Big Horn Sheep. [I think it's disgusting that foreigner's pay up to $70,000 for a permit to kill one of these beautiful animals.] Near the summit I crossed an area only a foot wide with a drop on either side of 50 feet. I continued to scramble over loose rock and around Cordon Cactus until I disturbed a nest of Yellow Jackets. As soon as I saw them I laid down until they relaxed back into their nest and was stung only once, on my ear. As with the first trek, I came within a few feet of the summit, but just couldn't reach the summit. A plus was the view: our Palm lined camp; Isla Carmon and Danzante islands offshore and Puerto Escondido, a port originally developed by the French.

Except for the physical effort, climbing up a mountain is less difficult than climbing down. One reason is that climbing down you frequently can't see where to place your feet. A couple of times I asked myself, "*Did I really come up this way*?" It was frustrating and dangerous to place my weight on a rock and have it disintegrate. In one rocky area the entire mass (including me) began sliding down the mountain and I stopped my perilous descent by grabbing a bush. Another time I stepped onto a 4 foot diameter rock that broke loose and cascaded down the mountainside. Near the bottom I scrambled thru bushes and Acacia Trees until my arms and face were bleeding. Maybe these 'goal attainments' will eventually kill me.

After a few days rest I again attempted to reach the Mammoth, this effort to take two days if necessary. So on Trek 3 (although the 3rd was not the charm) I climbed up one of the several canyons feeding water from the mountains. After a short distance a gigantic rockfall blocked the canyon, however I climbed under some of the rocks and with the aid of a log, squeezed up thru a hole just large enough for me to pass. I came to a waterfall with a deep pool at its base, so had to remove my clothes; swim across holding my clothes and camera above my head, then scale the slippery rocks of the waterfall. I tried several routes but was unable to get out of this canyon. Finally I came to sandy area with vertical walls over 100 feet high; a Strangler Fig Tree that sent its tendrils down across the wall to the wet sand below; tracks of a Mountain Lion, then to a deep pool at the base of a 30 foot waterfall. I decided to camp and this became a truly delightful experience: the sound of the waterfall; numerous barking frogs and in the evening watching the stars thru the opening above, although I was somewhat concerned about the Lion.

CAMPING ABOVE JUNCALITO BAJA

Next day I climbed above the Strangle Fig and found passages higher and higher, however I eventually came to another vertical wall, Drats! Foiled again, so had to give up and return to camp on the beach.

Trek 4: Still determined to reach the Mammoth I figured that if I climbed to the summit at a lower elevation I could hike over to that cotton pickin' rock. So I started up Ligui Canyon and soon came to rocks as large as buses, blocking my passage. After several attempts I found a way to top all the rocks except a big one that extended out from the wall of rocks. This was one of those situations in which if I didn't feel invincible I'd never attempt to go higher, however I began crabbing over the rock while dangling backwards over a drop of 30 feet, to rocks below.

Later I came to where it appeared that I could reach the crest, so left the canyon and scrambled up the cliff wall, in one area shimmying along a shelf only 8 inches wide where a drop would be fatal. As with my previous efforts I came to another impassable area and had to return. Getting back down the rock fall was more frightening than climbing up. This was a 12 hour trip resulting in absolute exhaustion.

Later I heard that supposedly someone had told someone else that 'someone' had climbed the east side of the mountain, however I think this was a false claim that had become a local, urban legend.

I have this affliction (some say disorder) of setting a goal and pushing until I'm successful, so I planned to drive to the other side of the mountains and finally reach the Elephant/Mammoth. Everyone on the beach knew of my adventures, so, around the evening campfire some folks said they would accompany me. Next day this little caravan of vehicles drove the miles around the south end of the mountains; across Cactus festooned plains; splashed thru rivers and found a spot where I'd been told I could hike into the mountains. Members of the hiking group were: Mike, a genial Canadian; my friend Phil (Felipe) and a woman he talked into going for 'an adventure'. First we followed a streambed with green pools filled with algae resulting from grazing cattle. As we climbed higher the Cactus became more dense; the rocks larger and finding a passage up more difficult. Felipe has problems with his feet, so he and his friend turned back. The crest of the mountain didn't seem so far away, however whenever Mike and I stopped to rest we didn't seem to be much closer. Late in the afternoon it became apparent that we couldn't reach the crest before dark so we laid out our sleeping bags under some Strangler Fig Trees for the nite.

Previously (while hiking on a beach) I'd found an emergency flare and had told the folks on the beach that when we reached the Mammoth that nite I would fire off the flare. Obviously we were too optimistic about reaching the Mammoth, but I decided to set off the flare anyway. As I watched the parachute lower the burning flare into the forest I became alarmed, would the flare start a forest fire? Fortunately no flames erupted.

Early next morning we continued our trek up the ever increasingly steep mountain. Near the crest the rocks were almost vertical so we scrambled first here, then there, locating a way up, then to our extreme relief we finally reached The Mammoth. After almost a month I'd finally reached my goal!

HUMAN BODY ON BEACH IN BAJA MEXICO

In 2005, while camping on a lovely beach near Juncalito in Baja Mexico I met two women from Europe who wanted to accompany me on a boat trip to view Whales, unaware that this would be an unforgettable adventure. We loaded **Rose Bud** onto the top of **Sammie** and drove across the peninsula to Puerto Adolfo Lopez Mateos where we launched into Boca la Soledad.

During winter months Gray Whales come into the shallow bays of Baja to avoid Killer Whales in deeper water, also to mate and bear their young. Annually they travel to and from Alaska to Baja California Sur, a distance of more than 6000 miles. Gray Whales were called Devil Fish due to their fighting behavior when hunted and are baleen Whales with origins 30 million years before present. These Whales grow to 50 feet; the calves are 13 feet at birth and drink 200-300 gallons of milk per day, with a fat content of 53%.

Since the tour boat operators are quite opposed to private watercraft, we headed north across the bay toward Isla Santa Domingo. We had viewed several Whales and their calves when we came upon mating Whales. [This process takes 3 or more Whales, as one male is on the opposite side acting as a 'mattress'.] I cut the engine and the wind began blowing us toward the thrashing mass of gigantic Whale. Keep in mind that our tiny boat was only 10 feet long. The closer we approached the more concerned the women became; Kirsten began to hyperventilate then exclaimed "**What if we floated over them; they became upset and toss us into the air?**" With no valid justification I assured her that this wouldn't happen and continued taking video. The wind continued to blow us into the swirling water, but soon, to everyone's relief, we were out of danger and the Whales joyfully continued in peace.

We decided to land on the island and hike the beach that was littered with Whale; Dolphin; Sea Lion and Turtle bones. Some or most of the animals died in fishing nets, then washed onto the beach.

After a ways I could see a huge boat mostly buried in the sand and examining the boat it seemed to have been a cabin cruiser about 65 feet long. Then walking about 100 feet south of the boat I was stunned to find a human body, not something you see every day. The person was mostly a skeleton although hair was evident on his head; his jeans and shirt were tattered and the skull looking toward the sky where I could see some primitive dental work. Evidently someone or a dentist tied a wire around a tooth; around the offending tooth and wrapped another tooth.

On the way back across the bay we watched some Whales 'spy-hopping' where they bring their upper body vertically out of the water and appear to look around.

GRAY WHALE SPY-HOPPING

I had been advised not to have any dealings with the police in Mexico and since I didn't speak Spanish I was hesitant to inform anyone of the dead body, however I met an American woman who ran a medical clinic on the beach. Alicia said that she would accompany me to the police station.

As we entered the front door my first sight was a policeman with a shotgun in his hands, now that got my attention. To my relief I soon realized he was just cleaning the gun. The officer said he'd have to contact some experts and for us to return in the morning.

Next day I met a diverse crew of Mexicans: 2 police officers; 2 forensic people from the capitol, La Paz; 2 boat operators; the American woman (Alicia) and for some obscure reason, the lighthouse keeper. Mexicans have always been masters of improvisation and this was no exception. They had 2 boats (Pangas) and an ATV that wouldn't fit in either boat, so they lashed a piece of plywood across the 2 boats and drove the ATV on top, they also use this technique moving automobiles.

The Pacific side was a little rough so we beached on the south end of Santa Domingo Island and walked a long ways up the sandy beach. Some of this party (especially the overweight policemen) was quickly tired after trudging thru the deep sand. About the time I became concerned that we had missed the body we came upon it. Looking at holes in the skull the forensic guys thought the guy had been shot. They bagged him; placed the body on the ATV, then into the boat I was riding. We pulled up to the tourist dock and were told to take the body to the fisherman's wharf, so the tourists wouldn't see the body.

Later Alicia emailed me to say they thought the body was from a man from Magdalena Bay who had been involved in a drug deal that went bad. [Afterward I heard that Alicia was severely injured in the crash of her ultra-light airplane.]

BEAR ENCOUNTERS

"What kind of men would live where there is no daring? ...nothing can be accomplished without taking any chance at all." Charles Lindbergh

Prior to traveling to Alaska (in 2000) I had had only three close experiences with Bears. While working for the Florida Game and Freshwater Fish Commission a Black Bear had been getting into someone's beehives, so the owner built a tall fence around his beehives, yet the bear climbed over the fence. So they put barbed wire on top of the fence and the creative Bear climbed a tree, leaned the tree over and came down inside, resuming his feeding on the honey in the beehives. The Game Warden (who had been in

David's Middle School class) darted that Bear. However this was his first darting experience; the chemical was too strong; the Bear wouldn't wake up, so they brought the Bear back to the office and placed it into a cage. Before leaving work I had gotten some Grapes; although the Bear couldn't sit up he could open his mouth and stick out his tongue, so I rolled him some Grapes. Now, overnite, I'm thinking I developed a friend like Gentle Ben that I'd seen in Disney movies, however that was definitely not so! Arriving early to the office I went to see my 'friend' and as I approached the cage the Bear growled and charged at me. If he hadn't been in a cage I'm sure he would have torn me apart. I don't blame the Bear he was just frightened, I blame myself for thinking that a wild animal is like a Disney movie creation.

Rip, Doug and I were camping at Pisgah National Forest along the Blue Ridge Parkway. Doug had locked his keys in the trunk of his car and had to remove the seat to reach them, evidently leaving the door agar. During the nite I heard unusual sounds; at daybreak I heard it again; got up and walked around the back of Doug's car. Two young Cubs bounded out of the car, just as a huge Momma Bear rose on her hind legs in front of me. With her outstretched paws she looked 20 feet tall. I just knew she was going to come down on top of me; however she turned to see her Cubs climb a tree; dropped to the ground and eased over to lead them away. A camper across from us (who had seen this) said he knew I was dead when she rose up in front of me.

An almost Bear encounter: Rip, Doug and I were backpacking into the Slickrock Wilderness of North Carolina, that adjoins Joyce Kilmer Memorial Forest. Hiking into the wilderness we met a Bear hunter who relayed the story of kid who was Squirrel hunting with a 22 caliber rifle; came across a Bear; shot the Bear who was more angered than wounded, so the Bear attacked the boy; opened up his chest and the boy may die. Slickrock has the highest rainfall east of the Mississippi, sometimes more than 90 inches/year. However, on the second nite, we assumed it would not rain so just laid our sleeping bags on the ground between Slickrock Creek and a vertical rock wall. During the nite we could hear the Bear hunter's dogs running a Bear down the creek toward us. No one spoke. Next morning we revealed that all of us were thinking: here is a pissed off Bear running down the valley; he runs into 3 guys on the ground with a creek on one side and a wall on the other, so takes his anger out on us.

Fortunately the Bear had climbed a ridge just before reaching us. Then it began to rain.

A side story: Linda and I had recently married and she had never been backpacking, so here we were with what she felt was an unholy amount of weight on her back. Slickrock is aptly named, since all the rocks are as slick as hot butter. We were wading across Slickrock Creek (only a few inches deep) when she slipped and fell backwards into the water. I still recall seeing her with flailing arms and legs yelling at me to help her up. Being the adventure photographer I dashed to shore; dropped my pack; retrieved my camera and return to take an action photograph. Linda failed to see the necessity of recording that moment and will retain that as a <u>Barry Black Mark</u> for the rest of her life.

One more story: Judy; Michelle (8 years old) and I made their first backpacking trip into Slickrock Wilderness. We had left the car a few miles down Slickrock Creek and the first nite camped along the creek. On the map the car was less than a mile from the creek, along Big Fat Gap and from the creek shouldn't take but a few minutes to reach, NOT! Before we arrived at the trail to the car rain began and continued to rain and rain. Our first shock was that the muddy trail up was almost vertical. After a short distance Michelle revolted and said she would hike back upstream to the trailhead and Judy was not particularly happy, so this was rapidly becoming a '**Barry Trip**'. Anyway, after what seemed like days we reached the car and discovered a flat tire. In a driving rain the jack slipped, shoving it into the mud and our Corvair slumped to the ground. After considerable effort I replaced the flat tire, then we drove to the Nantahala Outdoor Center with the plan to raft the next day.

On the Nantahala River just above the Center are Class 4 rapids, however when we drove by there was only a trickle of water thru the rocks, what else could go wrong! To our astonishment we discovered that the dam would release water next day at 10am, not something you see in Florida. We had planned to tent camp, however after the day's episodes we wanted a dry place to rest, but no cabins were available so we bunked with several smelly people in a room with multi-level bunks. After that misadventure Judy and Michelle actually accompanied me on other backpacking trips, including another misadventure on the Appalachian Trail.

On the way to Alaska (in the year 2000) Brenda and I stopped at the Teton Mountains (in Wyoming) and were hiking a trail around Jenny Lake. As we were returning we saw a Bear was standing in the middle of the trail. Immediately I was taking video, then to our extreme alarm the Bear rushed toward us. That's an action that stimulates a noteworthy adrenaline rush!

GRIZZLY BEAR

[Actually this photo is a Grizzly from Yellowstone, but is definitely a Bear.]

Brenda took a flash photo that scared the Bear who returned to his original position in mid-trail, but not for long. Again he stormed at us and when we stood our ground he backed off. I 'told' the Bear we needed to get down that trail, but he wasn't listening or didn't understand my 'Southernese' speech. Again he charged us, so I threw a tree limb at him; he abruptly reversed course and climbed a tree. Since the Bear seemed determined not to move off the trail we veered off the trail; began scrambling thru the woods and this Bear followed us. We could tell that the Bear was agitated because he would bite on limbs and occasionally growl. <u>This was **NOT** a comfortable situation</u>! After we got back on the trail the Bear came at us again and when we threw sticks at the Bear he would dash back up a tree, only to come back toward us. After what seemed like forever the Bear was distracted by a Marmot and sauntered off chasing the rodent.

This was a Black Bear although his fur was brown. In Southeast America Black Bears are almost always jet black, however out west they can be about any color from blond to light to dark brown. This presents a dilemma when confronted by a charging Bear. Authorities say that if you are charged by a Black Bear and they make contact, then you are to fight back because their intention is to have you for a meal. However if it is a Grizzly Bear you are to drop to the ground in a fetal position and protect your neck, because the Bear was startled or saw you as a competitor and (hopefully) once the Bear no longer sees you as a threat, the Bear will leave. A third scenario is a bluff charge, where the Bear charges you and at the last moment veers off. Now that would certainly result in soiled underwear. A real life problem could be: here is a huge Bear charging you and he is not black, so is he actually a Black Bear (so you fight back) or really a Grizzly (so you drop to the ground)? Fortunately I never had the 'opportunity' to be in this situation.

Knowing that when I got to Alaska I'd be out in the bush so read everything I could about Grizzly Bears. Some of the stories were absolutely horrible with the Bears dragging people out of their tents; ripping their tents open and killing a number of people. One woman, who survived, tells of the Grizzly actually eating her, resulting in the loss of both legs and an arm in this encounter.

In Alaska, I was camping along Montana Creek and walked to the mouth of the river where people lined the shore catching Salmon. It appeared that everyone was fishing only one side of the river so I ask why and they replied '*Look over on the other bank where there's two Grizzly Bears feeding on Salmon.*" Undeterred and feeling invincible I crossed the river on a railroad bridge; struggled thru the brush and hid behind a log so I could video the Bear. The Bear before me was catching Salmon that were so plentiful he would playfully toss some in the air. Then he began walking toward me and I became 'somewhat concerned'. Near the log he angled off a ways, but still kept an eye on me. The Bear lumbered past me then into heavy brush and trees and was I determined not to go into those bushes where that Grizzly was lurking. So I waited for quite some time; the Bear didn't reappear, so I waded across the waist deep river to what I felt was safety.

Back at camp I saw where people were leaving ice chests containing freshly caught fish outside their RVs so warned one person that from everything I'd read this was worst thing you can do around a wild Grizzly. I was told that these two Bears down the river have been hanging around for a long time; stayed on 'their' side of the river and no one worries about them. OK, I'd like to believe that, but I'd also been told there was a tooth fairy that would leave money under my pillow.

Early next morning (probably around 4am) I was out taking photographs and when I came out of the tunnel under the railroad (on our side of the river) there was a larger Grizzly eating Berries who immediately stood up looking at me. The books I've read recommend holding your hands up high so you look bigger, then the Bear would slowly move away. Sure! Well I followed this suggestion, yet the Bear stood his ground. Being determined to explore along the river I cautiously moved closer and to my relief the Bear finally lumber off into the woods.

I remained determined to get some video of Grizzly Bears so hiked into Denali State Park where there were fresh Bear tracks and scat along a muddy trail. I mean these tracks were gigantic and I tested the scat and it was still warm. Now I was violating all the rules of safety; the wind was blowing; I was not making any noise and crept along the trail hoping to find a Grizzly Bear (at a distance away) so I could get some video. The worst thing you can do is to startle a Grizzly Bear because their first reaction is to attack, whereas a Black Bear will usually climb up a tree.

Well I never did find a Grizzly (and none found me) so went on into Denali National Park where people were seeing Grizzlies everywhere. You're not allowed to drive into the Park so had to take buses and I took several bus trips without seeing a Grizzly, although people in other buses continued to tell me how they just saw one or more. Finally the bus stopped and a Grizzly Bear walked right along next to the bus; looked up at us, so I finally got my video. Other than their immense size what impressed me were the huge claws that clanked on the rocky surface.

At Denali National Park you can drive your RV into the Park only if you were camping at the Teklanika campground. I was camping there and as I was returning to camp one evening I saw a Moose beside the river surrounded by Wolves who had injured the Moose's leg. I figured they wouldn't allow me out of the bus to take photographs, so planned to come back there after the last bus, around 10:00 PM. Here it is in July; it's snowing and as I hiked out of some bushes a Wolf also dashed out of the same bushes. This Wolf was in a subservient mode with the ears and tail down and immediately ran over to the Alpha Wolf who was watching the injured moose. I waited to see what the Wolves were going to do and observed that when they approached, the Moose would move out into the center of the river. Around midnight and it's still light, I returned to camp; got up at 4:00 AM and walked back down to the bridge where the Moose remained by the river. Previously there had been three Wolves around the Moose and now there were six. I watched the Moose for a long time; the sun came out which seemed to invigorate the Moose; caught a bus still looking for more Grizzly Bears and on my return the Moose was gone.

After a couple of weeks I returned to Denali and was told that the Moose had come out of the Igloo Forest; been killed by the Wolves and (as is usual in summer) a Bear took over the kill from the Wolves. Later another Bear came to the kill; the Wolves became bolder; finally got a meal from the Moose carcass and someone had photographed this last episode. A year or so later I open a National Geographic Magazine and 'my' Moose was in that issue. So indirectly I have photographs in National Geographic Magazine.

MY SHARONA

Linda and I were looking for a boat or at least a big fiberglass hull to turn into a floating home. We knew of a large cruiser (**My Sharona**) sunk at the dock at Shell Point, but it was wooden. Later a friend (who knows wooden boats) said the hull was in great shape and appeared to be mahogany, but locals said a piling had punctured its hull so was unsalvageable. The owner had recently spent thousands of dollars fixing up the yacht, however now he was to be in prison for a long time for smuggling. Always ready for a challenging adventure I questioned the marina owner who said, "***Just get it out of here***". So I borrowed my Cousin Jeff's water pump; friend Randy's skiff and called my brother Dave to help. On a low tide, we began pumping and to everyone's surprise the boat floated. The 'plan' (which seemed so plausible) was to push the 48 foot boat 5 miles to the St Marks River, then 5 miles up to my Cousin Richard's house on the Wakulla River. The idea was for me to push using our aluminum boat (we called her **Al**) while David maneuvered with the other skiff. For a while the plan was working beautifully, however we were using much more gas than 'planned', so David and his friend Jessie would leave us and motor to Shell Island (on the Wakulla River) for gas. Well the wind began to build from the south, right into our face. By the time we were within a couple miles of the St Marks River; the waves were so high that **Al**'s bow was scraping completely up and down **Sharona**'s 8 foot transom. Finally it was no use, we were not moving forward, so tried to anchor. After several attempts the anchor finally set.

As the sun began to set, we waiting and waited for David's return. Dark clouds formed onshore and Linda became concerned. Knowing my history she was fearful of another "Barry experience'. I matter-of–factly reassured her: ***"The winds are from the south, no problem.***" Well just about that time a strong northwest wind began rocking the boat. As darkness approached Linda (naturally being skeptical of my authority) said the clouds looked pretty dark. I said, ***"Don't worry; it's just a cool front.***" We turned on the radio to here repeated announcement of a tornado alert, now Linda became somewhat distraught. From the north the waves began to form nasty peaks in the shallow water, then 'snap', **Al**'s painter broke and into the darkness, off she goes. Fortunately the wind had temporarily returned from the south. We had no gas; no way to return to shore; no food; no warm clothes and we were in a huge rocking boat with tornados on the way. As darkness enveloped us we found some dirty 'croaker' sacks and tried to lie down and sleep. As **Sharona** rocked from bow to stern the diesel fuel in the bilge sloshed from end to end, emitting an aroma that made us gag, but it was better than trying to sleep outside in the rain. Of course sleep didn't ensue and every few minutes I'd look out and imagine the faintest hint of sunrise. I repeated this all nite until the horizon finally began to lighten.

At sunrise David returned, saying that yesterday they got to the mouth of the river and the sea was too rough to ferry gas out to us. [Indicative of a passed era, David didn't have enough money to buy gas cans or gas, so charged it with just his word.] Luckily we found **Al** washed up on shore, so continued our trip up the St Marks River. That was the beginning of many interesting adventures including moving **My Sharona** down to the Florida Keys.

After towing her from Shell Point and tying to Richard's dock (on the Wakulla River) we returned to Tallahassee and next weekend returned to find her on bottom. Fortunately the water was only 4 feet deep, so I swam to the stern; stuffed some rags in the exhaust pipes and again using Jeff's pump, refloated her.

Removing the huge engines became a nightmare. First I thought I'd be able to dismantle the engines (6-71 Detroit diesels) using my tools; so I jacked an engine, inch by inch, then began removed external parts and soon realized that this was NOT going to work. There was a friend nearby, Charlie Davis, who had a crane; I removed a section of roofing over the engine; moved **Sharona** under the hiway 98 bridge; Davis positioned his crane on the bridge and as he hauled up one of the engines he swung it around and almost collided with a passing car. He finally removed both engines; a huge generator and we were relieved that the Highway Patrol hadn't come by.

Another time I asked my brother Joe to come up from Ocala to help us removed a fuel tank and that it would only take half a day. Well he arrived on Friday and we struggled ALL weekend removing that 500 gallon metal tank. By late Sunday we were exhausted and covered with oil and grease, from head to foot.

I also recall Joe coming up to help clean the inside of **Sharona;** she was up on the marineways (rails) at Mike Marshall's Marineways in St Marks; we borrowed a high pressure water sprayer from the Davis's; sprayed all weekend and by the time we finished Joe and I were completely covered in diesel fuel; grease and resembled tar babies. Also, on Saturday I slipped in the grease and gashed my arm on a nail, however, since we had to finish the task, I just wrapped my bleeding arm and worked throughout the weekend.

Now that **Sharona** was relatively clean, although desperately needing a paint job, I pulled her down the Wakulla River to St Mark (using Al) where there was to be a boat parade. We gathered a gaggle of people; hung clothes from lines around the boat; put up a sign "America or Bust"; entered the parade as a Haitian refugee boat and won a prize.

Finally we needed to paint her hull so had to push/pull her 5 miles down the Wakulla to the Gulf of Mexico and across to Shell Point where she was lifted from the water on a Travel Lift. Linda and I spent hours applying a coat of blue paint to her hull and painted her bottom with antifouling paint.

PAINTING SHARONA AT SHELL POINT

BELIZE

<u>An adventure that fortunately didn't happen:</u>

When in my 50's (on **The Rose**) I had solo sailed to Belize and set a goal to backpack across the country from San Ignacio, across the highest mountain (Victoria Peak), then back down to the coast. Packed 5 days of food; British topo maps (I'd gridded out for my GPS) and an EPIRB for real emergencies. [A side story: An EPIRB sends a signal to a satellite indicating your position and that you need assistance. A friend in The Keys (aware of my wild adventures) gave me an EPIRB for my trip. A few years back an all-woman group was hiking to Mt Victoria; a woman broke a leg; they transmitted a signal on their EPIRB; the satellite sent a message to a ground station in Miami Florida, who contacted the British forces in Belize and a helicopter extracted her within hours. Now that's technology not available to past explorers.]

Took buses from Placencia to San Ignacio and visited some friends, the Zuls. Heard from their friends, "***Oh no, you can't make it walking across the country***." Each person would have their reason: either a Jaguar would eat me, or a Fer-de-lance would poison me or a pack of Peccaries would tear me apart. I did talk with a local (originally from England) who said I could make it across the mountains, but once I got into the rainforest it would become impenetrable. Skeptical of that advice, yet quite determined, I headed out.

[Belize had been under the British rule for 200 years when it was called British Honduras; just a few years ago Belize had become an independent country; Belize has a dispute with Guatemala over a road to the Caribbean coast; their neighbors have threatened in invade them, so British troops were stationed throughout Belize, conspicuous when you land in Belize City where Harrier jets are stationed around the airport.] Well I entered an area where the British troops were training the Belize Defense group and they would not let me pass, so that ended an almost adventure that certainly would have become another Barry Trip.

It was a couple weeks later before I came to believe the advice about the impenetrable jungle. I was miles up the Monkey River (in my 10 foot rubber dinghy, **Rose Bud**) looking for Howler Monkeys. After searching all day I found a sandbar to camp for the nite. [Preparing for this trip (since it would be in the tropics) I bought a tent that was almost all mosquito netting. I expected the weather to always be warm or hot and even the front 'door' was netting. But I did take one of those emergency blankets that folds up to about 2 inches square.]

Around dark I could hear Howlers across the river; a good sign and nearby a camp of Mayans in grass huts, not so good. I'm not normally paranoid, but here I was in a foreign country; many miles from any village, among natives I had no knowledge of. Everyone here carries a machete and I'd recently heard of disputes that ended with severed heads. Well, in the nite I had an increasing fear that the people in the grass huts might attack me and my plan was to use my pocket knife to cut the back of the tent and flee down the river. As nite set in the temperature began to drop and drop and I was becoming cold. Finally I found my emergency blanket; opened it (for the only time in many years) and the aluminum fell off, leaving me with a thin sheet of plastic, so I shivered the remaining nite. [Locals later told me this was one of the coldest spells they'd had in many years.] Although the temperature was only in the low 50's I was not at all prepared, just wearing a bathing suit and T shirt. In the early morning hour, mostly awake and shivering and true to my paranoia there were footsteps just outside my tent. I was all prepared to escape from the assault that never came.

Rising at daybreak I found Tapir tracks encircling my tent. I grabbed my video camera and intended to follow the animal into the jungle. This is where I finally understood what the guy from England was trying to tell me. In this jungle you could cut all day with a machete and not make a kilometer. How that huge Tapir got thru I have no idea, but I could not.

By the way Tapirs (locally called Mountain Cows) have poor eyesight and sometimes dash into the jungle, hit a tree and are knocked unconscious. Also, when I had last visited Belize I found a Tapir track with a Jaguar track superimposed in it. Did that Tapir become lunch?

EAGLE HARBOR

An interesting day and nite at Eagle Harbor or a flirt with disaster

A ship is safe in the harbor, but that is not what they are made for. William Shedd

The story began in the 4th of July weekend as Linda and I sailed from Shell Point (near Tallahassee) into Eagle Harbor (on Cape San Blas near Port St Joe) in our sailboat, **The Rose**. In a desperate need of ice, coke and butter we realize our cash funds were left in the car in Apalachicola. Undaunted we anchor behind the State Park store; row ashore with a Tupperware container of change turned green from the salt air; a checkbook and no ID or plastic money. The store attendant accepted our story, so with a check we purchased a few essentials.

By candlelight we eat a delicious dinner of: scallops (freshly retrieved from the bay); the previous nites salad and French bread all prepared by Linda, the then willing crew. On our way to the beach we talked with John, Silky and friends who were anchored near us. John and Silky also work for the Florida Department of Environmental Regulation.

We had looked forward to a fresh-water shower and the result was a matter of perspective; to me it was a refreshing outdoor experience, although I mistakenly remembered the shower as being indoors, however, to Linda this was "*What else could go wrong*!" This statement was just a little pessimistic, but unknown to us at the time, before the night was over her comment had undeniable validity.

We walked along the pure white sand beach; picked up a few sea shells and chased Ghost Crabs. [In this area are some of the most delightful beaches in the world. They are composed of pure, quartz sand that squeaks under your feet; the high sand dunes are festooned with Sea Oats; knarly, demented Oak Trees and the clear greenish water fades offshore into turquoise blue.] We rowed back to **The Rose** and procrastinated about moving into deeper water. However, since the sun had come out (after raining off and on all day) we just crashed where we were anchored. Maybe I should just say we were tired and went to sleep, rather than crashed!

Well, somewhere around 'Dark 30' I was awakened by the sound of thunder and the sight of considerable lightning. I got up and again considered moving the boat into deeper water; however this storm seemed to be moving north of us, so I snuggled back into bed.

Around midnite we were rudely awakened by a tremendous blast of wind; thundering rain and almost continuous lightning. Before I could get thru the companionway hatch we were blown across the narrow channel onto bottom. As I entered the cockpit a bolt of lightning struck close-by; Linda had her hand on the side of the boat and was slightly shocked; I was looking outside and for few moments was blinded; I draped a foul weather jacket over my shoulders, then started the engine. The wind was furiously blowing to at least 40 miles per hour and we were hard aground from the stern. I surveyed the situation and was relieved that we had missed the rock jetties at the entrance to the marina. The incessant lightning flashes lit the sky like day, however we could not move into deeper water.

In moments the waves were amazingly high from a fetch of only 200 feet and the surface of the marina was more like a violent sheet of spray than a windblown harbor. For a while I sat in the cockpit with rain blasting at my back, wearing nothing but the jacket, hardly worried about *The Rose*, she was 'safely' on the bottom, but somewhat concerned about the lightning striking my exposed anatomy. Finally the boat started to move and for only a fleeting moment it looked like we could pull off bottom and into the channel, no, Aeolus (god of wind) realized what was happening and sent a mighty blast of wind (possibly 60 mph) that soundly put us back on bottom. Now there was nothing to do then but shut down the engine and wait. Fortunately we were at low tide and since the waves couldn't become high enough to damage the boat we only had to wait until high tide.

In a few minutes, the wind calmed as rapidly as it had come up, although it remained at a considerable velocity of about 20 mph for 15 minutes or so. During that time I developed a plan to set our sails and try to pull off bottom, but just as I moved the wind suddenly dropped to a gentle breeze.

I gave a few minutes thought to the boat *Aphrodite* (from Shell Point) who was to meet us on their way back from Panama City. Were they sailing offshore in that storm? It could be especially serious for them.

Well at an angle about 45° we tried to sleep. Soon *The Rose* began to move so in my optimistic way I assumed we were coming up already, then we realized we had healed even more, evidently it wasn't quite low tide. I couldn't find the tide tables; tried to sleep by hanging my butt against the galley cabinet and of course Linda slept through all of this. She is truly amazing; she could probably sleep standing up on one leg, on a rock, with the Budweiser in hand.

After a while the wind shifted causing the dinghy to again begin banging against the side of *The Rose*; so I got up in the rain and tied the dinghy. When I returned to the cabin I finally found the tide tables that indicated a very ample high tide at about 6:00 AM. Now nothing remained but to wait out the tide and try to sleep. It appeared the worst storm had passed so I <u>assumed</u> it would probably just drizzle the night away. NADA!

Soon the wind shifted <u>toward </u>the east, when we anchored the wind had been <u>from</u> the east and anchor was set in that direction. This violent storm had come from the exact opposite direction sending another deluge of rain. Since we were close to the rock jetties this was not a favorable direction if we came off bottom.

I must have dozed off and was awakened by the keel bumping on the sandy bottom. It was about 3:00 AM and we're going to be off bottom sooner than expected.

Then I notice lightning on the horizon, but again it seemed well north of us. As I waited I noticed Linda was still sleep; the boat moved more upright and the electrical storm moved closer. Now there was also lightning to the south. If the storms would only hold out for a few minutes we would be off bottom and into deeper water. Suddenly the wind began building from the northwest and we must move, now! I called to Linda; jumped into the cockpit and started the engine. At first the rudder was stuck in the bottom; fortunately the building waves allow the engine to remain in water and the wave motion allowed us to finally extract ourselves from bottom. Now everything began to happen at a frantic pace and as Linda got to the bow the rain and wind arrived with a vengeance. The wind was fierce and the engine was hanging at an angle and I wasn't sure what was wrong, but expected it to fall off any minute. As we got into mid channel Linda yelled out that the dinghy was filling with rain water and was about to sink. We must get out of the channel and into deep water, so I slowed our speed as Linda fought to keep the dinghy afloat. As we approached John's boat the inevitable happened, the dinghy submerged, then passed under *The Rose*. The almost constant flashes of lightning were enough to see into the clear water as in daylight. I could see the dinghy under the water heading for the engine and us being blown toward the two anchored boats before us. True to Murphy's Law the dinghy painter snarled into the prop, so I had to dive overboard and frantically untangle this mess.

I idled the engine and instructed Linda to pull the dinghy forward with all her might. Of course at this moment the engine died, so as Linda struggled with the dinghy I attempted to restart the engine. The starting rope kept pulling out and not engaging, which didn't surprise me too much since it seemed that the elements were determined to cause disaster. Finally the engine started and I backed up enough to allow maneuvering room between us and the other boats. I had envisioned us snarling on their anchor lines, entangling three boats together. Then I realized that the other sailboats anchors had also pulled, driving them toward the Bay. We finally moved past the other sailboats, as our wooden dinghy again banged into our newly painted hull. In mid-harbor I dropped the anchor, then immediately realized they were being blown backwards so fast that the anchor was <u>surfing on the top of the water</u> and again we were rapidly approaching shallow water. I was just about to dash back to the engine when the anchor line became taut. What a relief!

I played out more rode and sat there for a minute until I realized the sky was again bursting with lightning flashes. I didn't like the idea of being a bow perched lightning rod so crawled back to the cockpit and surveyed the situation. The waves were much higher in the bay, but the anchor held fast and the other boats were clear, so our situation was improving. Well, Not! The wind rapidly shifted and we were now directly windward of the other boats. With each flash of lightning my imagination put us closer and closer to them and our fate. Being at the mercy of the elements we retrieve the air horn ready to warn the other sailboats, then waited. Suddenly the wind shifted 180 degrees changing our direction so rapidly that again the dinghy came alongside. Now the question was, did the anchor reset or had all that frantic effort been in vain? The lightening became less intense, the rain slackened so we sat there waiting to see if we were stationary or again drifting.

The storm from the south passed to the east and the wind again shifted direction. <u>This was getting to be a little too much</u>. I considered motoring out into the bay toward St Joe Paper Company, but the wind was rapidly dropping and we seemed to be soundly anchored. The remaining hour or so before sunrise was spent in fleeting moments of sleep.

I have experience similar storms, even near life threatening coral reefs, but lightning is something I'll never get accustomed to. I have control over my boat and my actions, but I feel so helpless in the dominating force of all powerful Thor.

Overall the only damage was a bent motor mount and scratches on the hull paint. However this damage was minor compared to the possibility of being blown into the jetties; colliding with the other sailboats or being offshore during that blow.

Such was sailing. For every episode such as this we have had hundreds of pleasurable, even breathtaking, sailing experiences.

THE ROSE AND SANDY YOUNG'S DINGHY

WELL, THE HURRICANE WAS IN THE WAY

I'm way too adventurous to be considered ordinary. Mario Tomasello

In 1998, while working for McGlynn environmental consulting firm I was to meet with some folks in Baton Rouge; hurricane **Georges** had just bashed The Florida Keys and was expected to strike New Orleans. I figured that I'd head west and skirt the hurricane, north if it stalled or south if it move on through. I never thought that I'd <u>drive right thru the middle of a hurricane.</u>

Note: I am driving a 1987 Toyota pickup truck with a topper.

On I-10 I left Tallahassee in clear skies; rain began around Panama City and the wind picked up around Pensacola. Later the rain came in violent squalls. As I approached Mobile Alabama I could see flooding along I-10 and was convinced that I wouldn't be allowed to cross the Mobile River bridge, however when I arrived there was no one stopping me. Matter of fact I couldn't see anyone else on I-10. I had been concentrating so much on maintaining control of my Toyota in the gusting winds that I just hadn't realized that no one else was on the Interstate. I now saw that police were blocking people from getting onto the Interstate, guess I just slipped 'thru the crack'. Alone I crossed the bridge in a wind that was gusting to over 50 mph. West of Mobile the wind really picked up; billboards were flying across the hiway and in places I'd have to dodge limbs and debris on the roadway. On the radio it appeared the hurricane would not strike New Orleans, but they weren't quite sure where the center was located or where the eye would make landfall.

By now the wind had begun to gust at hurricane force and it was becoming difficult to keep her **Tonja** aligned on the road. Up on the Pascagoula River Bridge the gusting wind became perilous, so I slowed a bit and hugged the bridge railing. Since I was in an area no longer protected by trees and near the hurricane's eye, the gust must have been over 100 mph. Just past the bridge the wind shifted 180 degrees, so I was very near the eye, although I didn't see it. **Georges** had come in at Biloxi, moved just inland and then followed I-10 to Tallahassee.

By now the gust were subsiding and the rain eased. There was debris along the Interstate, but not like west of Mobile. After I-59 I began seeing other traffic and by the time I arrived in Baton Rouge the sun was shining. So I traveled from sunshine, thru the middle of a hurricane, back into sunshine; a truly exciting and memorable experience.

HALF DOME

(REMINISCENT OF MY MT. WHITNEY ADVENTURE)

Adventure is worthwhile in itself. Amelia Earhart

The magnificent Yosemite:

El Capitan

In October of 1999 I entered the Wawona Tunnel (video camera running) anticipating a spectacular view of Yosemite National Park. My first disappointment, the Valley was completely shrouded in morning fog and smoke. In the 1960' (in California) I remember that newscasters would list the specific amount of smoke and fog, avoiding the 4-letter word: SMOG. However that's what this is, Californians are so much in denial. Recently I heard the term 'seismic event'; this is to avoid the denial word: Earthquake.

There were 11 fires burning in the Park, two caused by campfires and the others by lightning. [East of the Mississippi most fires are human caused and out west most caused by lightning.] On down into the Yosemite Valley I drove, trying to rejuvenate my excitement; Bridal Veil Falls was barely showing itself, but where was Yosemite Falls, one of the highest waterfalls in the world? The next day I discovered that Yosemite Falls was typically dry this time of year. The joke was that the LA Aqueduct Authority had drained all the water and would open the valve in the Spring. This isn't too far from the truth since most streams in the Sierra Nevada Mountains are intercepted for water by either Los Angeles; San Francisco or the Central Valley. This wouldn't be so serious if they were more responsible; however Californians waste a tremendous amount of water. It's not unusual to see irrigation water running along the highway and in Los Angeles the summer streams results from excessive irrigation of lawns and golf courses. [By the way, all the trees, shrubs and grass in the LA area survive with water from the northern mountains. Before it was settled, Southern California was a desert and as far as I'm concerned we would have been better off if it had remained a desert.]

Photo is Yosemite Falls in the Spring:

YOSEMITE FALLS

Well, for the next few days I hiked; took Ranger walks and experienced evening Ranger programs at the Yosemite Lodge. There was a Ranger here who started in 1931, Dr. Carl Sharsmith. A woman tourist questioned him: ***"I've only got an hour to spend at Yosemite, what should I do, where should I go?"*** Carl finally found the voice to reply and said, ***"Ah lady, I suppose if I had only an hour to spend at Yosemite I'd just walk over there by the river; sit down and cry."*** Yosemite is truly a wondrous American treasure, a confirmation that National Parks are America's Greatest Idea.

Early one morning I waded into this pool and snapped a photo of The Cathedral.

I'd been there for a few days and was running out of new or exciting things to do. In a way it's a curse, but I can't just lie around camp in a hammock or piddle around The Village, I require activity and adventure. So I decided to climb Half Dome, now I had a goal.

Half Dome rock dominates the eastern end of the Yosemite Valley; is 8842 feet above sea level; its sheer wall drops 2000 feet to the talus slope below and from the summit it's about a mile to the Valley floor. Yosemite Indians (the Ahwahneechee) called Half Dome, Tus-sa-ack, after the principal character in one of their legends. In the stains of the wall (with a little imagination) you can see a woman's head in profile; some say it's Tus-sa-ack herself. Half Dome is the most common, single symbol of Yosemite National Park, now my objective!

HALF DOME

I'd heard that the cables were down on Half Dome, but unfortunately really didn't know the meaning of that statement, however would soon find out.

The trails here are rated by difficulty: from easy; to moderate; strenuous; very strenuous and Half Dome- extremely strenuous! On Sunday I visited the Wilderness Center to obtain an overnite permit. Again I heard the Ranger say, *"**The cables are down**."* Not really knowing what I was talking about I said, *"**That doesn't bother me**."* then the Ranger responded, *"**Cool**".* I mistakenly <u>assumed</u> that the cables were on top to keep old farts from falling. Little did I know that this misconception could be no further from the truth.

Sunday night I was packed and filled with anticipation. I wanted to leave early on Monday because a Bear had been seen around Vernal Falls. I left before 7:00 AM and took the John Muir trail. The Mist Trail is shorter, but has hundreds of rocky steps. The overall round trip is about the same as Mt Whitney, 18 miles, but here the altitude is lower.

There were piles of horse poop on this trail, which I found offensive. I had already filled out a questionnaire stating that "***Horse shit on the trail was not my idea of a rewarding wilderness experience.***" I'm certain that John Muir would also find this offensive.

Reaching Nevada Falls I was delighted to see some flow, although a guy from Santa Cruz told me this is the least he's ever seen. For a while I talked with a couple from Holland who had backpacked the 25 miles over from Tuolumne Meadows. It's interesting that (on the trails) most of the tourists I see are foreign, mostly Asian or European. But rarely do you see Asians on the backpacking trails, most are northern Europeans, commonly Germans. It's also interesting that Blacks account for less than 1% of the visitors in National Parks I've visited. Doesn't that say something about their "cultural priorities?" Another observation I've made is that most Californians don't make eye contact. I verbally greet everyone who makes eye contact and almost all are foreign or from the east. I saw this avoidance behavior in LA and think it is an indication of an overcrowded, ailing society.

At Nevada Falls I lay in the sun, soaked (actually just momentarily dipped) my feet in the ice cold stream and ate some nuts and Berries. Looking toward Half Dome all I could see were shear walls. Again I mistakenly <u>assumed</u> that the trail would follow switchbacks like on the way to Mt Whitney. [For those who don't know, switchbacks are zigzags in a trail necessary to climb steep areas.] I talked with a guy who said that last year at this time it rained for a week. I'd been in California for three months and have yet to see rain.

On I pressed, thru Little Yosemite Valley, then steeply up thru the forest toward Half Dome. A few days before a campfire started a forest fire and a crew was still mopping up. At the Wilderness Center I was told that above Little Yosemite Valley there was a water source. After climbing for half a mile a flowing stream could be heard, however I <u>assumed</u> again that the stream crossed the trail, but no. Later a firefighter assured me there was water above. After climbing thru the burned, smoldering forest I became concerned because I certainly didn't want to go back down to the Merced River for water. Hearing running water to the north I left the trail and finally found a cascading brook. With my newly purchased water filter I filled 3 canteens with Giardia free water.

[Giardia is a protozoan that causes extreme diarrhea that can last for weeks and can be fatal.]

Further up again I met the guy from Santa Cruz and talked about RV's and me traveling alone, then he said "*Maybe you'll find the woman you're looking for on Half Dome.*" I replied, "*I'm sure I won't find her on the Internet.*" I had been told that camping above 7600 feet was prohibited, but how would I know when I reached that elevation? In the past, people camped on top of Half Dome and had killed (for firewood) 4 of the 6 trees. It's a shame that more and more wilderness places are being closed due to human abuse. For example the parachutists (BASE jumpers) had a good thing going, leaping off El Capitan, they became irresponsible now it's prohibited. However you can still hang glide from Glacier Point, but it's tightly controlled.

Around the Valley I heard it said that an illegal BASE jump was to occur on Friday and that the people would be arrested. [BASE stands for: building, antenna, span (bridge) and earth.] Couple of years ago a Navy pilot landed on a rock that ended his career, so after that incident BASE jumping was banned. One factor that makes the jump dangerous (in the 3600 foot drop) is that you don't have time to deploy an emergency chute. This June a guy made an illegal jump and while evading Rangers drowned in the Merced River. On Friday (as I left Yosemite) there were Rangers in the Valley below El Capitan. Five jumpers leaped off, the first 4 successfully parachuted to the Valley floor where their equipment was confiscated; they were briefly jailed and fined about $2000. The fifth jumper 'Bought the farm.' She never opened her chute. People in the Valley were yelling "*Open up! Open up!*", but that didn't help. The jump was to protest the ban and show how safe BASE jumping is. She was a 60 year old woman from Santa Barbara and had borrowed someone else's chute because she didn't want her parachute confiscated. On this chute the D ring was located at a different place and she never pulled it. Her husband was photographing the jump and slumped over his camera repeating, "*If only she had her own gear.*" Several years ago I saw a movie in which Bruce Willis said, "*Assumption is a mother of all fuckups.*" That woman assumed that the D ring was in the same place as hers. Bad assumption. No second chance.

The trail became steeper and steeper and nearing Half Dome I was becoming a little tired. I ask a guy about camping areas higher up; he replied that he didn't think there were any suitable places, so I decided to pitch my little tent on an almost level spot next to a Ponderosa Pine. This was the only 'flat' spot in the area that was big enough for my tent. Just behind my tent the cliff dropped for a couple hundred feet, no sleepwalking here. I couldn't drive tent pegs into the ground (mostly rock) so placed rocks inside the tent as in the Mt Whitney experience.

Since I didn't anticipate the hike to Half Dome as being very eventful (little did I know) I planned to get on top near sunset and stay until dark to video the mountains under Moonlight. The plan was to leave for the summit around 4:30 so I lay in my tent; read more John Muir experiences and thank goodness rested. After about 3:00 pm I didn't expect to see anyone coming down, otherwise it would be after dark before they got back to the Valley. As I was about to leave, what should appear, but 'A woman from Half Dome'; an attractive, obviously adventurous woman. She and her "climbing partner" had climbed the south flank of Half Dome and she said, **"He was going to stay up there."**, although I really didn't understand where he was to spend the nite. She was one of those energetic, friendly young women who elicited my immediate interest. She never said friend, or lover or buddy just 'climbing partner' and they wanted to continue climbing but **"Unfortunately I got a job in Vail for the winter, but in the Spring we will continue climbing."** She wore a T shirt; shorts and I commented on her chill bumps. The temperature was cooling rapidly and it would be well after dark before she could get back to Curry Village. She said, **"I have a headlamp, I'll be OK."** I hoped she made it back OK, then she said something peculiar. She said that climbing down Half Dome was "***intimidating***". I thought that strange for a woman who climbs faces of cliffs. It was only a short time before I fully realized what she meant.

That conversation put me behind schedule, however as I started up I saw the potential of a great photo if I could get in line with the sun behind Half Dome. So I left the trail and scampered along the side of the hill to get into position and then had to wait for the sun to lower, also delaying me. Now it was necessary to set a rapid pace. Hurriedly I scaled The Shoulder (a smooth, rounded rock dome) that was steeply up then down; fortunately steps had been hewn from the solid rock surface. Crossing The Shoulder I could see two micro figure's on top of Half Dome. The two people were silhouetted against a setting sun and it looked like a photo from Outdoor magazine.

Descending to the face of Half Dome I was indeed intimidated! The emotion was almost shock, never expecting this in a National Park. Before me lay an <u>almost vertical rock wall</u>! I was panting from a hurried exertion and for few moments thought, ***"I'm not going to do this!"*** I had not prepared myself psychologically for this. Now I saw what they've been saying about the cables being down. The cables were down, that is not removed, however the stanchions and steps were removed so the cables lay against the rock wall. In the summer the steps and stanchions make climbing the rock wall much easier and safer. Since snow would break the stanchions, they were removed just a week before I arrived.

At the base was an almost comical site, a jumbled mass of gloves, mostly tattered gloves of all sizes, more than 100 pair. The sun was rapidly setting, so I began the climb. After 30 or so feet I was panting for breath and had to stop. I questioned, ***"Can I really do this? What if I get most of the way up and my hands failed me in fatigue?"*** Well, on I pressed, 15 to 30 feet at a time resting in a few places where I could set my boot. A 'lifetime' later I could see there was a long stretch of smooth rock with no place to rest. Now I was gasping for air and my arms quite fatigued, since catching my breath while hanging on to the cable was not allowing me to rest my hands. Near the top, to my extreme relief, the rock wasn't as steep; I had to crouch over and pull up to keep the cables at knee height. Pulling up on the cables was even more tiring to my arms. The last 50 feet to the top was not as steep, so I let go of the cable and scampered up the cliff wall staying above the cables in case I slipped. Later I was told the wall was only 300 feet although it felt like an eternity to me. I'm not sure of the angle of the wall, but it seemed to be almost 75° in places.

On top I moved onto relatively flat ground and laid on the cold rock to catch my breath and rest a bit. However the sun was rapidly setting and after a short time I had to get up and take some video. Unfortunately the Valley was shrouded in a deep, bronze haze. [In Summer the cool, clear winds come off the Pacific Ocean at San Francisco; pass Sacramento; then south along the Central Valley and up to Yosemite. By the time the air gets here it is unhealthy and pollutes the Valley and all that are here. What a sorry testament to mankind, a force he couldn't have foreseen corrupts John Muir's paradise.]

Although my legs felt weak and sore I walked around the summit and took photographs. [It's interesting that these domes were formed miles below the earth and uplifted during mountain building. Later the overlaying sediments were eroded away and this release of pressure caused the rocks to crack in layers. This process is called exfoliation, as the rock comes off like the skin of an onion, forming domes. At one time the vertical face of Half Dome was thought to have been scowered by glaciers; later evidence indicates glaciers failed to reach that height in this area. Actually the glaciers cut rock from the base of Half Dome and the wall collapsed into the Valley.]

Looking to Glacier Point I could see camera flashes. On the way down next day I met a couple from Tuscaloosa Alabama who (from Glacier Point at sunset) had seen an "ant" on top of Half Dome. That ant was Barry.

The Sierra-Nevada Mountains are very young mountains as mountains go, whereas the Appalachians are among the world's oldest, at 500 million years. Over that time period the Appalachians have eroded down so that the tallest peak, Mt Mitchell, is only 6684 feet. Whereas the young Sierras rise abruptly from the Owens Valley (to the east) to peaks around 12,000 to 14,000 feet and have been rising almost an inch each year for several million years.

The view across the Sierras was awesome. Over on North Dome I could see two campfires and another looked as if it was near where I was camped. I quickly absorbed the splendor of the moment and prepared to start down.

My plan was to wait until after dark and get some video of the Moon. I hadn't previously considered the descent to be dangerous after dark, so now I began to reevaluate. I'd have to use both hands going down and to do this my little MAG light would be useless. Should I leave before dark? Well, Mother Nature settled that question, darkness was rapidly upon me and the temperature was dropping just as fast. I really didn't want to back down those cables. It wasn't that I was frightened; I was just exhausted; had an eventful day and just wanted to be transported into a bed.

With considerable reluctance I grabbed a cable in each hand and began my backward descent. By now the only light was that of a half Moon. I had to look between my legs to see 'ahead' although there was little I could see. The situation was precarious enough; I didn't want any surprises, like stepping into to a crack or off a ledge, so tried to hold the MAG light in my mouth, but that didn't work for long. Down I would back, until I could feel the strength of my hands waning, then I would hug the wall to rest, usually where I could get a foothold.

In the nearly vertical area I had a real scare. There are two parallel cables in two sections, so with my left hand I reached for a cable that wasn't there. As I located the second cable luckily my right hand held fast, so I resumed my awkward backpedaling. I really didn't like the insecurity of changing cables. This reminded me of my vertical caving days when I'd switch from one rope to another while suspended 100 feet in the air, sometimes in the total darkness of a cave. Here there was no choice, I couldn't hang and rest in my seat harness. I keep going down hoping my footing remained secure. Relief overwhelmed me as I saw, a short distance away, the jumbled pile of gloves.

A Ranger had warned me about the dangers of getting lost in the darkness and possibly falling over a cliff, now I saw what he meant. The Shoulder area loomed above, white in the Moon's glow, with the silhouette of a small tree or bush here and there. Each side of The Shoulder dropped at a steep angle to almost sheer cliff faces thousands of feet down. With my inadequate MAG light I scrambled up and down thru the brush, frequently having to backtrack. The trail itself was usually clear of loose rock, but just off the trail the grains and pebbles of granite were like roller bearings.

Off The Shoulder I passed through a relatively flat area interspersed with large Fir trees. Again I could see the campfire below, but it wasn't near where I was camping. It was a few hundred feet below, to the north of the face of Half Dome. Now I was back into loose rock, then realized I was thoroughly lost. I knew I was going down toward the south face, but should be going further north. After turning back and forth for a while I located the trail and after a distance (further than I remembered) found my tent.

I wasn't warm and was extremely tired so prepared for the nite. I expected Bears, so placed my Bear-proof food container 20 feet away so I could watch it: both cameras were ready and I left the tent flap open so I could photograph the Bear or Bears. A brief reading of John Muir and I was out. After a short time I was awakened by what sounded like a Bear coming up behind the tent, but it was just the east wind. The winds in the mountains are different from what I'm accustomed. I've yet to see a windy day in which the wind blew steadily, even the infamous Santa Ana winds comes in blasts. One minute it could be blowing 40 miles an hour and the next be breathless. What I heard was a blast of wind coming up the mountain. This east wind from the desert brought somewhat warmer.

I had an inflatable pillow which I raise higher by placing a rock underneath and once in the nite my head slipped off and struck the rock. Also the ground wasn't level, so I had to occasionally scrunch back onto my sleeping pad.

At first light I was up, viewing the mountains as just black silhouettes. What was remarkable were the two, very bright morning 'stars', one Venus and the other, Jupiter. This experience was breathtaking, however I felt disconcerted that the sun would rise and spoil the predawn magic spell.

Sometimes in everyone's life they think 'What if I could start over; who would I be and what would I have done differently?' Powerful experiences as I was living caused me to regret that I missed so much in my life. Sure I challenged; tested myself; had many, many great adventures and shared many of those with my wife. But I have the capacity for so much more. Few people have a desire or capability to experience 'the edge'. For most of my life I professed, ***"To experience life as close to the edge as possible to death as this is the only way to live a life to its fullest."*** I recall trying to explain to Connie that adventure and exploration was in my blood, the compulsion controlled me. My childhood was filled with daring explorations and adventures that to most people seemed extreme. In my second grade I ran away from home with a plan to walk to Savannah, get on a ship and explore the world. In middle school I read books on exotic places and animals and then fantasized about traveling there. In the sixties I was still planning to sail round the world. Australia was an attempt to discover the pioneering world lost in America's past. I would have been in my element in those pioneer days: exploring the next mountain; heading to California for gold; finding headwaters of rivers; discovering the unknown... The years working for the State of Florida were squandered years. First there was a five year plan to cruise the Caribbean on our sailboat; then divorce; then an imprudent relationship with a young woman, Sheree. Years with Linda weren't without adventure though. In my past, if nothing else, I could have been career oriented. No, I'm too much of a dreamer, a doer, an explorer. Most of my life I wanted to rock climb and I'm disappointed that I missed that challenge. I could've been one of the climbers spending the nite suspended on the face of El Capitan or Half Dome. I could've explored the high country of the Sierras and Rocky Mountains. In Florida I had searched for the cave no one else had discovered, out here I could've climbed the mountains no one else had climbed.

Being up here (among 12,000 foot peaks) in the enchanting time before sunrise will always remain as a consummate memory in my mind. I was filled with a delightful wonderment. Then came the serene Alpine Glow as the sun embraced the mountain peaks. As John Muir would say: "*A noble experience.*"

After taking some video I returned to my sleeping bag. My plan was to get to Nevada Falls around noon so the sunlight that would illuminate the waters as they cascaded 600 feet to the rocks below. So I napped, not expecting anyone up there before 10 am or so. However around 8 am I heard someone hurriedly passing my tent. Peculiar, I thought, where had they spent the nite?

I slowly packed, started down around 9:30, then sauntered through the forest. Walking slowly I absorbed the serenity of the wilderness and the animals within. After a while, two firefighters approached me and asked if I'd seen the injured climber. I said "*No, but suspected that the campfire I'd seen was where he had spent the nite.*" On down the trail I talked with some Germans who were hiking to Half Dome. They seem so interested and informed about this country and so many Americans are so ignorant.

As with my trip down from Mt Whitney, people would ask "*Did you summit*?" Before this trip, not reaching my goal had never entered my mind, but I'll have to admit that when I saw that wall and those cables on Half Dome I briefly had second thoughts.

At Nevada Falls the Ground Squirrels were pests as they leap for your pack and hover for a handout. It's against Federal law to feed wild animals, although too many people do. Against my better judgment I went back up 3/10 of a mile to the Mist Trail. It cuts a mile or so off the trip down, however this trail was very steep, with hundreds of rock steps. But I wanted to see what this trail was like and abhor backtracking or repeating trails I've already experienced.

In many ways my body ain't what it used to be, and now I was exhausted. From James Michener's memoirs I recall the statement concerning people my age *"**If you wake up some morning without pain, then you know you've died**."* Therefore, waking up this morning in considerable pain was not at all undesirable, I was alive. Backpacking is painful, but that fact isn't going to deter me. Going up the primary pain is in my calves and shoulders. Going down it's my knees and toes being jammed into my boots, compounded by a heavy backpack. My feet, especially my right foot hurts most of the time. My feet are too wide for normal shoes, so I've never had shoes that properly fit. I thought, when I get back to LA I'm going to buy some boots that fit!

Well the Mist Trail was as expected, long stretches of rocky stairways that were murder on my feet and knees. I had to be careful to place my foot straight ahead or the twisting in my knee would result in considerable discomfort.

Just below above Vernal Falls I stopped for lunch and read some Muir. A Ground Squirrel kept nosing around looking for a handout, then disappeared. When I looked around I could see him rolling my apple away! He was already 20 feet away and I felt like giving the enterprising Squirrel a treat, but resisted feeding him.

I could hear a helicopter on the other side of Half Dome. Later I discovered they did rescue the injured climber from the ledge near where I had seen the fire.

From the top of Vernal Falls you must traverse a sheer wall on a narrow trail cut into the wall that is about one person wide, where I had turn sideways, with my backpack over the edge, to allow a couple pass by. The 300 foot falls was impressive, in Spring it would certainly be spectacular. After that wall there is long stretch of rock steps shrouded in thick mist.

[When I returned to Yosemite in 2011, just after we passed these steps, a guy fell to his death.] On down there were some short stretches of uphill, which rekindle the pain in my calves. After the bridge it was still a mile and a half and I was really becoming weary. I wanted to stop and rest, but more importantly, wanted to be back to **Maybellene**. So I plodded on and arrived back to my campsite at 3:30 pm.

Thus ended what was expected to just be a routine hike. However it became an adventure worth savoring and writing about. A continuing legacy of grand adventures and I enjoyed it thoroughly, however in the future I hope to share adventures with a compatible woman.

PS The next day I again met 'The woman from Half Dome.' Jessica was coming from the Curry Village store and said that she had been worried that the injured climber was her 'climbing partner', but she could see him on the face of Half Dome above the rescue helicopter. She saw them summit at 2:30 PM and was getting food to prepare a special dinner. She invited me to their camp in the Sunnyside campground, called Camp 4 by the climbers. This site has been used by climbers for years and is now on the National Registry of Historic Places.

When I arrived at Camp 4 I was exhilarated by the expanse of small tents; smelly clothes and gear hanging to dry; climbers crouched in groups planning the next day's climb; the smell of campfires... This reminded me of the annual TAG Cave-In held in Northern Alabama. I can relate to these people, they are self-confident; energetic; adventurous and obsessed with the challenge and personally rewarded thru their accomplishments. It took me years to realize that (unlike me) most people don't value of setting difficult goals and reaping the personal rewards.

Jessica was making tortillas, so with a jar I helped her roll some flat. While in High School she had spent time in Chile; later in Mexico and Honduras after hurricane Mitch. Her climbing partner's father runs a mountain climbing school affiliated with the religious group; she worked there and evidently that's where she met her 'climbing partner'. Also there were two climbers from England camping with them.

Kevin her 'climbing partner' and an Englishman returned to camp about dark relaying the story of the injured climber. They were below two climbers who were into a rapid ascent. Someone yelled "***Rock!***" followed by a scream of pain. A rock had fallen and broken the shoulder of one of the climbers. When Kevin got to them a guy was crumpled up in pain and had to spend the nite and half the next day with a shattered shoulder. Kevin and his friend spent that night on a ledge on the vertical face of Half Dome.

Soon they were planning a trip for the next day, to take food and water to a ledge on El Capitan; come back; gorge themselves with food and begin climbing El Cap the following day. EL Cap is the highest granite face in the country at over half a mile. Oh yes, Kevin received a care package from his girlfriend (including soap and gummy bears) so that explained Jessica's relationship with her 'climbing partner'.

Afterward I attended the evening program at the Lodge where the speaker, Bob Corbin, talked about the 55 times he has scaled El Cap as well as assisting Mark Wellman, the paraplegic Ranger in his climbs of El Cap and Half Dome. Mark had to perform 7000 arm pullouts to get up El Capitan in seven days' and due to rain and storms it took 13 days to do Half Dome. Bob showed the spectacular NBC documentary of Mark's treks and their visit with President Bush. The longest time Bob spent on the face of El Capitan was 14 days. For some obscure reason two Frenchmen wanted to set a record for time being on the rock face, two months, not an adventure that would interest me. Midway through the program a streaker ran through, followed by a guy with a flashlight. Haven't seen that in a few years.

On to the next adventure.

Later, at Death Valley, I met a man whose daughter died in a fall from Half Dome. There have been 6 deaths there since 1995, including 2 while I was there in 2011, a record year in which 17 people died in Yosemite National Park. I just discovered that this hike is one of the 10 most dangerous in America. Obviously, when I decided on this adventure I knew nothing about the effort or danger, not that this would have made any difference.

MYSTIC FALLS: ONE OF THE MOST BEAUTIFUL WATERFALLS IN THIS WORLD

"To conquer without risk is too triumph without glory."

Well it's August 17th 2011 and Brent, Steve and I plan to rappel Mystic Falls, near Silverton Colorado. We hiked from Butterfly Falls to the top of Mystic and I took photos of Brent, Steve and Alena rappelling down. Looking down it looked like you could rappel all the way without getting into the waterfalls; however Brent slipped on the mossy rocks and disappeared near the bottom of the falls. When he didn't reappear I was somewhat concerned, then rationalized that he had air behind the falls. He finally reappeared, swimming across the pool. Alena had some trouble in the bottom of the falls getting her harness unhooked and she also spent an unnerving time submerged in the falls. Brent was so concerned he swam out to help her. Steve had the same problem as the two before him, being in the full blast of the waterfall attempting to unhook his harness. After Steve got down and swam across the pool I drove around, then hiked up to the lower falls to take photos of them rappelling down the lower falls. Leaving Alena to take photos we then drove back to the top to rappel down.

Not being familiar with their rappelling gear I was somewhat apprehensive as I backed over the 125 foot cliff face.

BARRY RAPPELLING MYSTIC FALLS

About three quarters of the way down, no matter how much I tried not swing into the falls all efforts were fruitless. I swung into the falls, swallowed some water and didn't know if I was in or above the pool; as I tried to get free of the rope, water was battering upon me and the sound was deafening. I had a moment of serious concern that I would drown or fall into the rocks below. However I was having trouble breathing and needed to get out of that maelstrom. Finally I swam free of the falls and sucked in a welcomed breath of air.

Brent and I waited in the cold spray for Steve to rappel down, then began setting up to rappel down the lower falls. By now the adrenaline had worn off and as soon as I entered these falls I was not warm, also the rocks were slippery causing me to swing back and forth in the falls. At the bottom I waded across the pool and into a cave behind the falls. After getting out of the cold pool I was shivering, with chill bumps the size of eggs.

After they got down we hiked very steeply up to the top of Mystic Falls. Since I knew the route I was leading and past breathless, but just had to keep up a fast pace. It's one of those testosterone things. I mean they were in their 20's and I was 70 and had to keep up the image that 'old guys rule'.

SHARKS AND SEA CREATURES

Several miles offshore from Tallahassee I was spearfishing and violated the cardinal rule: don't keep bloody fish near you. Since the water was deep I didn't want to keep coming up to the boat, so stuffed some fish in my wetsuit top. I was thinking this is 'Not a good idea' and looked up to see that an 8 foot Bull Shark is heading right toward me. In some rocks I hugged the bottom and still the Shark made a B-line for me. To my extreme relief he passed directly overhead as if I wasn't there and I was quite relieved and grateful. I removed the Grouper from my spear; dropped them to the bottom and swam up to the boat, keeping an eye out for the shark. Years later (while spearfishing) I would hand the fish to Linda so could take them to the boat. It took a while for her to realize the danger (so after a while) she refused.

In Australia (in the early 1970's) I was working with the Dolphins and aquariums at a tourist attraction along the Gold Coast at Tweed Heads. They had captured two large sharks, 12 to 15 feet long. In Australia they call them Nurse Sharks and we call them Sand Tigers. They were distinctive and menacing looking in that from their mouth spouted a bouquet of needle sharp teeth. The attraction had a show where a diver would go into the tank with a fish on a skewer and feed the big sharks. In the tank were other sharks, Jewfish, Moray Eels; and other toothy marine life. [By the way, now the politically term for Jewfish is-Goliath Grouper] One day the diver was sick so I said "*I'll do the show*". So into the tanks I swam, with my skewered fish and carefully watching the two big sharks. Well, a smaller Wobbegon Shark about 5 feet long decided he was hungry, rose, unseen from the bottom; grabbed the fish <u>and</u> my hand. As blood clouded the water my greatest concern was what the Sand Tigers would do. Fortunately they didn't seem to be interested in me so I swam to the edge of the tank. Then I noticed, through the portholes, the wide eyed gawks of the spectators who anticipated seeing me being devoured by the circling Sharks. Two day later that Wobbegon Shark died (really, I didn't do him in) and amazingly he "bit" me again. While placing a stick in his mouth for a photo my hand slipped and he bled me again.

SAND TIGER SHARK

Later, while snorkeling near Cook Island, I reached into a crevice for a Lobster just as a Wobbegon Shark rose from the sand and snapped at my moving hand. Since I was snorkeling, if the Shark had connected I would be trapped in the rocks and would have died.

Also in Australia, I was collecting tropical fish for an Aquarium where I worked. Trying to maneuver a very venomous Lion (Turkey) Fish into my collecting bag he zapped me. Fortunately I have a high tolerance to venom and pain. Later an extremely venomous catfish stung me. Now **that** really hurt.

As a side story: While collecting tropicals with another guy (using a Hooka) the air stopped flowing. Judy had turn off the compressor when she saw a kid get hit by a boat. He had been spearfishing next to us and the boat propeller cut into his back. I drug him to shore, however because the medics wouldn't go into the water for him, so we had to take a stretcher and get him into the ambulance. The propeller had cut into his kidneys. Afterwards his mother thanked me and later she called to say he had died.

While attending Ocala High School I occasionally visited my Aunt and Uncle in Miami. I would take the train and since my Father was with the railroad and known throughout the system I could travel free and get away with carrying a big speargun on trips. At my aunt's it always seemed that some calamity would occur. On a diving trip I was messing with a Stingray; he zapped me in my hand with his tail barb, producing excruciating pain! I can still remember the pain moving up my arm into the side of my head. On the 10 mile trip back to shore (to keep my mind off the pain) I cut the Stingray into tiny pieces. At the Hospital they really didn't know what to do so give me a tetanus shot and wanted to keep me overnight, however I got Louise to change their mind and allow me to return to her house. Louise jokingly said she should stock her swimming pool with Sharks; Moray Eels and Stingrays, so I would be safer than out in the ocean.

When I returned home I still had an open wound in my hand. We were crossing the Ichetucknee River; I spotted a Rattlesnake; we followed him to shore where I carefully put a paddle across his neck and picked him up. (You must handle them carefully or they die before you sell them.) The snake twisted his head around in my hand and venom ran down my hand, just past the open wound. If the venom had gotten into the Stingray wound it could be as if he had bitten me.

While working at Marineland of Florida (as Curator of Animals) I was shocked by an Electric Eel. The Amazon Eel was over 3 feet long and could give a shock of several hundred volts. It had air in its swim bladder and I was inserting a hypodermic needle, removing the air to allow it to swim, rather than float on the surface. Although I was wearing rubber gloves, somehow it gave me unforgettable jolt.

When I was in High School I'd visit my aunt and uncle (Louise and Earl) in Miami (actually, Perrine). One summer I was spearfishing off the jetties at Government Cut. Lacking experience in salt water I was just <u>a little</u> apprehensive. All of a sudden realizing that I was in water where I couldn't see bottom; there was a strong current and between me and the jetties was a Barracuda that looked 10 feet long. [Those huge ones are called Cuda Bears] He just eyed me as his toothy mouth seemed to size me up. I just pulled in my legs and let the current carry me out his sight. Later I heard that nearby someone had been shot with a speargun. The shaft hit them in the chest and of course the barbs opened. He was transported to the hospital with shaft protruding from his chest and survived.

While in the Air Force, stationed near Sacramento California, I went on a dive trip to the Farallon Islands (offshore from San Francisco) and one of the divers was bitten by a shark, but didn't lose any limbs.

When I worked at Marineland I was spearfishing among the coquina rocks at what is now Washington Oaks. The rocks were covered with algae, eaten by Sheephead fish and these are tasty fish. A friend and I were in the water with very limited visibility and I felt a swish beside my legs and assumed it was him swimming close to me. But when I surfaced he was several yards away, then I could see the fin of a Shark between us. Not a pretty sight!

MY MOMENTOUS MACHETE MISHAP

At 57, while working for an environmental consulting firm in Tallahassee, Shannon and I were cutting transects thru a forested area in order to document the survival of planted trees. I had been cutting all day with a machete and within minutes of finishing for the day the machete hit the side of small trees and ricocheted into my knee. Shannon asked if I was OK and I replied "**Yes**", hoping there was no real damage. After a short time the amount of blood let me know it was worse than I wanted. Shannon said we must go to the hospital, but I wanting to minimize the episode saying, "**No, let's just go to town and I'll get some butterfly bandages**". She insisted, so in an attempt to locate the hospital in Marianna she stopped at a Fire Station. Now to them blood was a cause to practice their skills, so four of them rushed out and to my dismay ripped my pants leg and began bandaging the wound. Before they did any more damage we headed to the hospital.

There I sat in the emergency room bleeding, with little Johnny with an ear ache and Sally with a sore throat. After some time, trying to not completely cover the floor with blood I asked when I could see a Doctor. *"Oh, you're next"*. In the hall, a not very observant "nurse" took my blood pressure and temperature then asked, *"What seems to be the problem?"*, as if I was there to get an aspirin for a headache. I pointed to the blood which saturated by pants leg and was across the floor. She exclaimed, *"Oh! I see, we need to get you to a Doctor"*. I thought, *"Yes lady I needed attention quite some time ago"*. Once in a room they washed the wound with a saline solution and after a while a Doctor came in and began to rant about the people who were building his house. He said: *"They were slow, not careful and totally unsatisfactory..."* followed by several expletives. My immediate thought was, *"This guy is really upset. Do I really want him stitching my leg?"* He approached with a needle and I expected him to give me a shot of pain killer into my leg. No! He bent over and shot into the side of the wound which was now pooched out on both sides. I have a high tolerance for pain but that REALLY hurt and I told him so. He didn't reply, obviously thinking of ways to waylay the house builders. To my relief he walked to the other side of the table. I was thinking *"Well that's over"*, just as he stuck the needle into the other side of the wound. Still complaining about the workers he pulled out a staple gun and set 10 stitches to close the wound. That was the first time I'd had staples and asked *"How do you get them out?"* He said they had a special tool. My thought was, *"It's probably designed to inflict more pain and if he is the one to remove them, I hope he is in a better mood"*. Since it didn't hurt I said I didn't need a pain killer, and returned to where we were camping.

By the time my wife arrived the pain had set in and I REALLY needed something. Finally they got a codeine drug which put me to sleep. The next day, since I intended to complete our work task, I refused to take a drug that made me sleepy. So for the next two days, while we identified surviving plants, I drug my aching leg through the forest and continued whacking with the machete. Our boss was an Engineer and not blessed with people skills. On replaying the episode his unsympathetic comment was, *"**This might raise my insurance rate**"*. This was the second time in three months that one of us had been injured. Shannon had ripped her hand crossing a barbed wire fence. Since most of our work was in wetlands (from Louisiana to Florida) it always amazed me that not one had been bitten by a Moccasin or Alligator thereby really raised his insurance rates. Anyway, when I got home it really pissed me off that he was so insensitive. I could have taken a week off work, yet I took no time off and suffered thru the completion of my job. The next day I told him so, but his reaction wasn't particularly sensitive.

NATIONAL PARKS: AMERICAS' GREATEST IDEA

There are no words possible for me to express my appreciation for the existence of America's National Parks. They were created by Americans who had a philosophy quite different from the commercial conservatism I see today. The idea of a National system of pristine national treasures for all Americans (The People) was unique in the world and is a clear example of liberal socialism for the masses. Conservative influences opposed the park system at every turn and continue to lobby for privatization and eventual destruction of <u>America's Greatest Idea.</u>

I have visited almost all the major National Parks, many, several times. However what I consider as a visit is certainly not what most people profess. When I'm in a Park it is not to just drive thru and take photos from the car window like I see so many people do; I hike the trails; drive all the roads; climb the highest peaks; attend almost all the Ranger talks and spend hours or days out in the hinterland absorbing the serenity and beauty.

<u>A few experiences in</u> **National Parks**: **Yosemite**, by favorite National Park. I first visited there in 1961 when the Firefall from Glacier Point was still being performed; I've climbed Half Dome; watching BASE jumping from El Capitan; hiked Yosemite Falls and Glacier Point trails in snow; explored Tuolumne Meadows; visited all the major and some minor waterfalls and enjoyed numerous Ranger programs. After a day out exploring I really enjoyed sitting before the fireplace in the communal hut in Curry Village.

Bridal Veil falls is just one of the wondrous waterfalls in Yosemite.

BRIDALVEIL FALLS

Zion (my second favorite Park), first visited in 1975. After not visiting for many years I was on the shuttle bus; many people were getting off at Angels Landing, so I joined them. I really didn't know what was before me, however I could see an absolutely vertical rock wall 1500 feet high and several people were heading that way: Angels Landing

I befriended a German guy (Johnny, named after Johnny Ringo) who
told me that the early settlers knew it was impossible to climb this rock
pinnacle, so said only Angels could reach the top. Now I'm thinking, whoa,
what have I gotten into. We started up a steep trail cut into the side of
the sandstone wall; thru a narrow crack, then came to Walter's Wiggle,
a series of 21 switchbacks, straight up the rock wall. Arriving at Chicken
Crossing I saw that several people could not bring themselves to cross the
narrow passage, maybe they had heard that 6 people had recently died

in falls from Angels Landing. The crossing is certainly intimidating; you must walk on top of a rock 'bridge', only inches wide with a drop on both sides of over a thousand feet! After this was a steep scramble up to the summit. The view from the summit was spectacular.

I've hiked almost all the trails; slogged down the Virgin River for 14 miles; visited the stunning Subway and poked around in the backcountry, all actions shared by only 1% of the visitors. I regret not taking up rock climbing; however, being raised in Florida didn't provide much opportunity to even find rocks.

Organ Pipe National Monument in southern Arizona was an unexpected delight. Since it was a Monument and not a National Park I incorrectly assumed it wouldn't be as grand, boy was I wrong. [Later I discovered that the only difference between the two is that Monuments are designated by the President and Parks are authorized by Congress.] However, a surprise was the fence between the US and Mexico. I had driven a long, loop road thru the hills and came to a dilapidated barbed wire fence and a gate that was lying on the ground; I had expected at least a 15 foot chain link fence. Recently that changed after a Ranger was shot and killed by a drug runner. This Ranger was one of the many who choose to become a Park Ranger; top of his class in college; outstanding athlete and caring father. Evidently the drug runner wasn't attempting to kill the Ranger because he was shot in the leg, however the bullet hit an artery and he bled out.

Speaking of Rangers (Forest and Park Service): These are some of the finest public employees in this country, partially because most <u>choose</u> to take on that responsibility and philosophically support the overall concept of National Parks. Many are over-qualified; work for meager pay, yet enthusiastically perform as if it is their own Park and it really is. To these Rangers, employment is not just a job, it is a responsibility and privatization would yield people who just desire **<u>a job</u>**. To allow the conservative movement to privatize the Parks and continue to cut funding would be a catastrophe for The People's Parks.

Utah to me has the most delightful and interesting natural diversity of any other state and has 13 National Parks and Monuments: **Dinosaur; Bryce Canyon; Vermillion Cliffs** (mostly in Arizona)**; Zion; Canyonlands; Timponogos Cave; Arches; Grand Staircase-Escalante; Capitol Reef; Natural Bridges; Hovenweep; Cedar Breaks and Rainbow Bridge.**

One of the best for exploring is **Staircase-Escalante:** this Monument is filled with slot canyons (Zebra my favorite); desert landscapes; waterfalls; Indian pictographs and petroglyphs; deep canyons and adjoins the Colorado River. I recall sitting in Zebra Canyon, waiting for the sun when a Rattlesnake emerged from the sand just inches from my butt.

Zebra Canyon

At **Canyonlands** marveling at Mesa Arch at daybreak; camping along the White Rim trail; Native American ruins and Newspaper Rock in the Needles area; camping in The Maze and marveling at the ancient Pictographs in Horseshoe Canyon.

Holy Ghost and consorts at Great Gallery

Green River in Canyonlands NP, Utah.

In **Arches** I recall taking video through Delicate Arch during the eclipse of the Moon; exploring Fiery Furnace; climbing up into Double Arch; the Devil's Kitchen with my grandson; a clear nite at Turret Arch and Balanced Rock at sunrise.

World's longest free standing arch in Arches NP, Utah.

Then there is the majestic **Yellowstone** (the world's first National Park, established in 1872); inside the world's largest active volcano and has within its bounds over 70% of the world's geysers. However most people visit the Park for the animals and it's sometimes called the Serengeti of the Americas. I've been there many times; hiked and backpacked many areas and each visit is always been a fresh adventure. I've had close encounters with Bison; frustration attempting to photograph Grizzlies; backpacking to Heart Lake and climbing down ice covered steps to Lower Falls. A high point was when Janice and I spent the nite in the Old Faithful Inn.

Surprisingly the most visited Park is the **Great Smoky Mountains** and I've hiked over much of the more than half a million acres. This Park has more plant diversity than most places on this planet and is the only major Park that doesn't charge an entrance fee. I recall one nite when a Skunk came into our tent; the nite Michelle told us she had candy in the tent as Bears ripped open other backpacker's packs; Alum Cave and an ice covered trail to Mt LeConte.

Originating near the **Smokys** is the **Blue Ridge Parkway** (administered by the Park Service); 469 miles of winding road thru the Appalachian Highlands; beautiful stone bridges; vistas and is a genuine tribute to the CCC (Civilian Conservation Corps).

Back out west is the **Grand Canyon**, too big to comprehend. Although **Grand Canyon** (from the rim) is overwhelming, I'm one of the 1% who has been into the canyon and that's where its real majesty is emphatically revealed. I've made several hikes/backpacking trips into the canyon, including to Phantom Ranch and one 30 miler that challenged my endurance.

The cliff dwellings at **Mesa Verde** are remarkable although (prior to the Antiquities Act) so many of the artifacts have been removed from America.

Then there is **Glacier**, soon to be called '**Once upon a time Glacier Park**', since within 15 years all the major glaciers will have melted. I mentioned this to a guy in Florida who responded that this talk was part of the Climate Change hoax, so I asked if he had ever visited the Park and of course he replied, "*No*". I understand there remains a Flat Earth Society, maybe this guy should join with the millions who also have their head in sand. It's easy to deny something you know nothing about or haven't made an effort to learn the truth.

If you have never driven the <u>Going-to-the-Sun-Hiway</u> you have missed a wonder of the world. I'll always remember the close up encounters Justin and I had with Mountain Goats on Logan Pass; hiking around Two Medicine Lake; the island in St Mary Lake and the Garden Wall area.

In Alaska is **Denali,** another Park jam-packed with wild and unusual animals and the tallest mountain in North America that is also the third highest mountains in the world, above the surrounding plain. This is where I witnessed Wolves attacking a Moose; backpacked into the tundra and hiked into the mountains to view the rare, Dall Sheep.

Trees so large that they defy the senses are preserved from logging in **Redwood** and **Sequoia** National Parks. For a past World's Fair a cutting from one of these trees was sent east where they were considered some kind of deception, a tree could not possible be that vast.

Another Park saved from development is **Acadia** in Maine that (in the turn of the last century) had been a playground only for the wealthy.

In Florida we have the unique underwater Parks, **Biscayne**; as well as **Dry Tortugas**. The **Everglades**, exciting to non-natives, however it is the only Park in the Americas where you can see Crocodiles. Also (at 60 miles) the broadest river in the world and it normally flows at only 100 feet each day. Here you can discover tropical plants such as Mahogany and Gumbo Limbo.

Death Valley (in winter) is a treat with highlights like: The Racetrack; Scotty's Castle; Warm Springs and Badwater Basin, at 282' below sea level, the lowest point in North America.

If you enjoy caves there is **Carlsbad** with one passage 120 miles long; **Crater Lake** known for its blue color and water clarity and **Capitol Reef**, a 100 mile gash in the earth's surface; The Wave in **Vermillion Cliffs**; lush vegetation and rare Roosevelt Elk in **Olympic** and the unusual trees of **Joshua Tree** NP.

A tragic shame is that many natural wonders have not been saved for The People, such as **Niagara Falls** and **Sedona** Arizona. Years ago Europeans berated Americans as uncultured for allowing Niagara Falls to be commercialized into a tacky tourist trap.

Bryce NP in Utah.

CAVING EXPLORATIONS

To understand the heart and mind of a person, look not at what he has already achieved, but what he aspire to. **Kahlil Gibran**

I know this sounds irrational for someone who has always been claustrophobic, but I've explored many, many caves, usually alone. When I was young a goal was to find a cave no one else had explored, although Florida isn't the best place to be caving. I guess the desire for adventure superseded the irrational fright. However there were many times when I would have to stop and 'gather my wits".

When I was 50 years old I became involved with the cave club at FSU. Some of these cavers delighted in getting into extremely tight situations. We were in Climax Cave in South Georgia, it was warm and I had to squeeze sideways through a very tight hole and it hit me, feelings that defy logic, all of a sudden I would be obsessed with getting out of there. Unfortunately with age the feeling surfaced more often. I can remember a couple of times while SCUBA diving I would have to unzip my wet suit to allow cold water to wash away the anxiety. This was when I was in the Research Diving Team for the organization that assists in creating artificial reefs. While conducting surveys I recall diving in cold water with zero visibility, without anxiety. Interestingly I never recall feeling claustrophobic when I wasn't overheated

While living in Tallahassee a cave that really caused extreme anxiety was Glory Cave in South Georgia. The decorated part of the cave is uniquely beautiful in that the formations are translucent; however they are marred by careless cavers who walked on some of these formations. Over time, this mud would become permanently impregnated into the formations and destroy their unique splendor. With the FSU cave club I journeyed on 3 trips into Glory to clean the formations with toothbrushes and water. So, to reduce my chances of becoming claustrophobic I'd be last in line, but not on one of these trips.

This is a cave gated by the Florida State University Cave Club and is located on private property. In the farmer's field you climb down into a sinkhole, then into a perfectly normal cave and walk for some distance within a

20-30 foot wide, horizontal shaft with a 10 foot ceiling. Then you come to the apparent end of the cave, there you slide head first into what is called the Birth Canal, a 2 foot wide, muddy clay tube going almost vertically down. [This is where the cave had once been blocked by mud and clay, then water carved a narrow passage to lower levels.] After the Birth Canal you crawl almost 25 yards thru a muddy tunnel about 24 inches or so wide and sometimes 15 inches high. Going in I was last among the group of 20, mostly from a cave club in Atlanta. [Later I discovered that a Tallahassee friend's daughter, Gail, is a member of the Atlanta club.]

At the end of the workday somehow I became mixed into the group (not at the end where I desired) and found myself squirming in this small tunnel with someone's boots inches from my face and someone else inches behind my boots. We were hot and steam rose from our bodies and my mind created extreme anxiety, but I held together and concentrated on counting the pebbles in the mud just under my nose. What a relief climbing back out of what became a narrow, claustrophobic challenge.

A side tale is that inside the cave I met an attractive, adventurous woman that excited my interest. She had sustained a back injury from a mishap in Ellison Cave near Chattanooga. [This has the deepest, unobstructed, in-cave, pitch in continental America at 596 feet and was particularly difficult because you are sometimes immersed in a cold waterfall. A few years ago a guy became stuck in multiple ropes in the falls and died of hypothermia. In 2011 two University of Florida students also died after being stuck 'on rope'.] Anyway, in the darkness it's difficult to tell when you reach bottom; on the wet rope she rappelled too fast; landed too hard and injured her back. I was anxious to talk with her after we exited the cave. Back on the surface the farmer's wife had made us cookies; then we changed into clean clothes and drove to a local restaurant. Sitting around the table I couldn't find the woman who interested me. Finally I realized her identity and in the light of day looked completely different for how she appeared inside the cave. She appeared more like a troglodyte than a beauty.

I regret not ever 'doing' Ellison cave. Twice I was set for this adventure; however both expeditions failed to occur. Too bad, that would have been a magnificent quest.

Of interest to me are the stories by club members about coming out of caves late at nite; going out to eat and have locals claiming they were devil worshipers going underground performing all sorts of strange rituals.

A Halloween tradition of the FSU cave club was to crawl under the FSU campus. For this experience there were about 10 of us, including Linda. Thinking back I find it difficult to believe she did this unless she just wanted to do something exciting with me. First we walked thru an underground drainage culvert and entered a pipe about 2 feet in diameter. The objective was to get to the steam tunnels, but I'm not sure who was leading or whether they knew the way. My worry was that one of these pipes came from a chemistry lab that dumped acid or something worse. After some time we came up thru a manhole at the swimming pool and several of us had had enough. I understood that some crawlers ended up in Landis Green and never did find the steam tunnels. Sometimes I really wonder about why I do some of the things I do. As my family would say, 'Oh, that's just another Barry Trip'.

As a kid (in Ocala) I was always trying to find the cave that no one had explored. Near my home there was a small sinkhole. I dug and dug, but never got it to open into that magical cave. One cave that comes to mind was in what was called Roosevelt Village. You went into a big sink; thru a small hole and into a large room with a stream running thru. Wading along the stream there were small passages out from the sides. In some you could look down into deep pools, into crystal clear water that gradually turned blue with depth. We found lots of 30 million year old marine fossils, but one was special. It was a complete Blue Crab. This Crab looked so real that at times it seemed as if it could walk again.

Claustrophobia is a form of anxiety that runs in my family and it took me over 60 years to realize how it originates. When I was an infant my crib had a lid, to keep out the insects. I think this may have originally stimulated my condition, although my siblings also share this condition. The first episode I recall was in Waycross Georgia, when I found myself under a mass of midget level football players. Throughout my life I didn't let this restrict my adventures. As a youngster while exploring caves, when I became stuck or in a tight place I would close my eyes and think rational thoughts until my paranoia subsided. For some reason temperature accelerates the anxiety. I have always been active, for example after school I was never on the couch watching TV, I was running in the woods; building a fort; digging tunnels; searching for caves etc. Sometimes I'd just run. In school, if the subject or presentation wasn't interesting to me I would drift off into my imagination. Looking back, during those years I would remark that I had a short attention span. While in college I would sometimes study with a group and know the subject better than most, however during the exam I'd become anxious and 'go blank'. They would make A's and B's and I'd make a C. Judy and I divorced after almost 20 years and found that I couldn't concentrate, while hundreds of images and words hurdling thru my brain. Of course this was extreme anxiety and still I didn't recognize it as such. Although having a certain amount of anxiety is normal and is an integral component of normal fight or flight behavior. Now there is a 'politically correct term for what I've had all my life, ADD (Attention Deficit Disorder), or at this point in my life: AADD (Adult ADD).

In the FSU club several of the cavers (not speleologists, meaning profession researchers) were into vertical caving. That's where you rappel down a free-standing rope and climb back vertically up the same rope. Most of this is done in pits (sinkholes) and understandably is called 'doin' pits'. At the bottom, many pits have horizontal caves that can then be explored. In Tallahassee we trained on ropes tied in a huge Oak tree; followed by a test with club members and finally it was time for my first, vertical caving trip. The name of my first pit was **Neversink** (in northern Alabama) and was about 200 feet to the bottom and we did it twice, once at nite. Later (I believe this was my second trip to TAG: the area where Tennessee, Alabama and Georgia join) on a hillside in Tennessee we had been doin' pits all day; it began to rain, but we continued (the physical exertion keeping us warm) but darkness was falling, so we headed down. [Let me explain that I was 50 years old and the other guys were in their 20's. After a day of caving I was a bit tired. Also imagine the gear: a backpack heavy with climbing gear; carabineers, food and water, canvas pads, helmet, lights and batteries and over your shoulder 100 to 300 feet of climbing rope]. Now the cold rain is really coming down and it's almost dark. We are climbing down a vertical, 30 foot cliff; I grabbed a rock I thought was stable; it wasn't and I fell. Fortunately I fell into a tree below and only slightly sprained my ankle. I'm not normally a macho guy, but do have a certain old guy image and hate to be dependent on someone else. My buddy, Gary, volunteered to carry my rope, but I declined. By now water was sheet flowing across the ground, thankfully the deeper streams gave temporary relief to my painful ankle. However, as we crossed a newly plowed field my boots would stick in the mud and produce some unkindly pain. We finally got back to my VW bus, with a heater that failed to warm us. Arrived at camp only to discover the wind had blown over my tent, even though I had placed extra weight in the corners. Much of our sleeping gear was also wet, including my sleeping bag. Two of the guys chickened out, then returned to Tallahassee and Ron left his tent for me to use. Half of the floor was a puddle of water, but I was tired and believe I actually slept.

In the morning the temperature was below freezing. I recall my wet jeans crackling when I pulled them on. They wanted to do one more cave, **War Eagle**, and I didn't want to hold them up. When we arrived at the site a fierce north wind was blowing and the chill factor had to be near zero. My ankle hurt so bad I had to crawl up the hill to the cave. Now this cave has a difficult lip and is a real bear to get back over, however the cave was supposed to be spectacular. Against better judgment I rappelled in, not knowing if my ankle would allow me to get back up the rope. The drop was around 80 feet and inside was a huge column shaped like the space shuttle. The floor was muddier than I wanted and since I'd have to crawl I waited there in the relative warmth of the 50 degree cave. As I heard them returning from up the stream I began to climb and to my delight I could hold my ankle at an obtuse angle that wasn't too painful. But the flowstone at the lip was a real challenge. The surface was smooth, like hard plastic, and to move forward (overcoming my full weight) I'd struggle to lift my Jumars off the surface. Eventually I survived, crawled back down the mountain then we drove back to Tally. That night I kept thinking: '*Is this really fun?*' And sometimes, '**Really,** *why am I doing this?*'

A few years ago I was told that a 'risk gene' had been discovered, so I've determined that I must have it. People with this gene are: thrill seekers; pursue novelty actions and are rewarded with systemic dopamine. Some studies also ascribe: enhanced sexual enjoyment; a tendency toward multiple sex partners and a liberal predisposition. Of course genetic predisposition doesn't guarantee that a person will exhibit all these characteristics, however I am guilty.

SCUBA DIVING ADVENTURES

You can either be a victim of the world or an adventurer in search of treasure. It all depends on how you view life.

I began swimming at age 6, continuing being a 'water rat' all my life. When I was 8 or 9 I began snorkeling with mask and fins and in my teens experienced scuba a few times, but didn't have my own gear until I was in the Air Force. At that time I could use my limited funds for flight lessons or purchase scuba gear, either could certainly lead to adventure. However I chose scuba partially because a friend and I had discussed diving for gold in the rivers of the Sierra Nevada Mountains, east of Sacramento California. We had gone into the Sierras; successfully panned some gold, so our plan was to buy a small dredge and seriously retrieve gold from the rivers. Well, as fate would have it, just as we bought our scuba gear he was transferred to a base in Oklahoma. Soon dredging for gold using diving gear became very popular (as well as profitable) and I still see folks dredging in the rivers of the Sierras.

The nearest suitable diving to Mather AFB was in Lake Folsom (the one that Johnny Cash's song made famous) and where Judy's family lived before the dam. I recall 4 dives, all different and noteworthy. One was when I ran out of air and surfaced far from shore in an electrical storm. My overriding thought was that I had a metal lightening rod strapped to my back. Another trip was with the woman I was teaching to scuba dive. The third followed my construction of a high powered spear gun, built using an aircraft fire extinguisher filled with 2000 psi of air. As a test, I shot a Bass; the shaft sailed thru the fish; disappeared and was forever lost. The last dive was with another guy and we were going deep; however around 80 feet he began to suffer from nitrogen narcosis and became disoriented. I ascended a ways with him; he seemed to be OK at that depth, so I continued down alone. I don't recall how deep I dove, but it was more than 150 feet.

I was diving in the American River (near Sacramento); surfaced and was almost run over by a car. It was one of those amphibious cars that just happened to be in my way, or was I in his path? I recall diving for Crawfish with the dive club at the base. This was in the cold water just below the Folsom dam where I discovered that the Crawfish here are a quarter the size of Florida Crawfish. Then there was diving at Sloughouse on the Consumnes River and a trip to Baja Mexico. On that second dive, just out from shore the bottom dropped out to more than 100 feet where these spires of rock rose from the depths below. All of a sudden something blocked my vision and my first thought was I was being swallowed by a Shark, however it was Sea Lion. I did spear a Sheephead fish, which became a meal for the 3 of us. On our way thru San Diego we ended up in jail, but that's another story.

Then there were a couple of really cold dive trips for Abalone up the coast from San Francisco, one leading to my marriage to Judy, previously described. For much of my adult life the only real suit I owned was a wet suit, I guess that says something about my priorities and interests.

When we returned to Florida Judy and I lived in a fantastic house over the Santa Fe River at Poe Springs, I mean the water was below our porch. I dove that area of the Santa Fe so many times that I knew every log; rock and spring for miles. The Santa Fe is a world renowned location for Pleistocene fossils and many were under our porch; ancient Horse, Camel; Manatee and just down river were two perfect Mammoth Teeth. [Unfortunately David dropped one of the teeth and Michelle's friend dropped the second tooth.] Most of my diving was in the Santa Fe; Ichetucknee and Suwanee Rivers for fossils and Indian artifacts. To the Paleontologists (at the University of Florida) the most interesting fossil I found was from a flightless bird, the Terror Bird. Later I discovered that a High School friend from Ocala was first to discover bones of the Terror Bird. Although I didn't know it at the time, but Donald and Ben had been diving this area the same time as me. Also I moved many rocks from the mouth of Poe Springs in an attempt to gain entrance to the cave there.

Several places along the river have what we call 'sucks'; places where part of the river flows in sinkholes, then into to the subterranean water system.

76

Below the Lake City Bridge I recall swimming from water less than 2 feet deep; over the edge of a suck where the void seemed bottomless, an experience that elicits a bit of apprehension. Usually the water flowing into the suck swirls like a bathtub drain, fortunately sluggishly. Just downstream there is a deep hole in the limestone bottom that locals claim is bottomless, of course I had to check it out and it is not more than 20 feet deep.

Upriver from the Lake City Bridge is where the entire river disappears underground before reappearing at The Rise. The Santa Fe isn't the only river in Florida doing the disappearing act, the Aucilla river (near Tallahassee) also plunges into the limestone karst; periodically reappears; rises just below where the Wacissa River enters, then continues on down to the Gulf of Mexico.

This area of North Florida is the center of cave diving in America, so the opportunity beckoned me. Since I didn't have anyone to accompany me I was a mite unsafe or looking back, extremely foolish, when I'd dive alone with one tank; one light; no safety line and usually no one knowing where I was diving. I also took additional chances like diving a cave on the Ichetucknee River where I'd have to remove my tank; push it before me and wiggle thru a narrow opening. Obviously I survived however during one year 23 divers didn't make it out alive. I was at Gennie Spring just after 3 guys from Tampa had drowned. In a cave you don't get a second chance, these guys made a big mistake and an incorrect assumption. In that cave you swim thru a narrow, but wide opening over piles of rocks, then drop down to the passage level. Actually what you first swim over is where the roof had collapsed. Well, they had a safety line, but kicked up bottom silt, first mistake. So when they returned to the drop-off, in the poor visibility they could see the safety line in between the rocks and assumed there had been a cave-in, fatal mistake. They used all their air trying to dig their way out when all they had to do was swim up just a few feet and safely exit. The wife of one of the divers was so distraught that she sold her husband's dive gear to the first person who'd give her a few dollars.

Directly across from our house was a small sink that dropped down 20 feet to a cave. I built a platform above and planned to dive the cave, thinking it connected to Poe Springs, however (in 1964) a hurricane passed thru; the river rose 18 feet (3 feet into our house) and by the time the river cleared we had moved to Tallahassee.

After I completed Community College (in Lake City) we moved to Tallahassee where I entered Florida State University. Of course I continued to dive, in rivers and the Gulf of Mexico. I met two math professors from FSU and we dove sinkholes in the area, searching for caves. I recall one cave containing pure white, blind Crawfish, with red eyes. We dove in some extremely turbid water because we knew that once you reach a spring the water would be clear.

Later I volunteered to be on the Research Dive Team for OAR, Organization for Artificial Reefs. One episode I recall was during training; Richard and I were together; approached a concrete pipe and inside was a huge Jewfish [now called a Goliath Grouper] weighing more than 200 pounds. As I looking at the fish from one end, Richard was at the other end trying to coax the fish out in my direction.

With OAR we surveyed sites for the location of artificial reefs; assisted with the deployment of the reef material and had contracts with several counties to assess the success of the reef by identifying natural growth and fish.

We would spearfish off-shore, however we'd have to boat out 12-15 miles to reach 30-40 feet of water. Without electronic gear they would drag me behind the boat so I could locate a rocky bottom. Around that time I had spoken with a guy from Steinhatchee who had a towable submarine and told me about a Tiger Shark that rammed the craft, trying to get him out. So naturally I kept an eagle eye, fore and aft, for any approaching Tigers. I think I previously describe my Shark encounter when I was diving around some rocks and had bloody fish in my wet suit.

Also I spearfished off the rock jetty at Panama City; sunken boats off Cape San Blas [I recall when I dove on a sunken shrimp boat and that evening saw that the waters were seething with a congregation of Hammerhead Sharks]; many dives in the Wakulla; Aucilla and St Marks Rivers; a couple of springs around Ocala; down in the Florida Keys; some Springs and caves in North Florida and off-shore at K Tower.

I had taken **The Rose** out to K Tower which was placed by the Air Force to record dogfights by jet fighters. Of course the sign said not to tie to the tower, but no one was around. So here we are spearfishing then spy a large orange AF boat rapidly approaching. As they neared the tower we expected lots of yelling and serious trouble, however, to our relief they lined the decks and began fishing. There were some Amberjack nearby so I speared some and handed them up to the people on deck, after fishing they removed the recorders from the tower and zoomed away.

After returning from Australia Judy; Michelle and I settled near Cutler Ridge south of Miami. [Interestingly our 2 year old daughter heard us say Miami assuming this as the singular version of 'Your Ami'.] David and his wife Diane came down and met us at Big Pine Island (in the Florida Keys), where we camped. Out in their boat we were spearfishing and through the clear water spotted Grouper, so as we jumped in the ocean, David tells the women to drop the anchor. There were Groupers everywhere, so soon we both had speared one. We surfaced to see the boat drifting far away; I left my fish with David and swam toward the boat to discover that they had indeed thrown the anchor, but it wasn't attached to the boat. Getting back into the boat I began searching for David, however the sea had kicked up a bit and we couldn't see him anywhere. Eventually we found him and returned to find the anchor.

We returned to Tallahassee and for a short time I was associated with the FSU dive club, although I really didn't like the macho atmosphere. The State Archeologist approached the club to recruit some divers to look at a gunboat in the Apalachicola River. A dredge had discovered a Union gunboat and the State wanted the serial numbers from the boiler. A group of us anchored over the wreck site and this 'super diver', who wore 12 knives; 16 watches and depth gauges and every bell and whistle he could find in a dive shop, floundered off the stern of the boat and was rapidly swept away by the swift current. Rather than diving, he panicked; his perception narrowed to getting back to the boat and he almost drowned. We screamed at him to swim to shore; finally he lost his obsession of getting back to the boat and managed to get to shore, just a few feet away. I said let's stop this foolishness; go upstream; tie the boat to a tree and work back down a rope to the boiler.

In 1984 I organized a trip to the Bahamas for my siblings; spouses and friends. Well the 14 of us terrorized the island of Eleuthera and snorkeled the reefs around the island, mostly for fish; Conch and out of season Lobsters, locally called Summer Crabs. The only scuba we did was from a dive boat and the boat operator didn't have enough buoyancy compensators so I just put a scuba tank in a bag over my shoulder. I recall Patty and I diving deep to face a large Grouper and Joe fighting off a gaggle of Grouper with his fists. Evidently other tour boats fed the Grouper and they would aggressively approach divers, so Joe had to smack one on the chin. Overall this trip to Eleuthera was a hedonistic adventure: with wrecked car; unholy amounts of rum; nude bathing and sun burned buns.

After several years in Tallahassee we moved our fleet of boats to the Florida Keys expecting oodles of great diving in clear water, however the reefs have degenerated and the visibility wasn't like it was 40 years before, when I first dove there. Our first winter there was frustrating because this was a particularly windy year and the visibility was dreadful. The clearest water along The Keys was at Looe Key, off Big Pine Island. Other dives involved my sister Patty and her kids (Pete and Sara) who came down and we dove the reefs at Looe Key, using my hooka outfit.

In our marina at Coco Plum was a treasure hunting boat that had located a Spanish wreck just off-shore. The galleon had rolled in the shallow water depositing artifacts every few hundred feet. As far as I know he failed to discover a treasure, but recovered some coins; swords and platters.

I was diving at what is called a Nigger Head, Oh, currently that's not politically correct. I was diving at a coral head; could see a huge Green Moray Eel; was looking deep into the coral for his head; looked up and just inches from my head was the Moray opening and closing his mouth exposing his needlelike teeth.

I recall diving with Linda off Key West; under a ledge I had discovered a large Nurse Shark; wanted to show her, so led her down to the ledge and as she peered under she was only inches from the Shark. Really I didn't mean to frighten her, but that didn't prevent her from scolding me and she will remember that episode until the day she dies.

Just off Coco Plum I had speared a Grouper and as I was swimming back to the boat a large Barracuda darted by and sliced off half the fish. I really didn't want to give up the half-fish, but if you have ever looked into the eye of a large Barracuda and observed his assortment of nasty teeth you'd agree that I did the right thing by leaving him the remaining fish.

In 1991 I solo sailed to Central America for the adventure and exploration, however ever present in my mind was the Spanish treasure I'd discover. I'd fantasize how the treasure would allow me to fulfill my wanderlust by exploring the world; find that cave behind the waterfall on a deserted island; visit archeological sites in far corners of earth; dive the reefs and ships of the South Pacific; boat the entire Amazon River; go on many Africa safaris and on and on, always searching for my next great adventure.

I had bought an underwater housing for my video camera and while visited Belize was told that this full moon was when the Groupers gather to reproduce. I'd seen this phenomenon on a Jacque Cousteau show where thousands of Grouper gather in a small area of the reef. I sailed out to an island (actually an atoll) to where the Groupers were to perform, however the sea had kicked up and anchoring was a chore. Thrashing around in **The Rose** I put my camera into the case; dove the 40 feet to the bottom; there were Groupers everywhere, however the problem was that I could see water filling the case, so rushed to the surface where the waves were really tossing me about. I tried to pull the anchor chain, but it was stuck and no matter what I did would not release. I donned my diving gear dove back to 40 feet and removed the chain from a clump of coral. Back at the surface again I tried to pull the anchor, no luck, so this was becoming ridicules. I returned to the bottom; untangled the chain and carefully laid it out in the sand and this was finally successful. Quickly I motored behind the reef and washed the video camera in fresh water and alcohol, I didn't know what else to do. It made a feeble attempt to come back to life, but soon could see that this was fruitless. Evidently, in the rocking boat, I'd gotten a strap over the O ring that prevents water from entering the case. So, at the beginning of my year-long expedition I'd lost my only camera.

I dove some reefs off Mexico's Yucatan Peninsula, then some reefs off Belize, where I took a couple of young women from England on **The Rose** and was warned by the chief of the boat guides that I was not to do that again or else. He said, ***"I know where you leave your sailboat at anchor."***

Also I dove along reefs along the southern shore of Roatan in Honduras.

One of the best dives in my life was on the north side of Guanaja with a fellow sailor who had been a Pan Am pilot. This was along a high wall with a deep overhang where shafts of sunlight streamed thru. He had dived all over the world and also said it was one of his best dives.

Off Guanaja I was diving at nite and suddenly something covered the front of my mask and that always gives you a start; however it was just an Octopus who was just being friendly.

An advantage to being a scrounger is that I could always get seafood, so I'd shoot some Grouper; catch Crabs and Lobster; take them to other sailboats and they would happily prepare dinner. One nite was on a Catamaran from the Cayman Islands and what a meal: hors d'oeuvre of Shrimp on a huge platter; broiled Grouper and Lobster and dessert, all served with wine.

Another dinner was on a boat with a friendly couple who were at least 70 years old who had sailed from Washington thru the Panama Canal and were heading up the US East Coast via the Intracoastal Waterway. They had gone to the Settlement (on Guanaja Island) for fresh hamburger; the full moon was rising over the ocean; the water crystal clear and there was a slight breeze rustling the Palm Trees on shore; there was ice in my rum drink and they served me <u>The Cheeseburger in Paradise</u>.

After leaving Guanaja I dove off the north shore of Roatan, then sailed overnight to Lighthouse Reef (off Belize) where I dove 140 feet in the Blue Hole. This is the sinkhole were Jacque Cousteau anchored the **Calypso** and dove with submersibles.

I also dove off Isla Mujeres but didn't make it off-shore to see the sleeping Sharks.

After an eventful sail from Mexico to Dry Tortugas (near Key West) we anchored; I went for a dive and saw Lobsters so big they were scary. Although this is a National Park I had to have one Lobster and it was so large that it lasted for two meals.

After getting back to Tallahassee Linda wanted to be in the Bahamas for Christmas and that resulted in the end of 18 years of adventure in **The Rose** and with the loss of my diving gear the last time I scuba dived.

HORSETHIEF AND BEAR CREEK

HIGH ALTITUDE BACKPACKING WITH JOE, CHARLIE AND BARRY

Do not follow where the path may lead. Go where there is no path and leave a trail. Marial Shrode

The year following the 'discovery' of Silverton Colorado by Michelle and me, next year my goal was to spend the entire summer. In Silverton there was a business, The X Club, mostly catering to the extreme skiers. I had heard about backpacking to Chicago Basin and quizzed Michael, the owner, about hiking there. Since I had just arrived from flat Florida he suggested a less difficult backpacking trip, Cimarron Creek, the trip that almost killed me. So I still wanted to get to Chicago Basin and considered it during subsequent visits. Last year (2011) Joe and I drove to Missionary Ridge, above Durango, and he suggested we backpack into Chicago Basin and backtrack out because he couldn't take his dog, Charlie, on the train. Well next year I proposed that we backpack into Chicago Basin and hike the 14 miles up the railroad tracks back to Silverton. While Joe was backpacking in Alaska I finally computed the miles and the trip would be 40 miles, further than I wanted to go. So I proposed an alternative trip: from north of Capitol City; along an old cattle Driveway; then over to the Horsethief Trail and across Bridge of Heaven.

Joe committed to the backpacking trip; even though it has been raining every day for a while and I was not excited about hiking in the rain, however I agreed to go, rather than waiting. We dropped Tonja off at the tunnel just after Bear Creek and Joe drove us past Ouray and several miles up into the mountains. The trailhead was in an Aspen Forest, over 9,000 feet in elevation. On the map there were several streams and we <u>assumed</u> water would not be an issue, so didn't carry an adequate supply. After crossing several stream beds it became clear that this area (of similar elevation as Silverton) had little snow and no water. I think the warm air from the lowlands (where Grand Junction lies) caused the snow to melt early.

The trail steeply swithbacked up the mountains and we were rising 1000 feet per mile! Around noon we struggled to an area above the treeline and talked with some day-hikers who pointed out the mountain we had to get over to reach Bridge of Heaven. We were now approaching 12,000 feet and in the thin air I had to constantly pant to get enough oxygen.

When I would take a drink of water there would a moment of panic (as if I was suffocating), because just a moment without panting didn't provide enough oxygen to this Florida boy.

Again we started steeply up and I was hoping that the trail passed around, not over, the mountain before us. However this was not to be so. We came to a creekbed; I was exhausted; Joe was also tired so we rested and gazed up at the saddle, hundreds of vertical feet above. Slogging up that trail I could not keep a steady pace and was reduced to 'baby steps. By the time we arrive at Bridge of Heaven (elevation: 12,368') we were above almost all the nearby mountains.

Bridge of Heaven

To the south was Red Mountain Number 1; to the west the Yankee Boy road; to the north the lowlands toward Montrose and 5000 feet below, Ouray. Unfortunately clouds almost covered the sky; there were fresh tracks of Big Horn Sheep, but none in sight. Also we couldn't determine how we were to get across the mountains to the east, they looked much steeper than I wanted. I had <u>assumed</u> that the trail was relatively level down to Difficulty Creek. Wrong again!

When I lived in Florida I considered 10,000 feet as an extreme height. Linda and I jumped from an airplane at 12,000 feet. Now, here I am hiking above that elevation.

Took some photos and were relieved to start down, <u>very down</u>. After swithbacking steeply down the mountain we crossed a meadow and, to my chagrin, started up again. Passed over a tributary of Cascade Creek where we hoped to find water, however it too was dry. Now the clouds had darkened and thunder reverberated throughout the valleys. We came to a flat area, suitable for camping, but really needed water so continued along the side of a mountain. I did get a great photo of Joe and Charlie (his dog) as rain began to fall.

Soon we passed steeply down to Cascade Creek and were extremely disappointed to find it very dry. This is a major creek that feeds a huge waterfall above Ouray, yet it was dry as a bone. I was totally exhausted and really wanted just to find a level place to camp, however there wasn't a flat area anywhere nearby. I suggested that we dig in the creek bed to see if subterranean water might be there. It was strange that there was no snow at this elevation, yet around Silverton considerable snow abounded. Before us was another saddle at 12,240 feet. Now I could barely walk, I wasn't that winded, but it was that my legs were pooped. I suggest that Joe go over the saddle and look for water, but he wouldn't leave me. After what seemed to be hours we reached the crest and plopped down beside a sign for the Weminuche Wilderness. I was getting headaches from lack of water and my throat felt like the skin was falling off. Then we heard what sounded like running water. Sure enough, off to the south, we spied a small waterfall. Rejuvenated, we started down; found a shallow creek and finally found an almost level area to pitch our tents. Now it was 6:30 pm and we had traversed only 6 and a half miles in 8 ½ hours! That's less than one mile an hour.

Over Joe's new alcohol stove (made from a beer can) we boiled water for instant potatoes and by 7 o'clock I was in my sleeping bag. As soon as we lost the sun the temperature precipitously dropped to 42 degrees and I was somewhat concerned whether I'd be warm enough in the nite. My socks were wet, but I didn't have the energy to put on a fresh pair.

Somewhere in 'dark 30' I awoke, probably 5 am as usual, and could hear Coyotes howling nearby. My plan was not to get up until the sun hit my tent. So finally the sun arrived, I got up and immediately the sun hid behind some clouds. Typically the mornings are clear, so this was not a good sign. After a while the sun broke free, we had oatmeal; hot chocolate; packed and left around 9 am.

At a fork the trail sign had been knocked down so it was not clear which trail was the correct one. When we arrived at Difficulty Creek we had assumed we must head up that creek, however it turned out that this was not the actual creek, but a tributary. Still not certain if we were on the correct trail we hiked up to what appeared to be Difficulty Creek. Looking up to the saddle from where we started it didn't look too difficult, however that was another false assumption.

Along the way were fresh Elk tracks and scat and animal trails along the slopes, but no Elk; Big Horn Sheep or Deer. Again I was barely moving. If I had been alone I would have stopped every couple hundred yards, but Joe was pushing ahead although he was also tired and at intervals briefly rested. [Note that Joe is 30 years younger than me.] By the time we got to mid climb I could see that this was NOT going to be a 'walk in the park'. We moved away from the creek and slowly trudged up the steep mountainside. Now the clouds darkened and thunder 'welcomed' us. It was now urgent that we get over the saddle before the lightening arrived. We were well above the treeline and, next to Florida; Colorado has the most lightening caused deaths. Joe was apprehensive about the lightening and was really pushing to get over the top. I was less concerned, since I've never before been struck by lightning and I told Joe to go on over the top, but he stayed with me. A very frigid wind preceded the storm and felt like it would blow us off the mountain. We were relieved that most of the lightening passed to the north. Note that we were at 12,600 feet, twice as high as Mt Mitchell, the highest mountain in the East. As we passed down the south side, even darker clouds approached. At this elevation hail is common, so we hiked up a steep, rocky area to get behind a rock cliff and just as we arrived the hail began and the lightening rocked the mountains. One strike bolted off a nearby mountain top.

Next we followed a relatively level valley with recent evidence of the passage of a large number of Sheep. [In summer, Sheep are allowed by the BLM to graze in these mountains, attended by Peruvian herders and their dogs.] To the east was Wildhorse Peak at 13,266 feet. Again, as we neared the crest another electrical storm passed nearby. We were relieved to find a sign that indicted the direction to Bear Creek.

I have no problem while hiking on level ground with a 35 pound pack, however as soon as I start up the difficulty level becomes punishing. I have never seen what at first seems to be the mountain crest and actually be the top of the crest and this was true to that observation. I slowed trudged up the ridge hoping that it was the top and of course it was not, nor was the second, but finally the third ridge. I was really, really tired now, but could not rest. The storm with intense lightening was rapidly approaching and we needed to quickly get below the crest. Since there were no trees at this elevation we were the highest point, i.e. human lightning rods. A post could be seen to the south, so Joe was concerned that we were not on the correct trail. I assured him that the post was for the Engineer Mountain trail and this was the Bear Creek 'trail'. Actually you couldn't see a trail, just cairns here and there. Once over the crest (at 12,640 feet) the frigid wind was ferocious; to compound that nuisance, the cold rain came in sideways right into our faces; footing was a problem, due to the high wind and the loose shale rocks and I almost tumped over more than once. The lightening was now very close and we urgently needed to get below, however the trail switchbacked making progress down agonizingly slow.

Finally we got well below the crest; the electrical storm moved away, leaving only rain and we hiked along the headwaters of the Bear Creek. The plan was to camp in the trees below, where we would build a huge fire to dry our gear and warm our bodies. It was still a mile down to the treeline and was swampy in places, so our boots were not staying dry; then we came to an area where the trail disappeared and we waded thru water soaked weeds 4 feet high. This appeared to be an old roadbed from the mining days; everything was wet and soon my feet were soaked. At one point we had to jump over Bear Creek, no easy task with a backpack. Finally we came to the trees and a nice place to camp, but the rain persisted. Below was where a deep gorge came in from the south and the trail to Engineer summit. At this point we decided to just hike the final 4.6 miles and savor the warmth of the truck heater.

Going down I was surprised at how steep the trail became. We stopped at a log cabin, with logs hewn with an adz; where I suggested staying, but Joe was concerned that the building was leaning and could collapse; so we pressed on; now my thighs and calves were really hurting, but my knees weren't too painful. Next we stopped at the Yellow Jacket Mine to view the equipment. Below were multiple waterfalls and later along the trail were washouts and scrambling over wet rocks with a backpack was not without apprehension. In places it was hundreds of feet down to the creek, a slip could be fatal.

[You can see Joe in the upper right corner of the photo.]

LOWER BEAR CREEK TRAIL

The rain finally let up a bit, but the sky remained cloudy. Crossing a creek of slippery rocks Joe fell and hurt his shin that he had injured in Alaska. A little while later, as I was rubber necking, I stepped into a hole and tumbled down. By now I just wanted to get down to Tonja and get the heater going. In the first part of the trail we were a hundred or so feet above Bear Creek and later near the creek, then back UP! The last section of the trail was a narrow path at least 300 feet above the creek. My legs felt like they would turn to jelly and off the cliff I'd tumble.

We stopped for a rest and I really didn't want to get back up. My legs hurt from top to bottom and now my back was in pain. The last part of the trail switchbacked hundreds of feet straight down to hiway 550.

The only factor that kept me going was that Tonja was down there and soon I'd be still and warm. It was after 6pm before we got down, and then drove to a Mexican restaurant in Ouray for dinner, although I wasn't really hungry. Then it took forever to get up the rocky road to where Joe left his Toyota and 8pm before I returned to Maybellene and crashed.

Thus ending another adventure. Overall it was an enjoyable trip, but I'm not sure how many more years I'll be able to repeatedly climbing above 12,000 feet. Joe and Dean wanted to do a 4 day backpack next week but I declined. Not that I couldn't do it, but I didn't want them to go slow and have to wait for me and I was packed to go up to the Tetons and Yellowstone.

August 27, 2011

ROSE BUD FROM DEADMAN'S POND (Nova Scotia)

Destiny is not a matter of chance. It is a matter of choice. It is not a thing to be waited for. It is a thing to be achieved.

Jenny Bryant

[**Rose Bud** is my 10 foot dinghy that used to live with my sailboat, ***The Rose***.]

By 6:30 **Rose Bud** and I were on the water (in Deadman's Pond) at Bay St. Lawrence, Nova Scotia. I was somewhat apprehensive since the engine hadn't run since I last had it apart and ***Rose Bud*** hadn't been in the water since the last major patching. To have the engine die or ***Rose*** fill with water out in the Gulf of St. Lawrence would not be good, especially with the strong current out to the frigid North Atlantic, however I did take several flares in case we were stranded offshore. Everything looked good: calm wind and the waves not too high, so we motored offshore heading due north searching for Humpback Whales. Shortly the sea became confused (waves from all directions); then began to build and trekking became very uncomfortable. Soon the incoming waves were much higher than where I was sitting and beginning to break, so I decided to head back toward shore before we took a wave over the bow.

Saw some Whales near shore, but it was too rough to take pictures; then the wind really began to scream; we pulled up on a sandy beach, beside a scenic rock arch. Picked up pebbles and waited for the sun to get on the arch so I could take photos. The sky was clear until 8:30 and just as I was about to take a photo clouds showed up. To get out of the wind I motored on around toward Cape North. Decided to risk going thru a narrow cut, with crashing surf on the shoreside and a rocky island to seaward. So at the critical moment what happens, the engine begins to die; I leaped forward to pump up the gas and got her going before being blown ashore. Around the point were huge Harbour Seals, but they wouldn't approach the boat. Motored on east to the Cape North lighthouse, the farthest north you can go in Nova Scotia. Around the point I could see heads of about 50 Seals, but they dove as we approached. The wind continued to build and the ride back was a bitch. Didn't get as wet as expected, but sometimes **Rose Bud** was airborne and she would crash down with a spike shocking jolt. Then the clouds became thicker, I was cold, so cancelled the plan to motor down to Meat Cove.

BIRD ISLAND

Got on the water before 6 am, just as the sun broke into a clear sky and the sea was probably as flat as it ever gets. Got to Bird Island, actually 2 islands, and could see only a few Puffins. As in Alaska the multitudes of Kittiwakes were nesting in the rock cliffs, along with Cormorants; Guillemots and Murres. On the shadow side of the islands there were more Puffins, but almost all flew away before we got close. Here, Puffins are called Sea Parrots, which is more descriptive. Frustrated at not getting good Puffin photos, we slowly motored along the rocks, not too worried since the surf was subdued. Saw a couple of Eagles take flight from the rocks, with Kittiwakes diving at them; then headed toward St. Ann's Bay and straight into a building wind. I sincerely dislike pounding into a heavy sea, especially when **Rose Bud** comes out of the water and slams down with a jarring crash. Sometimes I can feel the collision in my back and neck. The real hassle was getting thru the tangle of Lobster trap lines. The ropes lay out across the water, sometimes for 30 feet and with the changing current and wind we picked up a few on the foot of the engine. In some places (at low tide) it's impossible to get thru this spaghetti of lines, some overlapping. Later I noticed the lobster boats running right over the lines. Earlier I had observed that the boat propellers are encased in wire, now I understand why. The Lobster fishery has almost collapsed, and it's no small wonder. There seems to be more traps than Lobsters. Like most fishermen, they overfish and now want the government to do something.

On the peninsula I walked along some beaches, although (tied to rocks on shore) keeping **Rose Bud** off the rocks was a chore. The wind dropped out a bit so we headed back to Bird Island and took more photos. Of all the birds the Puffins spook the first. I managed to get some halfway decent photos, but video from a rocking boat, with birds high on a cliff is less than ideal conditions. The ride back was bumpy, but not too uncomfortable. However loading the boat was a monumental hassle. Sometimes it goes smoothly and sometime not. If I had just a touch less strength I wouldn't be able to lift that heavy boat onto Sammie (my Suzuki Samurai).

HUMPBACK WHALES IN NEWFOUNDLAND

Rose Bud and I motored out into Witless Bay and were pleased to see the surface covered with birds and many Puffins. As we motored out to an island a pod of Whales surfaced nearby. We explored a couple islands in that area, then out into the North Atlantic Ocean. This water was COLD and reminded me that the Titanic sank just to the east of here. I was somewhat apprehensive, because the island would disappear behind the towering waves, but soon we were back along some islands, where on the east side towering waves crashed into the rocky shores. Returning to the original Island we motored real close to many Puffins, although getting good photos was difficult due to the confused waves. Suddenly a wave broke over **Rose Bud's** stern and wet both my cameras. This was not good, however the cameras seemed to be OK. In my travels I've gotten several cameras wet and they were not OK. [I just heard that OK originated in America and is now used throughout the world.]

We were just about to head back when I got a photo of a Humpback Whale breach.

The waves in the Atlantic had continued to build, so I was a little apprehensive about getting into the open ocean. However I 'needed' to get close to the whales. There was a whale tour boat nearby and I'm certain some of the people were alarmed to see this crazy guy in a 10 foot rubber boat out here among breaching Humpback Whales. I got some video of the whales as they playfully slapped their flippers and tails right next to *Rose Bud* and their breaches sending up torrents of water. I failed to consider that if a 50 foot Whale breached and came down on my little boat this would ruin my day. As I considered this option, a Whale was heading directly for my boat; just before he collided with *Rose Bud* he dove; I could clearly see his bulk slip below the surface just a few feet away. That certainly renewed my concern that I was a tiny speck in the North Atlantic in waves that frequently blocked my view of the tour boat or the horizon. However I didn't have time to contemplate what just happened because another Whale was approaching. I don't know whether the Whale was just being playful, but hoped he didn't dive too late and lift us from the sea. As with the first Whale he dove within a few feet of *Rose Bud*;

now all the Whales began moving into the bay, so I decided to return to shore. Not a typical day at sea.

A TREK INTO THE ROCKY MOUNTAINS

AND A FLIRT WITH DISASTER

We all live under the same sky, but we don't have the same horizon.

At age 62 (while in Silverton Colorado) I'd been going to the Explorers Pub (locally called the X Club) and Michael suggested some backpacking trips. One would be 5 or 6 days and being from Florida I was not yet acclimated to the altitude, since Silverton is situated at 9300 feet. So he suggested a 'warm up' hike, east of Ridgeway, the town where Chester of Gunsmoke fame had lived.

PRELUDE: First, I made some **assumptions** : (1) Michael said the trail was not steep, so I assumed this meant something less than a 1000 foot change in elevation. But this is from a guy who does extreme sports and was leaving for Nepal to backpack. (2) Ridgeway is at a lower elevation than Silverton, therefore warmer. I even took shorts. (3) Since it was June 9th and lower (i.e. warmer), the snow would be melted along the trail. (4) The trail would remain in a valley when I rounded the peaks at the south end of the trail. (5) The weather would stay the same as it had been all week, sunny. **All** these assumptions were entirely wrong, dangerously false!

THE ADVENTURE: Entered the Uncompahgre Wilderness at 9 am and the first mile or so (through the Aspens) was delightful. On my map the ridges to the east and west looked steep, but I had no idea that (for more than 2 thousand feet) they were actually vertical, however the craggy tops and waterfalls made them exceedingly scenic. For a while I passed thru an area with a jungle of fallen Aspens appearing as following a lumbering operation, but it was those very destructive Beavers that persistently gnaw and topple huge trees and only eat the tops and some limbs. [Speaking of Aspens, those are truly amazing plants. They can reproduce by cloning, so a whole forest may be just one plant. In fact they may be the world's largest organism and live for thousands of years! There is an Aspen forest in Utah with over 70,000 trees as one.]

After a while I encountered snow drifts across the trail, so I had to either scramble around in the woods or plow thru deep snow. Then, thunder, echoing throughout the canyon; this was followed by the pitter patter of hail/sleet, which periodically continued throughout the afternoon. However the real problem was the trail was going UP at a steeper and steeper angle.

After 5 or so miles I was becoming really tired. After stopping to rest I would have to pant for several minutes to get oxygen circulating back into my system. Now there were large areas where the snow entirely covered the ground and after getting to the other side of a deep, rocky gully I lost the trail. After a frustrating time I proceeded on up. As I trudged higher, my back was really hurting and the backpack seemed to gain weight by the foot. After about 7 miles I passed from the Fir/Spruce forest into a wide valley that reminded me of Alaska, both in topography and weather. The rocky river was braided; there were newly emerging grasses; patches of flowers; the air was now quite cool and there were numerous Elk and Deer tracks, as well as Bear scat. On this (what was called a 'relatively level') trail I had come up over 2000 feet. And it was obvious that no one had passed this way during this year.

Then I came to the remains of the Silver Jack Mine. Obviously it was destroyed by an avalanche, but something was amiss. The trees had fallen in the wrong direction, they lay up hill. Then, to my amazement, I realized that an avalanche had originated a quarter mile on the <u>other side of the river</u>; roared down the mountainside; crossed the river, then up about 300 yards where it crushed the mining complex.

Fortunately when I approached the East Fork of the Cimarron River there was a sunny interlude. I made sure my cameras were wrapped in plastic and found a limb to use as a walking stick. Since I knew the shock of wading in icy water I removed my boots and pants to allow my legs and feet to cool off. This seemed to be a good idea, but what does a Florida boy know. Reluctantly I stepped into the ice cold stream. Immediately my feet and legs were in shock. It's difficult to describe the numbing pain of wading in snow melt. Had to cross 3 braids of the swift river (some places almost crotch deep) with a bottom covered with tipsy rocks. More than once I was almost swept down the river. On the other side I lay in the grass and tried to warm my lower extremities. Finally, feeling returned, the adrenaline dissipated and tiredness returned.

Just above, the trail was obscured by a huge avalanche; there I learned something beneficial about avalanches. They produce tightly packed ice that you can walk over, whereas snowslides (or as the locals call them, slips) are soft snow that you sink into. Unfortunately the edges of avalanches are soft snow that you must plow thru, then jump up onto the frozen snow. The trail became steeper and I could see a herd of Elk above me. Briefly I envied an immature Bald Eagle who flew effortlessly over the valley. Oh, to be a bird. Next impediment was another stream that you could step over most of the year. But now I had to pile some rocks and leap and splash over, getting my boots and pants legs wet. I was still going up and was at an elevation well over 11,000 feet. The air was colder; my back was killing me; black clouds were racing over the peaks toward me; it was 7 pm, so I looked for a place to pitch my tent. Problem. The entire hill was water, sheet flowing over Tundra. Finally I found a somewhat flat, dry place in some trees.

During the nite more icy stuff fell from the heavens. I discovered that (at that elevation) you rarely have rain; what falls is either: hail, sleet or snow. Later I was awakened by what sounded like breathing outside my tent. After a while I rationalized that it was the wind rubbing limbs together. That thought was more soothing than the thoughts of a Bear ripping into the tent. [That happened to two friends in Tallahassee while backpacking in Alaska.] Overhead I could hear a jetliner and thought of the irony of those people in their warm seats, sipping wine, eating hors d'oeuvres, while a few thousand feet below I was being eaten by a Bear.

DAY FROM HELL

Got going at 7 am and for a mile the trail was relatively level and sensible. Saw some Elk; Big Horn Sheep and a pair of Mountain Blue Birds; then the trail abruptly turned up, extremely up! I was already weary and could make only a couple hundred yards at a time, before slumping down for a rest. Repeatedly I could see a place where I thought the trail might go (without going higher), but the trail proceeded eternally higher. I was surprised to see an English Sparrow alight on a rock nearby and while collapsed on the ground I also noticed a Caterpillar, some Ants, Flies and a Beetle. What a harsh life they live.

CREST SOUTH OF OWL CREEK PASS WHERE I BACKPACKED

Now I was over 12,000 feet and still going UP. This is the altitude that Linda and I parachuted from an airplane! At a point (which proved to be a half mile from the summit) all I could see were numerous sheets of snow. I was really in trouble now. Some of this snow was 10 or 15 feet thick and there was the thought of falling thru and not being found 'til spring thaw. Reluctantly I climbed higher than the trail to find snow that wasn't so deep and some rocky patches. Finally I had to commit. In first few feet of travel snow was up to my crotch, then, to my extreme relief, the top was frozen. However only a thin crust was frozen, so I gingerly crossed what was evidently an avalanche. The next one had a stream running under and I was quite apprehensive about falling thru the snow into the running water.

Had to cross about 10 snow patches to reach the summit, then complete shock! The valley below was completely **covered** in snow. I briefly considered turning back, but I detest backtracking and that would be accepting defeat. It was 11 am; I had covered less than 2 miles and had 12 more miles to go. On the north side of the pass I encountered a fierce, biting cold wind. An additional problem was that ominous, dark clouds were rushing in from the west; lightening was punishing the mountain tops and you do not want to be above the timberline in an electrical storm. I imagined that if I was hit, and my heart stopped, I would drop, chest first on a rock in an attempt to revive the pumping.

Most of this snow was not packed or frozen, so I had to plow thru it. But in a few places it was topped with a thin covering of ice, so I could sit on my butt and slide down. Of course between the icy places I'd have to trudge through snow where I'd sink 2 or 3 feet. The biggest danger was crossing over the streams running under the snow banks. In places I could find where the stream was snow free and could jump across, not an easy task with a heavy backpack.

Further into the valley the snow became deeper and lacked an ice crust. I was exhausted, but there was no place to stop and rest. I had no idea where the trail was, so followed the snow covered bank of a stream. The snow drifts (particularly behind trees or logs) were frequently 6 to 8 feet deep. To keep from sinking too deeply, as I sank into the snow, I would bend my knees. This was a completely unique experience for someone from Florida. Every time it looked like I'd soon be out of the deep snow I'd come to an impassable canyon and have to climb up a steep bank, then back down into the blanket of snow. My boots were wet and my feet frozen, but at this point I had no choice but to proceed down. Now there was no way to go back up, so what could be worse? It began to hail! Big hail stones. Well, I thought, at least it wasn't rain. Of course, since the elements were trying to kill me, soon it began to rain! As the valley became less steep there were patches of snow free rock and an occasional avalanche I could climb over or slide down. Of course the rocky places were not gravel, but a solid covering of 6 to 10 inch round rocks. I ended up on the west side of the Middle Fork of the Cimarron River and on the other side could see a post indicating the trail, however there was much more snow there. Where I was there was less snow, but stretches of water soaked, muddy Tundra and inside my boots were now sloshing with snow melt. My back was in extreme pain. It wasn't my lower back, but muscles pulled back by the weight of the backpack. When I could, I'd walk hunched over like The Hunchback of Notre Dame.

As I neared the big waterfalls I debated crossing to the east onto the trail, but there was very deep snow there and I didn't want to cross the river. **Bad mistake**. As I climbed above the canyon the snow again became deeper, softer and was adjacent to the 200 foot vertical drop to the river. As I plowed thru the snow my concern was that if the snow slipped just a few feet I'd be carried over the edge to my death. Occasionally I'd sink chest deep in the snow; there was no way to push myself back up so I'd have to lie down and roll out of it. Again I was exhausted, but there was no place to rest. At least my upper body wasn't that cold, I was burning too many calories.

Passing the deep canyon I found a spot free of snow and slumped down for a brief rest. Then, more determined than rested, I followed an animal trail down into a deep gully and up the other side. As I reached the top and while panting for air, what do I see but a whole forest of trees devastated by an avalanche. Before me was a wall of uprooted trees, in some places stacked 10 feet high and tangled with limbs. I was utterly worn out and absolutely shattered! Where I could, I would walk across the top of the trees, not an easy task with a heavy backpack. I considered that if I slipped I might be impaled by a stob or break all my arms and legs and no one would look for me on the west side of the river. In some places I would crawl (on my hands and knees) under the tangle of trees. Finally this was becoming hopeless, so I stumbled down the very steep canyon wall to the river. After a very short distance there was an impassable vertical wall on my side of the river. I was so fatigued that (without removing my boots) I just waded across the river; then came to another cliff on that side. After a few more crossings, and more than once almost falling into the icy water, I came to a waterfall. So I decided to climb the extremely steep east side and somehow locate the trail. This bank was exceedingly steep, so sometimes I'd been on my hands and knees. I could only make fifty or so feet at a time before I had to rest and one time think that I fainted. Again I ran into a landscape of uprooted and shattered trees. I ripped my jeans; cut my leg and the limbs were trying to rip everything from my backpack.

Finally I found the trail and collapsed for a needed rest and dumped the water from my boots. My spirits were buoyed by being on the trail, going down. However at the Porphyry Basin Creek I lost the trail in the snow. I headed down to the river, but the trail wasn't there. So it was steeply back up, several hundred feet, to find the trail. Scrambling up the steep slope I was sometimes crawling on all fours. More than once I'd just collapse on my stomach and lay there panting. I was so cold and wet and I was totally given out. Passing over the top of a rise there was no trail, but another forest of devastated trees. I screamed to the forest, "***Where is the xxx trail!!!***" After a couple hundred depressing yards I found it. Following the trail remained difficult due to the snow, muddy bogs and flowing streams, but I kept moving downhill and if I wasn't so tired I'd have been elated. The sun would occasionally pop out, followed by dark clouds and usually hail or sleet. I didn't care, I was wet; in a numbing trance and reduced to taking baby steps forward-'one step at a time'. Around 6 pm I reached the road, which was back down at 10,000 feet. That day I'd only traveled 8 ½ miles, but on the most difficult trek of my life.

Now it was ONLY 6 miles to where I had parked. I left my backpack and began walking. Even the released load didn't cure the pain in my shoulders and back. The day before I had met a guy from Oklahoma and hoped he was looking for me, but no. After 23 miles, at 9 pm, I got back to Sammie in a dazed state. I had extreme difficulty lifting my legs to get into the Suzuki. Other than profound exhaustion I had 2 problems: my gas gauge was below empty and I had to drive UP to get my backpack.

Miles are agonizing long when the fear of giving out of gas causes you count by the seconds. I figured that if I could make it to my sleeping bag I'd be OK. However, if I ran out of gas on the way up I felt that I would not be able to walk back up that mountain. After those few minutes of being still my legs stiffened and when I got out (to retrieve my backpack) I almost collapsed. My entire body ached and my legs resisted movement. In the darkness I had trouble finding my pack; almost fell into a muddy bog; considered crawling into my sleeping bag and spending the nite there, but a stronger impulse said 'You really want to be in your bed tonite.'

To save gas I coasted down the 5 miles to the river. Even with the heater on *high* I had chills. On I pressed, up to Owl Creek Pass and 21 miles to Ridgway, during which I coasted most of the way. This was somewhat frightening, since it was difficult to concentrate; keep my eyes open and sometimes I'd be going too fast and slide to the outside of curves, with ominous blackness below. Around 11pm I got to Ridgway, just hoping there was a gas station which accepted credit cards. I had less than a half a gallon of gas remaining.

Now the big challenge: getting over the mountains between Ouray and Silverton, along one of the most dangerous hiways in America. There are many 10 mph curves, with no barriers, no shoulders and from the very edge of the asphalt it drops hundreds of feet to the canyons below. I stopped a few minutes in Ouray to rest; thought I could sleep a few minutes; couldn't, so headed on over. At midnite I finally got back to Maybellene (on Mineral Creek). My body was so exhausted that I couldn't warm up and alternated between spells of freezing to hot. I guess my body was nearing the point of 'shut down'.

OBSERVATIONS: (1) I still have strength in my legs, but lack prolonged stamina. It just ain't as easy backpacking as it was at 25 years old. Also, backpacking in the east was **way** up to 6000 feet, not almost 2 1/2 miles as here. (2) I've always searched for personal challenges and this was a most excellent one. I was adequately prepared, with everything but endurance, and survived. There were wrong decisions, but hindsight is 20/20. (3) I'm delighted that I had this adventure and it was an undeniable learning experience.

OCALA FLORIDA

Mom would take us all over the county and drop us off to go swimming; caving; camping or boating. On one such outing the car became stuck in the sand at the KP Hole (on the Rainbow Run) and tore up the transmission. I recall wading down that river and a Bream swam up into my bathing suit. Another time I caught a huge Snapping Turtle. It was considerably larger than any they had on show at Ross Allen's Reptile Institute, so I thought I could sell it for a veritable fortune. When we got there, they looked in a book and said 'Snapping Turtles $2.00', obviously that was for little pet turtles, not my giant. Dejected I released him into the Ocklawaha River.

An experience that stuck in my little boy's mind was watching a Turtle lay eggs in the sand at Rainbow Springs. Water in Florida springs flow at 72 degrees; as kids we'd swim all day and now it's traumatic to get into that cold water.

Another memory at Ross Allen's involved an Elephant. When I was a kid several of us were lined up along a fence watching the Elephants. All of a sudden an Elephant picked up a pile of hay and dropped it directly on MY head. I know that Elephants have a phenomenal memory, but I had certainly had not done anything to that Elephant to justify his disrespect, maybe his eyesight was poor and he confused me with some mischievous boy.

We had a 1950 Chevy; Mom took a sewing class on Tuesday evenings; Dad was usually out of town, so I would 'take out' the car for an hour spin. We were squirreling thru people's yards around the Woman's Club pond and David said there were no obstructions just about the time I perched the car up onto a culvert. Being industrious and frightened we manage to extract the car and get home before Mom returned.

Another memory at Ocala High School was the skepticism exhibited by the teachers. Since Middle School I have been fascinated by space travel and read every book I could find. I recall writing stories that spoke of: weightlessness; escape velocity and methods to land on the Moon, however teachers told me it would be 50 years before humans were in space. Well, in just over 10 years humans were indeed on the Moon, if you discount Area 51.

Religion was somewhat tragic for me and my family. My father was what is called a fundamentalist, not exactly extreme, however unwavering. When the doors of the Church of Christ were open we were there-twice on Sunday; Wednesday nite; summer camp and vacation Bible school. The lessons taught were filled with sin; fire and brimstone. I was always one to ask questions and I failed to receive rational or satisfying answers. Fundamental religious beliefs center on a person being born a sinner and all their life fighting with the influences of the Devil. I didn't see myself as having sin, although I felt guilty at times. We were to fear the Devil, yet I saw no evidence of such a supernatural being and the arguments seemed irrational and unsupportable. As with so many people I've met, I burned out on religion and chose to feel good about myself and continue to question. Now I see why what I call 'feel good' churches have become so popular, replacing fear with good feelings about oneself.

From my experience, all religious fundamentalists are profoundly conservative; leading to fear of the unknown and paranoia. During human evolution there was selective pressure for some people to be more conservative and some to be more liberal. Liberals are those who are open to new ideas; more tolerant; prone to explore and were more likely to die in the process. However the advantage to the group was that new living areas were discovered; new plants and animals harvested and new tools invented.

The advantage of being conservative was that they didn't take risks; didn't explore (i.e. feared the unknown), therefore were less likely to be killed by some unknown beast or hostile environment, so that at least part of the group would survive. The disadvantage was that the population stagnated; was replaced by more progressive peoples and (as history has clearly shown) populations that become more conservative (resisting change) were cultures that failed to survive. Therefore, as a population becomes more conservative, the risk of failure is increased, as is currently happening in America.

Secondly, few scientists are conservative due to inherent difference in their brain that causes them to select for evidence, whereas conservatives favor belief without evidence. Scientists (as opposed to conservatives) are basically skeptical and not prone to: faith based beliefs; conspiracy theories; alien encounters; proclamations without evidence and supernatural beliefs.

Overall this is why most religious fundamentalists are conservative.

I do recall a consequence of this fear of the devil, generated in my exposure to religion. As an early teen I was sleeping on the porch in Ocala, dreaming about doing something that was leading me to hell. Sounds became louder and louder and louder and just before the 'devil' jabbed me with his pitchfork I bolted awake. To my relief it was a passenger train going by, blowing its horn for the crossing.

In later years we thought it prudent to expose our daughter to both sides of the religion issue. However, when she came home from bible school frightened that the Devil would get her, we stopped letting her go to church. Fundamental religions have this distorted belief that the Devil is actually an entity that affects people's lives and they use this as a device to discipline children. Rather than saying "***Be good to others because that's the right thing to do.***", they say "***Do right or the Devil will get you!***" That is a philosophy of fear that is unfounded, perverse and produces tragic consequence for many people. All religious dogma should be replaced by a simple commandment- **Do unto others and you would have them do unto you.**

Summers in Ocala my brother David and I would sleep on roll-away beds on the front porch. One nite as I lay half asleep I heard a noise from over the hill. As it became louder I sprang up from my bed to identify the source. The noise became louder and now there was a red light flashing thru the mist it created. The movie "*War of the Worlds*" was fresh on my mind and I became convinced it was aliens attacking our neighborhood. Curiosity became alarm as 'it' crested the hill. Now it was a machine, emitting a 'deadly fog', with flashing lights and a tremendous roar! The closer it approached, the louder and more menacing 'it' became. My imagination had overloaded, *"**This was the end**!"* It was very near the house before I realized it as a mosquito spraying truck.

As my heart rate slowed I saw the opportunity for a new adventure; so on nites the mosquito sprayer came through our neighborhood we got on our bicycles and rode for blocks in this fog. Unknown to us they sprayed DDT with diesel fuel as a propellant, not a good mixture for kids to be breathing.

To compound the toxic ingestion, later, when Brother David would come home on leave from the Army he brought military insect spray. The civilian version probably had 5% DDT, this stuff was more than 50% DDT and we sprayed tons of it in our tents and all over us. I'm not sure there were lasting effects, however a few years later I managed to reproduce, with mixed results.

As an early teen we were in the Ocala National Forest; found young Flying Squirrels in a rotten tree; pushed the tree over and as it fell I caught a squirrel who immediately imbedded his teeth in my finger and it really hurt. I sat on a log; squeezed him around the neck, just wanting his teeth out of my finger. Finally he let go; I forgave him; took him home and for a while kept him as a pet.

Just a few other animal bites: While in Honduras I was bitten in the leg by a big German Shepard. To prevent infection a local woman put lime juice in the punctures. While Scalloping I would almost always catch (for a few minutes) most Puffer Fish I'd come across. More than once they latched onto my finger; the bite was uncomfortable, but didn't hurt that much. I've also been bitten by many a scallop, the worst being one that was inside my bathing suit. As a kid (in Ocala) while in the Rainbow River a Bream ran up into my bathing suit and finned me. At the Miccosukee Coop I was working on the roof of a house for Brian and ground a fuzzy caterpillar into my leg. I must have gotten his entire toxic load; over the next couple of days the pain worked up into my chest and was seriously painful. I vowed if the pain got any closer to my heart I'd go to the Doctor; it didn't, but it took several days to subside. I've been bitten my many snakes; a Kingfisher; a Scarlet Macaw; Stone Crabs; a horse; a Toadfish; a Bat and even a boy in grammar school.

There was an abandoned, underground cistern across the street from of our house in Ocala that was obviously just waiting for some adventure or catastrophe. Repeatedly I threw gasoline into it before we got the desired reaction, an explosion! And it was a mighty one; it rocked the windows for several blocks. It knocked us back from the top of the cistern, but none of us were seriously hurt. People ran out of their houses to see if a bomb had exploded, or (since this was the Cold War era) an atomic bomb, or Barry again. But it was just Barry.

While living in Ocala a friend's parents had a house on Island Lake. Lance and I would dive in the lake using a compressor with a hose clamped between our teeth. The art was to allow excess air to escape without allowed water to enter.

On the island I recall that we met some girls from a girl's touch football team in Ft McCoy. One of the girls was someone I'd really like to play touch with.

That reminds me of touch football in our neighborhood. Gay was a girl my Brother David's age, but fully developed for her age. We couldn't wait for another chance to play touch football with her. Later her father paid me to shoot Turtles in some water filled lime pits on his property, although I never understood why I was killing the Turtles, but money is money to a teenager.

At a party at Paul and Kathy's (on Black Creek) near Jacksonville, I met a nurse from Jacksonville and we planned a rafting trip on the Chattooga River, the location for the movie ***Deliverance***. I was living in Tallahassee so we planned to meet halfway from Jacksonville. She drove a 260Z car and on the way to meet me received a speeding ticket; she was upset so wanted me to do all the driving; as we entered the mountains I really got into the handling of her car, so began to test its capability by doubling the speed limit on the curves. I was having an exciting time and to my surprise she seemed to be sleeping. I was thinking, Wow, what an adventurous woman, here we are screaming around mountain curves and she is napping. Later (from her friend) I discovered that she was not sleeping, but was scrunched over in abject terror. Later we rafted the Chattooga and of course the raft hit a rock and flipped.

In Ocala my sister Mary Lou would have a huge Halloween party, with over a hundred people attending. Linda and I came down from Tallahassee without telling her and at Mom's we wrapped Linda in gauze (as a mummy) with 'blood' around her neck as if I (as a Vampire) had assaulted her. We finally had to tell my siblings who we were. However, being recognized wasn't a problem for David and his girlfriend Sherry, they came as Adam and Eve without clothes or even leaves. Brother Joe came in a raincoat as a flasher, with a huge dildo.

A couple of friends had traded a Wild Hog they had shot, for a 30-06 rifle and 1500 rounds of ammunition, a dangerous action for teenagers. On Halloween we rode around in a convertible shooting out street lights.

There was a hill (called Blueberry Hill) near town where couples would park and make-out. I recall us, from the hill, shooting behind Cows across on the next hill to get them to run.

One of my all-time favorite places is Juniper Springs, in the Ocala National Forest. Some of the springs are constant showers of boiling sand; so as kids we would cautiously sink into these boils and be pushed to the surface by the force of the spring. Of course now you are not allowed in the spring boils.

Most summers all I would wear would be a bathing suit, therefore some were well worn. I recall jumping from the Oak Tree above the head spring and my bathing suit split wide open.

JUNIPER SPRINGS

One time we waded way down the spring run, then realizing that it made a long curve away from the head spring, so decided to take a short cut back. The deeper we get into the swamp the more vivid our imaginations became. Not only were there Bears watching us, but also those things that hid in the dark and go bump in the nite. After quite some time we knew we were lost so headed back, but which way? I've always had somewhat of a photographic memory. For example when things really impressed me, such as an Army tank, I could get back home or school and bring it up from my memory and draw it in realistic detail. Anyway this characteristic allowed me to recall certain trees and stumps and got us back to Juniper Run.

Many years later, on a canoe trip, Linda and I had taken a side stream; came around some bushes and there was a huge Gator about 10 feet long on the bank, within 5 feet of us. There wasn't room for him to get into the water, so he hesitated and we quickly passed, then the Gator bolted for the water in a mighty splash. The next year a swimmer was killed by a Gator in the same area, probably the one we had witnessed.

On another canoe trip, while snorkeling, I found part of a Mammoth tusk sticking from the mud bank. There were some other bones around and I intended to return, but never did.

Many years later Damijan and I were canoeing in a section of Juniper Run that was only 6 feet wide and perched on a log (barely 3 feet away) was a rather large Gator that got her attention.

Along the Silver River (down from Silver Springs) Monkeys are living in the wild. Back then there was a tourist excursion down the river on the Jungle Cruiser to where some Tarzan movies had been filmed. You received a free trip if you didn't see the Monkeys. In that area was the Tarzan Tree; more than once we would be there, the Jungle Cruiser would come by, so we would jump for the entertainment of the 'snow birds'. Lance tells me that one time we covered ourselves with mud, than jumping from the tree to the delight of the visitors.

Afterwards a couple of my friends and I received Whammo slingshots for Christmas. then decided to shoot at some Monkeys. We walked in from the hiway, so they couldn't catch us by boat and as we were shooting at the Monkeys the Jungle Cruiser arrived; we hid behind some trees; Lance Davis was a red head and the Jungle Cruiser captain yelled out *"**Red!****Red**!"* He was calling to a particular Monkey, but we thought he saw us so we took flight and the guy yelled, but didn't pursue us. Don't be alarmed I don't think we hit any Monkeys.

In Ocala David and I faked sickness one Wednesday nite so not go to church. We sneaked down to the church; were looking thru the window; it appeared someone saw us; we dashed away across a neighbor's yard and were impaled by our necks by on a clothes line. I guess this was payback for our 'sins'.

While living in Waycross Georgia, after dark, we would tie a napkin mid-way on a string and extend it across the road. As a car approached we would wiggle the 'ghost' up and down and when the car screeched to a stop, run into the woods. In Ocala we did the same or sometimes we would stand on each side of the street as if they were holding a rope across the street. Most cars would pass on by but once in a while one would slam on their brakes, then we would take off running. Once we did the common prank of having someone in the truck with their leg hanging out, covered with ketchup. I also recall a bit of mischief beside Gay Camp's house. The City dug a ditch in the street and lighted flambeaus lined this ditch. We rolled some of the flambeaus across the street; the kerosene spilled and lighted the asphalt street.

Back then Negroes couldn't go to the regular Silver Springs, but could go to Paradise Park, on the other side of the spring. Near Paradise Park was a hole filled with gigantic Catfish. We decided to spear us one of those Catfish. Just as I speared a fish someone yelled, then chased us in a boat. Luckily we got away down the river in my speed boat.

We had a huge Hickory Nut tree across from our house. One day I came home from school to find someone on a bulldozer pushing down <u>my woods</u>, so I called some friends telling them to bring their BB guns; then we climbed the tree and began shooting at the bulldozer driver. It finally dawned on him what was going on and called to us to come down from the tree. Fortunately my mother came with Kool-Aid in appease the bulldozer driver. He said that at first he thought he was into a hornet's nest, then realized we were shooting him with our BB guns. We thought the issue was settled, however he called the police.

I think the police became familiar with our address, however later someone claimed that I shot their Cat with a BB gun and I had really been sick that day.

Well the end of my BB gun misadventures came when I shot our TV set. I don't recall why I did this, but I clearly recall my Dad wrapping the gun around the Palm Tree in our front yard.

I've never been much of a hunter, but as a teenager some friends were going to Gulf Hammock, so, desiring a new adventure I went along. I was the only one who shot anything, a wild Hog. When I got back to camp I explained how I'd tracked the hog; shot him once and he was a long way off. They asked me if I'd cut his throat and I said "***No, he was defiantly dead.***" I was showing my ignorance, they said I needed to cut his throat to bleed him out. One thing I recall is how good the meat tasted, nothing like domestic Pig.

We were camping in tents at Steinhatchee and the night before had been out gigging, however only speared one small Flounder. Upon our return we were too tired to clean the fish, so just lay the Flounder on a stump. In the morning I was awakened by a noise; looked out to see several wild Hogs nearby, then this huge Razorback approached; grabbed the Flounder and began chomping it down. In college I'd had just enough psychology to get me in trouble, so figured that if I jumped up and yelled this Hog would sprint away. Well I jumped out of the tent, yelled and the Razorback (with huge exposed tusks) slowly turned to look at me. Immediately I realized that this was not working for me and for what seemed like minutes could visualize this boar charging and ripping me apart. However, he swallowed the Flounder and to my extreme relief dashed off into the woods.

The vision of trauma from an attacking Razorback was fresh in my mind since a friend had recently been gored by a wild Hog. He was in the woods at nite; a boar came up behind him and ripped his tusks up the back of Donald's legs. Later I recall seeing the drain tubes from the gashes in the back of his legs.

AIRPLANE STORIES

I've always been interested in airplanes; as a kid I rode in my uncle Earl's Cessna and later (while in the Boy Scouts) a C-47 at the Jacksonville Naval Base. I also had models of the popular fighters of WW II and when I joined the Air Force wanted to fly jets. My fantasy in High School was to have been a P-51 pilot in the Pacific war.

My last real job was with an environmental consulting firm where I came in contact with a country 'boy' from Live Oak Florida. He told me stories about flying F-4 Phantoms in Viet Nam, however what was unique was the last planes he flew. After Viet Nam Pete flew B-58s (the first supersonic bomber); after taking off on a mission he radioed back to his navigator who didn't answer; the co-pilot checked and found him dead. A starter had exploded, sailed thru the fuselage and thur the navigator.

[My experience with B-58s was when I was in the Air Force tech school near Wichita Falls Texas. While they were being tested, a B-58 exploded just north of us in Oklahoma. They rounded up a bunch of Air Force and Army folks; put us in a line 5 miles across and we searched the area marking every piece of the plane with little flags.]

At some point a Colonel asked Pete if he'd like to fly over China, so Pete replied: "*If it was fast and high enough*." The Colonel replied: "*How about 80,000 feet at Mach 3*?" Pete enthusiastically said yes. Of course this was the super-secret plane, the SR-71 Blackbird. In the 60's the Blackbird was a plane that didn't exist.

One story Pete relayed to me was during takeoff. At the time they would takeoff fully loaded with fuel and be accompanied by a chase plane. As Pete rose from the runway he lost an engine and the chase plane ended up flying under the SR-71. Pete recovered control of his plane and said the real flying skill was the pilot of the chase plane. After this episode standard procedure was to take off with a minimal fuel load, then being topped off from a tanker flying above.

There were only 3 Blackbird bases in the world: Okinawa; in the mountains east of Sacramento California (Beale AFB) and in England. Pete was at the base in Okinawa when a Blackbird was late to arrive and it was clear that the pilot had passed the base. Flying at Mach 3 you can get a long way off in a big hurry. Communication codes were changed daily and this pilot could not be reached, so Pete told them to use yesterday's code, which they did and told the pilot to turn around.

Originally the SR-71 was not painted black and since the titanium skin flashed in sunlight I believe that many UFO reports resulted from pilots sighting the SR-71. Imagined a pilot in the 60's flying along at 500 mph, seeing a bright object zipping past him at Mach 3 (3 times the speed of sound) and naturally his interpretation is a UFO, although for the public to assume this was an alien spaceship defies logic. A couple of interesting facts about the Blackbird are: due to frictional temperature, during flight the plane increase several inches in length and it has stealth configuration even in the 60's.

While sailing in Mexico I met an American sailor who flew P-51 Mustangs during WW II. He said he hated Germans; was flying along one day; on a mountain top he saw a beautiful house with lots of glass windows, so he flew over and destroyed the house.

I also met a guy who flew the P-38 Lightening and in New Guinea was on the flight that shot Yamamota's planes down. Yamamoto was the architect of the raid on Pearl Harbor resulting in America entering WW II.

While in the Air Force (outside Sacramento) I would go home for Xmas on flight hops, space available flights on military planes. My first trip home, after getting my scuba gear, was very eventful. It began at Mather AFB with an ambulance transporting me out to the plane, I knew the driver. Flying in the plane (a C-123) was incredibly noisy, even though we were issued cotton to plug our ears. After hours of flight, trying to sleep and listening to various noises, including the 'weemp' 'weemp' of hydraulic pumps, I was suddenly jolted awake by a blast of cold wind. I was sitting on a bench and had loosened my seat belt, now I was hanging in space looking down several thousand feet to the desert of Texas. Unknown to me, cargo planes open their back door before they land. If I had slipped a little further down I would have landed before the plane.

We landed in El Paso and at daybreak a C-47 was to travel east to Huntsville Alabama. All nite three or four of us hung around the flight line trying to get some sleep. At first light the engines on the plane started and we knew we were going to miss the flight. We rushed across the flight line, me dragging a scuba tank, weight belt and way too much weight. Gasping and totally out of wind, I got to the plane to find they were just testing the engines and the plane wouldn't leave for another hour. The other guys went back into a building. Under the plane I sat, exhausted.

Mather AFB was primarily a base for training bombardiers and navigators, but had a SAC (Strategic Air Command) wing, that had their share of problems. One was a B-52 that ran out of gas and crashed! Evidently it had something to do with completing the mission, but it was a major boo boo for the taxpayers and ended some Air Force careers. The plane was named the **Miss Sacramento**, so they made a public relations effort by renaming another B-52 for the city of Sacramento. Well a while later this one ran off the runway and sank into the mud, but the public didn't know this. Later a B-52 and a KC-135 tanker were flying out from San Francisco and the pilot of the B-52 saw something unusual under the KC-135 and maneuvered under to take a look see. Well someone hit an air pocket and the tail of the B-52 knocked off one the tanker's engines and lost all its tail, just above the startled tailgunner. Both successfully landed at Mather and I was on the end of the runway marveling at all the "stuff" hanging from the planes.

The real crash that **could have been,** occurred in the summer. Early in the morning the temperature can be in the low 50's and later in the day in the 100's, or up to 118 degrees as it was one summer. The tankers are loaded based on the expected temperature of the air and runway and evidently they waited too long before taking off. The first tanker, loaded with thousands of gallons of jet fuel, took up **all** two miles of the runway. The second tanker saw this, so about 9000 feet down the runway raised his "bow" so far that the tail boom drug the runway in a shower of sparks. I was near the runway and just knew he would either explode in flames or go off the runway in a fiery crash. They became airborne after the end of the runway onto the overrun.

CASTLE DOME PEAK

The fast lane I am flying down is one with no end in sight, filled with reckless adventure and paved with dangerous delight.
Ashley Young

This is a prominent peak in the Castle Dome Mountains (within the Kofa National Wildlife Refuge) that can be seen from Yuma (Arizona) and beyond. The peak just screams out, 'Come climb me.' It is the remaining core of a huge volcano and as I was to discover, it and the surrounding mountains have 'passed their prime' and are covered with disintegrating rock.

As usual, the beginning of the mis-adventure began with optimism and confidence. After hiking along the dry wash for a mile or so I came to a canyon and the first obstacle, a high, dry waterfall. At first wasn't sure I would be able to scramble up, but made it without slipping.

Then, just around the corner, was a dam. It had been built (evidently by helicopter) for a source of water for wildlife, but was filled to the brim with dirt and rocks. I had been told to take a right fork and there was an arrow (in stones). Hesitantly (just past the dam) I took a right fork and after a ways it dead-ended. I then climbed over my first ridge- more like a mountain. On the way down I climbed thru several steep washes. Back in a wash (heading the right direction) I came to another deep canyon and an unclimbable cliff. I scramble up the side of the canyon, in rock that crumbled in my hands and rolled out under my boots. Since I wasn't sure where I was, I hiked on up to the top of that mountain; from there I could see 3 washes, but none seemed to cut thru the mountains. Scrambling down, the rock was so loose that some places were impossible to walk; the rock was generally between the size and shape of golf balls to marbles, so I sat on my butt and slid down on the rocks. I took the one wash that headed directly toward Castle Dome; scrambled over the ridge and to the right was a deep canyon heading off to the south. However there was no way to get down in that direction. I followed another ridge line (with patches of very red, rock); got Cholla spines in my leg and headed over that ridge. Where the cactus spine penetrated my calf, my leg began to cramp. This was not good. I had been thinking of what I'd do if incapacitated and the prospects were definitely not good.

Looking down into the next wash it seemed impossibly steep and I questioned if I would be able to get down. Not wanting to back-track I began my descent; I've never been in mountains that were so covered with loose rock and on this trip I fell down more times than cumulatively in my entire life. Sometimes I broke my fall with my outstretched hand, with bloody results. On this descent I fell many times and one time into a thorny, Palo Verde tree. At least I avoided more Cactus spines. The wash was very steep, then I came to a series of dry waterfalls that were impassible. I had to scramble along the side of the canyon, not knowing if I would encounter a sheer cliff. The last part (getting back down into the wash) was a scary (almost vertical) rock climb over rocks that frequently broke off in my hand. As I neared another wash I got caught up in thick, sticky brush. I really hate Acacia Trees, especially Cat Claw Acacia. These backward facing thorns rip your clothes and bloody your arms and legs. Finally I reached the wash that seemed to head for Castle Dome, but I was tired-very tired. I rested for a while; resumed my march (at a slower pace) and almost immediately come to another dry waterfall. Again the rock was so lose you could never trust that your boot would not slip. The wash narrowed to a couple of feet wide and was rocky and brushy. From there another ridge headed more steeply-UP. I was climbing over rock pinnacles, with vertical drop-offs to each side. At the next ridge I came to a dead end. There was no possible way toward Castle Dome. I'd have to back-track; it was late and I didn't know the correct return route and I was VERY tired. My calf was still cramping; my legs ached and I just felt exhausted. I could see that the wash (to the north) passed thru a flat plain; I knew I couldn't possibly go back the way I had come, so I decided to go the long way around.

For 3 hours I headed northeast in a gently sloping wash, and was relieved not to be rock climbing. But the wash was heading more and more to the east and I needed to go west, so began hiking northwest, across what looked like level ground, interspersed with Cholla and Ocotillo.

However was soon scrambling down into deep washes, running across my path. I was really tired now and the sun was rapidly sinking behind the mountains. I passed over a ridge and looked into the next valley for the road back to Sammie, but my optimism was thwarted. I passed another ridge and still no road; then across the valley saw what seemed to be a road, but was just another wash. I was not having fun. In mid-valley I searched for a possible way out and the only option was over a very high mountain range. I honestly didn't know if I had the strength. I said (into my video camera) *"If you don't hear from me, I'm here, shriveled up among the Cactus"*. On I trudge, higher and higher. Near the ridge, in the failing lite, I saw what appeared to be a mine and imagined a road. But when I arrived, it was just some unusual rocks. As I peered into the next valley I said *"If the road is not in that valley I'm in deep do-do!"* The mountains on the other side were too high and steep to climb; I was losing the sun and almost totally exhausted.

The rocky wash down was steep with many dry waterfalls, but I found an animal trail to follow. This trail led me into a deep wash where I laid down to rest. Now the sun was behind the mountains and it was getting colder. Finally I reached the valley, but had to traverse several washes crossing my path. I was almost to the west side of the valley and no sign of a road, but there was a canyon to the south that might allow me to get around the tallest mountains and was almost to the opposite side of the valley when (to my enormous relief) I found the road. After 9-10 miles, it was only a mile or so back to Sammie. Getting into her was déjà vu, the eventful hike in Colorado. I had to physically lift my legs to get up into the Suzuki, especially since she was lifted 4 inches. Now it was dark and that familiar body shivering began to take hold. I ran the heater full blast and after an hour got back to **Maybellene**. My foot (or rather my big toe joint) was excruciatingly painful. It must to a touch of gout. Before I fell asleep I thought, well that was one of the few goals that I didn't accomplish, but **<u>I'd never attempt that one again</u>**.

So what do I do the very next day? I found a better way to approach Castle Dome. It would be from the north, up the wash I had gone down the previous day. I figured the distance at 3 miles; figured I could reach the base within 2 hours and I would do it on Tuesday, after the pain subsided in my body.

The two subsequent days were anything but restful. Next day I drove all the way around the Kofa Mountains, a distance of about 100 miles. One objective was to 'ground-proof' the roads for the upcoming Quartzsite get-together. By the time I returned I'd had a year's worth of jostling and crashing and banging; even Sammie suffered, she ended up with a flat tire. During the day it was somewhat breezy, but the next day the wind howled like a banshee. The cold, north wind never dropped below 15 mph and there were gusts above 30. I tried to do chores, but just being outside was very uncomfortable. This brought the coldest nite this winter and if the wind stayed up in the morning I would not be able to climb Castle Dome.

Next day I left before sunrise, in 30 degree air; calm wind and a clear sky. It took an hour to drive to where the Wilderness began. From there was an uneventful hike along gravel washes to the base of Castle Dome. In 2 hours I hiked to a spot where (a few days ago) it had taken me more than 4 hours, but this time I wasn't exhausted, tired but not worn out. From this spot, Castle Dome was intimidating and really appeared to be unclimbable. The sides were covered with deep ravines; scree slopes and cliffs. Near the summit the cliffs became vertical and continuous. After a short rest I began my trek up, first along a wash, until reaching a soaring, dry waterfall. From there I scrambled up the loose rock: slipping and sliding. I wasn't too concerned with the instability of the mountainside because a fall wouldn't be too traumatic. As I made my way higher and higher, the slope became steeper and many times I found myself crawling on all fours. After a while the knees in my jeans had disintegrated and later my knees were bleeding. I'd have to zigzag across the face of the mountainside, looking for a reasonable way up, but finding a less rigorous place to climb became more and more difficult. Although I actively tried to avoid Cholla cactus I got a ball of it in my left leg; several spines penetrated my calf, which (as the last trip) began to cramp. Then I passed over a spiky ridge, then had to balance myself on shear pinnacles of rock, with steep drop-offs on each side.

Where the ridgeline opened a bit I stopped for lunch. I was a bit tired, but nothing like the past trip. From here it was more difficult to find a route up. I passed under an arch, and then had to scramble far to the west to find a way up. At first it appeared there was no possible way up, the only route I could see was an absolutely vertical rock climb. I really didn't trust this rock; I'd had many rock handholds just breakaway in my hand; now

I was in a place, that if I fell, it would be hundreds of feet down to my death, so became uncharacteristically anxious. I wasn't sure that I could get back down this way and I even considered turning around. In my past I've never been this stressed about heights. Have I become cautious in my later years or more vulnerable? As I inched my way up, I hugged the rock face and concentrated on not looking back and trying to block out the abyss below. Finally I got above that vertical wall and was near what I called The Penis Rock. To get there I had to crawl on my hands and knees up a continuous slope of loose rock. If the mass of loose rock gave way and slid down, there would be no stopping, before going off the side of the mountain. Finally I reached the Penis and had been told that from there was a 25 foot vertical climb to the summit. The problem was that rocks had recently fallen part way down, almost blocking the passage. The first rock was about 3 feet across and held a pile of rocks above. Not only was there the hazard of the rocks falling, crushing me, but it was a precarious scramble around the rocks. Finally I reached the last leg, a twisting climb of 50 or so feet to the summit. Once on top I didn't have my usual exhilaration of accomplishment, I remained apprehensive. Would I be able to get back down those frightening places? I commented (into my video camera) that I would never have thought I'd be on top of such a mountain at almost 65 years of age.

I remained on top for just a few minutes, it was now 2 pm and I had 3-4 hours of travel to get back. It's easier going up because you can better see foot and hand holds. Going down vertically, you are blinded and rely more on feel and luck. As I began my descent I found where someone had placed rock cairns to mark the passage down to Penis Rock, along a much safer route. After that, I followed alongside some rock scree until I came to a vertical cliff. This did not look good; I was too far to the west and there was no possible way down from here. At several places I peered over the edge, but didn't see a way down. Damn, I had to climb back up. I was really panting now and exhaustion began to set in, mixed with increased anxiety. I checked place after place and couldn't find a way down. This became serious. There were some places where you could climb down for a ways, but then it appeared impossible to go further. Finally I found a location that looked promising, however I had to hug the rock wall so could not see where to place my boot, so anxiety became extreme. I would lower my foot; find a rock ledge and hope it didn't break loose. After a hair-raising descent I made it below the worst point. I worked my way around further to the north, again finding several impassible cliffs and finally spied the arch. I was extremely relieved, but that soon faded as I saw that to continue down from the north was impossible. I needed to get to the ridgeline further to the east, but didn't see how. This was so frustrating. Coming up I could more easily pick a route, although frequently climbing up rock faces. But now the rock faces were more difficult to get down. After considerable scrambling and slipping over loose rock I arrived at the ridgeline. My knees and thighs were killing me.

After the ridge, I began another steep descent, over very loose rock. As in the previous trip, I spent considerable time falling on my butt and sliding down. Here I got some Cholla spines in my butt, which was literally 'a pain in the ass, to remove!' I was not having fun and cursed out, that I'd never again hike in these mountains, where it's less like walking and more like sliding down a pile of marbles. As the terrain leveled a bit, rather than sliding on my butt, I'd just stand and ski down with my boots, stopping before I gained too much speed. Then I was back in the steep wash, hopping over rocks and my knees felt if they would explode. It took me 45 minutes longer to get down, than to climb up Castle Dome. To get down into the wash and the way out, I had to climb one last ridge and that's when tiredness really hit me. From there it was down all the way. The only problem then was the knee pounding rocks in the wash. Finally I returned to Sammie a little after 5 pm, but wasn't nearly as exhausted as before.

SAILING IN CENTRAL AMERICA

Man cannot discover new oceans unless he has the courage to lose sight of shore. Andre Gide

I was sailing along the coast of Belize; a rain shower had just passed thru and all of a sudden I was surrounded by a cloud of flying insects. These were Termites massing to find a new nest site and they now covered **The Rose.** Frantically I closed all ports, hoping none decided to nest in my little boat, then as suddenly as they appeared they were gone.

The rules of the road (or rather, the sea) states that a sailing vessel has the right-of-way, however the practical rule is to give way to the largest vessel. This was tested while I was sailing between Roatan and Guanaja, in Honduras. On the horizon I could see a ship approaching; as the ship closed in I could see that we were on a collision course; as the ship neared I could see it was a large freighter with **Chiquita** (as in bananas) painted on its hull and I somehow thought she might veer from my path. But no, we would have collided if I had not tacked away, although I had to sail close by to make my point that I had the right-of-way.

My 'cheeseburger in Paradise'. I was near the Settlement off the island of Guanaja; befriended an elderly couple who had sailed from Washington state, thru the Panama Canal and were heading up the east coast of America. They had gotten fresh hamburger from town and invited me for dinner on their sailboat. The scene was absolutely idyllic; with crystal clear water; a setting sun over the islands and the gently slap of waves on the hull. I hadn't seen ice in a while and was delighted that they served rum and lime, with ice! I was overwhelmed and Jimmy Buffet would have been proud.

I was on an overnight, solo sail from the Bay Islands of Honduras to some atolls off Belize. Left Roatan around midnite so as to be near the atolls at daybreak; now I was trying to stay awake by watching the displays of bioluminescence; alongside the sailboat were gigantic explosions of light, resembling depth charges and here and there were long streaks of light from huge fish and pyrotechnic bursts from fish darting in all directions. Here I was, many miles into the Caribbean Sea alone and becoming drowsy. As usual I was attempting to stay awake to watch for approaching ships and as usual could not stay awake. All of a sudden something hit me in the chest, <u>inside</u> my foul weather jacket, causing an adrenaline shock as

I attempted to discover what was flapping around inside my jacket. With relief I realized it was just a Flying Fish. That kept me awake for awhile; eventually I fell asleep and at first light could see an island on the horizon.

During the day (on Lighthouse Island) I dove in The Great Blue Hole. This is where Jacques Cousteau took his little submarines and there is a famous photo of the Calypso suspended in this seemingly bottomless pit. My dive was to 140 feet to where you go under the lip of a huge sink hole. This was a bit deeper than a diver is supposed to dive with one tank of air. Fortunately nothing bit me and obviously I survived.

Sailing off-shore from Belize I needed to remove rainwater from my dinghy, **Rose Bud**. After placing **The Rose** on autopilot, I jumped into the dinghy; got her on-plane to run the water out and only then began to think: here I am butt naked in the Caribbean Sea; no one knows I'm here and if the engine died **The Rose** would motor away for hours, so decided it would be advisable to get back aboard.

After hearing horror stories about violent and prolonged weather along the coast of Mexico and Central America, I was really lucky. However one episode that was more agony than dangerous was as I was sailing from Guatemala to Honduras, south of the Bay Islands. I was heading east; an easterly breeze began early and by late afternoon the wind was screaming in my face and hammering thru the waves was frustrating and by the end of the day just plane miserable. Just before sunset I approached the rocky shore, searching for a small cove indicated on my chart. Apprehensively I motored thru a narrow cut in the towering rock walls into an idyllic paradise. Soon I anchored in an absolutely beautiful, protected Bay lined with Palm Trees; a sandy beach and Monkeys clambering in the trees.

The most dangerous weather incident was as I approached an atoll off the coast of Belize. A squall was approaching; I was lowering the sails as a shrieking wind and torrential rain descended and even with the engine running I could not pull up into the wind. I was near the atoll, in shallow water; through the rain I couldn't even see my bow and now I was being blown sideways (In Irons) completely at the mercy of the tempest. The awesome wind had captured me and any second I expected to be crashing into a reef. Fortunately, after what seemed like an hour (but only minutes) the most intense wind subsided; the rain slackened a bit so I regained control of **The Rose** and could now see we were dangerously close to a coral reef.

Later on I continued to survived, however my sailboat did not.

LAST SAIL OF THE ROSE

In 1992 I solo sailed to Mexico, Belize, Guatemala and Honduras for almost a year. Returning to Tallahassee Linda said we should sail over to the Bahamas for Christmas. Being unemployed and adventurous I said *"Sure"*. After returning from Central America I had given my sailboat, **The Rose**, a bottom job and repainted her bright red hull. The Honda engine needed new spark plugs; however the marina didn't have them and this became one factor in a long chain of events that led to a catastrophe and still elicits *"Well, what if?"*

I sailed her down the west coast of Florida; thru the Caloosahatchee River; Lake Okeechobee and down to Riviera Beach. Just before Linda arrived there was a very unusual storm approaching from the Gulf of Mexico. This was an intense low that you wouldn't expect in December. The winds blew up to 50 mph and were still blowing when Linda arrived. After she arrived we drove into south Dade County to purchase new spark plugs, delaying our trip by a fateful day.

The next day the wind was still up, but later the weather broadcast said the wind would drop to 5 knots that nite. Since we were trying to make it to Marsh Harbor by Christmas Day we decided to go for it. Out the channel we sailed, in 15 foot rolling waves. [Huge ocean rolling waves are not a problem as long as they don't break. While sailing, you can have 2 foot steep, breaking waves that becomes serious agony.]

Across the Gulf Stream we arrived near West End (Bahamas) just after dark; my chart indicated a light and an island, but we saw several lights so were uncertain as to the location of the channel. Unfortunately we were violating a cardinal rule of not approaching coral reefs in the dark. We slowly approached the coast, heard breaking waves so decided to take the safe action and anchor outside the reef.

True to the forecast the wind dropped to a breeze, but around 2 am it began to build. Within an hour it was gusting to 30; waves began to crash into my little 25 foot boat and later it gusted to 50 and waves began to break over the boat. The dinghy, which had a very heavy, Honda outboard, would flip over in a big set of waves and a few minutes later flip back over.

After a few more flips the stern cleat and a big chunk of fiberglass ripped off and the dinghy disappeared into the night. Now personal survival became a genuine concern. In the flashes of lightening you could see an ugly white line just behind us where the towering waves crashed into the coral reef. A couple of times I struggled to the bow adjusting the anchor rode to reduce the chance of chaffing. Down below it was impossible to rest; every few minutes a big set of waves would sweep completely over the boat slamming us across the cabin, then I became seasick.

At first light we could see a cut thru the reef and to our amazement we could also see the capsized dinghy behind the reef where the painter had caught in some coral. The sea remained monstrous and the winds at a steady 30 knots. I tied the anchor line to a float and tried to turn toward the cut, but the wind forced us toward the coral reef. The control handle on the outboard engine had been broken off during the nite, so I kicked the engine with my foot and we turned toward the cut; suddenly we were caught in a huge wave and were surfed toward the reef. The sailboat was now treated just like a surfboard as we rushed toward the cut thru the reef, completely out of control.

Under normal conditions there would had been ample depth to pass over the shallows, but we were on the down side of the wave that sent us slamming into the bottom. Suddenly we were bumping on the sand bottom, however that didn't seem to be a serious problem since I'd previously been on bottom. I said to Linda, "*Go below and check it out*". As soon as she opens the companionway hatch I know we were in deep trouble. I remember seeing rising water and corn flakes floating around her guitar. [Amazingly that Yamaha guitar survived two days underwater, as the case disintegrated and Linda still uses it.] Fortunately the radio was on the high side, so Linda radioed a *Mayday,* but no one answered.

Within a few minutes **The Rose** was pushed by the waves into deep water behind the reef and went down on her beam; we began swimming toward an island; the water was much colder than you would expect for the Bahamas and after swimming for a while we realized that we could walk. On the island we huddled behind some bushes to get out of the wind trying to keep warm and after some time saw a boat approaching. They had heard the Mayday. When the local Bahamians arrived we asked them to go over and pick up the dinghy. They said, "*No, mon it's too rough*". So they took us to shore; immediately went back out; picked up the dinghy and later demanded money for it. At the Jack Tar Marina the manager let us stay in a huge yacht until we could get some money. I had trouble getting someone to take me out to my boat because everyone was out catching Lobsters. By the time I finally returned to **The Rose** the keel had broken off and she was upside down. We cut a hole in her hull and I dove into the water to retrieve some of our belongings, someone had already removed the engine.

Later I visited the guy who had my dinghy and engine and he didn't want to be reasonable about compensation; however his wife had made cookies; gave us some and convince him that they would take a couple hundred dollars for the dinghy. However we couldn't get money because it was Christmas, then we had to wait another day for Boxing Day. We paid for the dinghy; found a dive boat who would take the dingy and engine back to Riviera Beach and the marina manager gave us a ride in his airplane on a shopping trip to Florida.

So this ended my 18 year adventures with **The Rose**. With her we shared experiences from purely hedonistic to sublime beauty. Now, when the wind blows I fondly recall the thrill of sailing: the glorious sunrises and sunsets; Dolphins surfing off the bow; peering down into azure blue of the Gulf Stream; anchoring off uninhabited islands; in tropical waters, gazing thru crystal clear water to the coral reefs below; being invaded by Termites in Belize; experiences with wives and numerous women; the Whale off Mexico that hovered beneath the boat and into endless memories.

SAILING ACROSS SUNSET

WARS; HUTS AND TREEHOUSES
IN OCALA FLORIDA

As an early teen I built a hut and a large treehouse. This treehouse was in a huge Oak Tree, had two rooms; a porch and to get down in a hurry a shoot-shoot. I don't know how the shoot-shoot received its name; it's just what my father called the apparatus. Now it would be called a zip line and has become quite popular. [So my father invented the zip line more than 50 years before they became popular.]

This Shoot-shoot was a long wire with a handle attached to two pulleys; there was a spring at the bottom and we would oil the wire to see how fast we could descend. Once that became boring we descended with two boys, this worked out OK because one kid could tumble to one side of the tree and the other kid to the other side. But when three kids did it the result was usually a tangle of arms and legs and at least some skin loss as someone usually collided with the tree.

However my main hut (i.e. fort) was built on the ground with sawmill lumber that still had bark on one side. Radiating out from the Fort were tunnels, built by digging a ditch and covering it with roofing tin, then dirt. In the trees there was a palisade to watch out for invading 'armies'. There was also a tower. I guess it's not unexpected but I did almost all the construction, however after completion all the local kids arrived to play.

As an early teen while living in Ocala we had all sorts of wars: using oranges; slingshots; rubber guns and then there were The Crusades when we made plywood shields (painted white and emblazoned with a red cross) and Palmetto swords. During one of these campaigns we allowed my brother and his gang to occupy the Fort I'd built; they ended up in the tower and we attacked. So with my sword and shield and wearing a GI steel helmet (without a liner) I fought my way up the ladder. Violating the *Rules of Engagement*, David, dropped a rock on my head knocking me from the ladder. Not to be outdone we built a fire under the tower and burned them out! They stayed until one of the legs gave way and the tower tumbled to the ground. War is hell.

Along this time a friend in my class came to do war with us, however we ambushed them by going up the street; hiding in the bushes and as they roared down the hill on their bikes we threw Palmetto spears into the spokes of their bikes. They walked home defeated and their parent's called my Mom about the damage we'd inflicted on their bikes. Some years later my daughter was attending the University Research School at Florida State University where it turned out that the Assistant Principal (those years ago in Ocala) was the kid leading the 'attackers'. At the time he apparently never made the connection, although years later Johnny and I discussed this issue.

When I was half way thru the 11th grade my father was being transferred to High Springs so we decided to give my Fort a fiery death. My Mom did the right thing by calling the fire Department to inform them we were going to have a weenie roast. We collected all the wood we could find and built a **proper fire**. Somehow I talked my younger brother David into entering via a tunnel and start the fire from below. As the flames rose higher and higher and the sound became a roar we became a little concerned, but not as much as the neighbors who rushed out of their homes. After seeing the flames soar above the treetops someone call the Fire Department. We were glad to hear the truck miss our street, although didn't consider that it may have irritated the firefighters. Finally they found us; roared up and began dousing the fire. A person we assumed was the Fire Chief lined up a few of us kids and asked, "**What's your name**?" The problem was that he was cross-eyed and none of us knew who he was looking toward, so we stayed silent. With obvious aggravation he repeated the question and got no reply. I think we smirked at his frustration and now he was really getting upset. Fortunately my Mother came out (as usual) to resolve the situation.

This Fort was where I keep my secret stash of risqué girl photos, the prize being the Marilyn Monroe calendar photo. Of course today people wouldn't even consider these photos as risqué. Later a neighborhood boy stole my photos, so I climbed a tree and could see him in his room looking at my treasures. I rounded up some friends; climbed the tree to see the family watching TV; sneaked into the house and retrieved my photos.

W we lived in Ocala we would build lead-to's roofed with Palmetto frowns. One thing we soon discovered was there was a construction skill we lacked. So, during a rain, at first we remained dry, however a few minutes later were drenched after the rain worked its way thru the frowns.

One nite about 6 of us camped in a lean-to (at what is now New Horizon) and stayed up late, after the moon set, maybe past 11 pm. As we lay there telling ghost stories something began crawling on top of the lead-to. The first comment was, ***"Oh it's just a coon"***. Then, ***"Well what if it's not?"*** Then, in our imagination, the sound became a monster or alien. Then someone said, ***"Phil, go out and see what it is"***. *"NOT me, you go!"* Finally I agreed to go and as I peeked around the edge of the roof it collapsed on top of us. We never identified the 'creature', or maybe it was the infamous Ocala Bigfoot?

RIVER OF LAKES

(Adventure on the St Johns River)

If there can be such a thing as instinctual memory, the consciousness of land and water must be deeper in the core of us than any knowledge of our fellow beings…. We cannot live without the earth or apart from it and something is shriveled in man's heart when he turns away from it and concerns himself only with affairs of men. Marjorie Kinnan Rawlings

To most people the river is simply, The St. Johns, harboring no history, certainly not one 10's of thousands of years old. Most never question how it originated; how it has changed over time and what is destined to be its future.

A quarter of billion years ago (when the Shenandoah Valley was becoming mountainous) Florida was under an ocean where marine animals came to dream. Although urban legend has it that people have found Dinosaur bones, 65 million years ago Florida remained under the sea. This was so until 20 million years ago, when the sandbars and cays that represent the early peninsula rose from the sea. The oldest and highest of these sand spits would evolve into the Central Ridge and farther north (thru Ocala and High Springs) immense limestone beds still chronicle this marine environment. During the ice ages the sea came and went, leaving ancient shorelines throughout Florida; later the warming interglacial periods cause the sea to rise and fall more than 300 feet. Eventually the 'St Johns Valley' became a vast salt water lagoon, the time was 100,000 years ago and the sea was 42 feet higher than today. After the last Ice Age, sea level lowered causing the sea to shape huge sand dunes to the east. Rivers from the highlands (e.g. Ocala and Gainesville) bisected these dunes in their search for the sea. A diminished example of one of these ancient rivers is Deep Creek, near Palatka, that remains 40 feet deep. Over time, the dunes became higher until they blocked these rivers causing an enormous lake, then water began flowing north to the Atlantic Ocean at present day Jacksonville. Until recently Native Americans could canoe from the Ten Thousand Islands (in the Everglades) to the mouth of the St. Johns, then on into the Atlantic Ocean. That is until the Corps of Engineers channelized the Kissimmee River and dug canals to drain the Everglades.

The early Spanish noticed strange eddies of water at the river's mouth, and called the river, *Rio de Corrientes*-'River of Currents'. It was the French Huguenots (led by Jean Ribault) landing here on May 1, 1562 who named the river *Mai*-for the month of May. Later the river was called *San Mateo*; then *San Juan del Puerto* (St John of the harbor), later corrupted to St Johns. The French erected a stone column at the river's mouth; the Native Americans (the Timucans) welcomed the newcomers and (thinking the French were honoring a phallic god of fertility) decorated the monolith with garlands of wild Magnolia blossoms. When the French returned in 1564 they built Fort Caroline, a half century before Jamestown. If this settlement had survived it would be America's oldest city, rather than St Augustine. However the Spanish wiped out the French at Matanzas Inlet (near Marineland) then destroyed Ft. Caroline. [St Augustine remained capitol of the Florida Territory until 1824 when it was moved to Tallahassee.]

As with most other rivers, the headwaters of the St Johns don't trickle from a mountain side or begin as a pond, but as a vast grassflat in Indian River County. The first discernible waterbody is Hell and Blazes Lake (just inside Brevard County) southwest of Melbourne. I see where the locals now call Hell and Blazes, Hellen Blazes.

The Seminoles called this river the Ylacco, meaning '*river of lakes*' or '*big water*'. This was corrupted to become: Welaka, a village near Palatka. The early Creek Indians were known to the Spanish as 'cimarrones'- "wild ones" or "runaways" and this became corrupted to yield: Seminoles. Believe it or not, but this was before Bobby Bowden.

Early European settlers left a dismal legacy; they saw a land ready to be subdued, believing they had a divine right to use the land for their purposes. Without consideration for future generations later settlers began draining the wetlands for the all mighty dollar. From 1900 until the early 1970 (when the environment movement began) the headwaters had shrunk from 30 miles wide to ONE mile. By then the 46 tributaries had become ditches; discharging waste and nutrients into the river. Without the cleansing effects of grass marshes, water quality in the river downstream suffered tragically. In 1980 the river had the 'distinction' of being on this country's list of most endangered rivers. However there is hope (thru efforts of environmental groups and governmental agencies) 235 square miles of the land in the upper basin has been reclaimed, mostly along the Kissimmee River. Lake Apopka is a classic example to human degradation of the environment. In the 1940's Apopka was so clear you could see vegetation in 10 feet of water. Today you may not be able to see an inch in the plankton-clogged water. Apopka feeds the Ocklawaha tributary, eventually dumping its nutrient load into the St. Johns. Nutrients are or act as fertilizer; turn the water green with algae and the reduced oxygen kills the fish. Many of the 3500 lakes in the St. Johns valley suffer from the thoughtless effects of man.

All this brings up the question of who, ultimately, can presume to own title to any land: humans, cows, fish? Marjorie Kinnen Rawlings pondered that same dilemma when she considered the little plot of land she lived on north of Ocala. *"Who owns Cross Creek?" "We are tenets and not possessors; lovers, and not masters." "It belongs to the wind, the sand, the rain, to the sun and the seasons, to the cosmic secrecy of seed, and beyond all, to time."*

Aborigine cultures, like those who lived in the river basin of Welaka, saw the occupation of the earth similarly, not as dominion, but as stewardship, therefore developed deep and mystical appreciation of the river. This was the first great river in North America to be explored by Europeans. The river valley covers almost 9000 square miles and the river is 3 miles wide at its broadest. From its headwaters, the river drops an anemic 27 feet in 310 miles, a drop of barely an inch a mile. [As comparison, the Virgin River (that runs thru Zion NP in Utah) drops 2560 feet.]

For years I'd wanted to explore the southern reaches of the St Johns River. I've always been intrigued by finding the origins of waterways. During the past summer Molly Ray referred me to a recent book by a guy from Sanford who wrote a journal of his exploration of the river. He included much of the history, vegetation and animal life of the St. Johns. In preparation for my exploration I talked with a boat Capitan at the Water Management District, in Palatka. He has explored the full-length of the river more than any other person and recently guided Wes Styles on the river for a PBS documentary. [A short time later Wes Styles (Florida's paramount cave diver) died in a diving incident.] They took a house boat to Lake Harney, then to the originating grassflats via airboat. The Capitan gave me a huge photo–map of the upper river.

On November 19th David borrowed Wayne's truck and drove me; **Rose Bud** and gear to Melbourne. [**Rose Bud** is my 10 foot dinghy from the ill-fated sail to the Bahamas in **The Rose**] I launched at Camp Holly, a fish camp along hiway 192. [Recently read a book about Fish Camps along the upper St Johns that discussed a life style that is long gone and I miss. The author states, "***The camps were never locked and canned foods were left in the event someone might need to take refuge or just ducked into camp to get out of storm.***" He tells of a fellow who finished running his air boat; his truck wouldn't start, so rigged a wire to the boat's accelerator, started the Air Boat and blew himself home. At home another guy had chained his outboard motor to a tree to prevent thievery. To get an early start he hooked up his boat in the dark and arrived at the river to discover, no boat on the trailer. Sounds like a similar David experience, when he lived in Gainesville.]

As I departed I could see that the river was 2 or so feet higher than normal and there were more Gators than I expected. [When I talk with people in western states they ask if I'm afraid of Alligators; I shrug and tell them I've swam among Gators all my life and the only one that bit me was one **I** grabbed. We used to go out on the Wakulla River and catch Gators, just for something to do. There have been less than 10 people killed (by Gators) in Florida (in the past 50 years. On the other hand, close to 100 are killed by insect bites, <u>each year</u>. In Florida you are more likely to be struck by lightning, than by the reptile the Spanish call *El Lagarto*- "The Lizard".]

OCKLAWAHA DADDY GATOR

Back in 1968 a Panther moved into this area around hiway 192, in early mornings (from the south) many people saw it crossing the road,. Evidently it bedded down for the day to the north of the hiway. Later, there was some high water (that may have flooded his 'bedroom') and the Cat disappeared.

Flooding is a periodic blessing that gives the fish a real 'shot in the arm'. They head into the flooded area to gorge on an abundance of new food sources. Locals say that (under these conditions) Large-Mouth Bass grow 10 or 12 inches during their first year and when these Bass return to the river channel (all fattened up) the fishermen will be also be delighted. Reproduction of birds is also stimulated and no doubt, snakes and Gators.

The river sinuously wound its way thru a vast landscape of Sawgrass; soon I was in Lake Washington and not sure where the river continued. [Indicative of its marine past the lake has a resident population of Southern Stingrays, mostly living next to freshwater springs.] I guessed correctly; took a narrow creek and motored on north, up to an earthen dam. Since the river was so high I thought I could ride over it, but nada! I discovered a mostly flooded airboat ramp, so pulled **Rose Bud** over and continued.

Winding our way north we crossed Lake Winder and I became truly 'lost'. Could not find a way out, but heard an airboat to the east. While searching for him I found the outlet. The river continued thru 6 foot high Cord Grass and an occasional Cabbage Palm.

Next lake was Poinsett, (west of Rockledge) where I passed some houses and headed northwest. After quite a ways it seemed I was going too far west, so turned back to the houses. Got to the end of a canal before realizing this wasn't the river. This is the closest the river will get to the Atlantic Ocean, until its final outlet to the sea at Jacksonville.

In the late nineteenth century, passengers who wanted to get to Rockledge would take shallow draft steamers from Lake Monroe, down the coast past the shallow Harney and Puzzle Lakes to the busy wharf on Lake Poinsett, then journey just a few miles to Rockledge aboard a stagecoach or buggy.

Back in the lake I traveled far to the west to finally find a channel leading to the SR 520 Bridge. Had stopped to video a large flock of Ibis when an obnoxious airboat roared by, scattering the birds. South Florida is 'ground zero' for the White Ibis population of the world. They made a comeback from when settlers hunted them for food, as 'Curlew'. In the early 40's flocks of 50,000 swarmed into Lake Washington to nest.

SLEEPLESS IN PARADISE

Since the river was out of its banks I was concerned whether I'd be able to find a dry place to camp, then I spied an island. From far off I was convinced that someone had to have a house on it, but fortunately not. However it was used by cattle as an open-air toilet, but I could live with that. It was only 2:30, but I decided to stop for the nite. I was so proud of my good fortune: such a lovely spot, with Palm Trees, flat ground and a view across the river to stands of Cypress. This was an idyllic paradise, **or was it**?

Locally the island is called PawPaw Mound and was used by Native Americans, likely for hundreds of years. The shore was littered with pottery shards. As the sun lowered in the west I tried to ignore the incessant airboats as they ferried tourist out to 'goo goo' at Gators and birds, animals that were rare to them. I figured, incorrectly, that by 5 pm or so they'd be gone. I was wrong, horribly wrong!

Around 4:30 I was just about to take **Rose Bud** out to explore and take photos when an airboat came screaming up and parked just a few feet from my tent. An ol' codger got out, as well as a young, local boy. The old man was 82 years old and looked 110. With a beer in hand, he bragged about his beer and 'ceegars' helping him live so long. I suspect that his contemporaries had already succumbed to their vices. His granddaughter has just been killed in a car wreck and someone was "heckling" him, although I really didn't understand what he meant, but neither did I understand much of what he said. True to most urban legends he was convinced there were only 2 rivers in the world that flowed north. For some reason he was surprised I knew the other was the Nile, but he refused to accept the reality that several major rivers flow north (including the Mackenzie in Canada); several, in Siberia and even the Ocklawaha. They pointed out the VAB building at Cape Kennedy, where Saturn rockets were assembled and flown to the Moon. [The Vertical Assembly Building is the largest single-story building in the world.] We talked for a while and then I took off exploring.

Followed the bellowing of cattle I found a group of six settling in to 'camp' on an island about 10 feet wide. Upon my return I built a fire and was reading when the two guys returned. It was almost dark and the old man was somewhat chilled. (I guess he hadn't drunk enough beer to keep him warm.) Although I was going to conserve the wood I'd collect, he piled most of it on the fire to warm his spindly legs. Just before dark we could hear shooting up-river. They said it was Duck hunters getting a jump on the season, which began the next day. After a while they left and I continued reading by the fire. Later (with my flashlight) I walked along shore, looking for creatures. All I found was few frogs and lots of pottery.

Just as I retired into my tent along comes several airboats. In the still of the nite those monsters are particularly loud and they just **had** to swing close to the island and shine their lights on my tent! After the stillness returned I was listening to the occasional screech of Owls; the melancholy 'moo' of Cows and mysterious splashing in the river. Then, right behind the tent I heard what sounded like someone trying to start an outboard motor, out of the water. My first thought was that they are so close, then the sound repeated and a sound (further off) answered. It was a Gator, a very big Gator, bellowing, just behind my tent. I lay there thinking about the rash of Gator fatalities this year and the almost 14 foot, 780 pound Gator someone killed last week, in Lake George. The record was over a thousand pounds. I heard splashing along shore and for a moment imagined a Gator ripping his way into my tent.

I think I may have dozed off when the tent lit up like daylight. Some @#&%# was just behind the tent with his million candlepower spotlight;

then he could not just taxi away, NO, he gave her full throttle and roared away like a screaming banshee kicking up leaves and sticks onto my tent. I fully expected some redneck to spin up on shore next to me and blow my tent away. I felt empathy for the animals in this area; they have no peace, day or nite. How do they sleep, or mate, or hunt with this infernal racket?

I got up and walked along shore again, fuming, then began thinking of the Indians who lived here, how they had eaten, had sex and probably died on this very island. In silent peace they probably also slept here, **something I was unable to do**.

In 1562, Jean Ribault described the early Native Americans as: smooth faced, hawk-nosed and tawny, *"all naked and of good stature, mightly fair and well-shaped and proportioned of body as any people in all the world. Very gentile, curious and of a good nature"*. As for the difference between the sexes, the men hid *"their privates with breechcloths of gaily colored deerskin"* and incised their skin with red, blue and black tattoos-while the women modestly *"draped their middle with Spanish moss"*. Thought to be godless by the later Spanish, these pre-Colombians lived in a world in which nature and its forces were exalted, in an ancient prelude to the transcendentalism of Emerson and Thoreau. However these beliefs went far beyond mere philosophy. According to the Spanish priest Francisco Pareja, the Native Floridians believed this about souls: each person has three: one is the pupil of the eye, a second is the shadow the body casts and the third is the image reflected in clear water. Upon death, two of the souls leave the body while the soul of the eye remains. So when someone returns to the burial ground they can learn from this soul.

The airboats continued throughout the nite! <u>What in the world were they doing at 3am?</u> It seemed that most of the noise was from the same 2 or 3 boats, probably just cruising the river and drinkin'. In the book I was reading the author stated reading (about Fish Camps): *"If there was a recipe for such adventure and misadventures, it consisted of only two ingredients: a plentiful supply of beer and a group of blow boats."* [Note: Airboats are also called Blow Boats.] Every time I thought there would be no more airboats and could get to sleep, here comes another one.

Later a motor boat pulled up nearby, evidently to allow a woman to go ashore to pee. It was 4am and surely the airboats were not to continue, but NO! Roar, roar. I lay there feeling like an insect on the runway of a busy airport, the airboats were that loud. They were violating my environment and I couldn't do anything about it; some just <u>had</u> to come close and continue shining their lights thru my tent.

Finally it was 5 am and I was sure I could get some sleep. So what's next? A motor boat on the other side of the island was clanking around for a long time, and then came around next to **Rose Bud**. I couldn't see a reason for him to come to this side, thought he might be drunk and mess with my stuff, so got out of the tent. As I was putting on my shoes he shone a lite on me and asked if he had disturbed me. <u>If he only knew</u>! He explained that he was a Duck hunter; has put decoys on the other side of the island; had been doing this for 25 years and was going to shoot from the island, 100 feet from me!

Lying there, I could hear some Sand Hill Cranes. Now it was 5:30 and any prospect of getting sleep was a lost cause. I strained to listen to a hum that turned out to be millions of Blind Mosquitoes aroused by the early light. So I got up as morning lite touching the eastern sky. Flocks of Ibis flew overhead and the edges along clouds toward The Cape glowed orange. Before the sun rose I'd had my cup of oatmeal and was ready to leave, hopefully, never to hear another airboat. Heard a sound across the island and as I turned 'on' my video camera, a couple of Bald Eagles flew away, just missed them. You could not pay me to live along this area of the St. Johns River. **I think airboat drivers will take their airboats with them to hell.**

Packed up; motored north and along shore videoed a couple of Sand Hill Cranes pecking the ground for breakfast. Later I saw a Bald Eagle eating a bird, probably a wounded Duck. Within a mile I passed under the SR 50 Bridge, where Marjorie Kinnen Rawlings and her friend Dessie launched their boat "*where the river was no more than a path through his grass*". In places, Water Hyacinths almost blocked the channel.

[Water Hyacinths are a plague to southeastern waterbodies. Their beautiful flower attracted a woman from Satsuma (near Welaka); who bought (in New Orleans) some of the South American plants, then released them in them into the St Johns River. Some waterbodies in the South are so infested by Hyacinth that boats or even canoes can no longer pass.]

Further north, the area reminded me of Humphrey Bogart in *African Queen,* tall grass for miles and countless streamlets. Still, there were a few Gators, lots of Ibis, Herons and more Anhinga's that I've ever seen. There were some Everglades Kites searching for Apple Snails and I spied a Caracara. [Cara is Greek for "top of head" and it is so distinguished in this way that the genus repeats the word twice: *Cara cara.*]

Rounding a corner I was surprised to see a Cow grazing in 3 feet of water; after reluctantly having his picture taken he swam across a stream to several other cows contently munching on the tall grasses. Further down the labyrinth of waterways there was a larger herd of cattle and a few feet away, a huge Gator. I stopped to video the Gator, just as he thrashed across the mud bank into the river. It certainly reminded me of pictures in Africa where the Crocs stalked Wildebeests.

In the 'middle of nowhere', on a small knoll, I passed a shack and several hunters with their airboats at rest. Far across the 'river of grass' I could see buildings, but no clear way to get there. After a couple dead ends I came to a small settlement of mostly rundown houses, some damaged by the hurricanes; passing under a low bridge (that could fall at any moment); explored the canals and for a while stopped to read in the shade of a tree. There were no clouds in the sky and rather warm for mid-November.

Moving on I was now in Puzzle Lake, it was true to its name; there was choice after choices as to which passage to take. I was correct on most, but finally found myself in an open area with no apparent pathway north and to the west were miles of cattle fence. Then I saw an airboat on the other side of the fence; considered that my best alternative and drove over the fence and again traveled north. Keeping to the west side I was able to finally get thru Puzzle Lake.

Marjorie Kinnen Rawlings described Puzzle Lake where the channel seemed to branch off "***in a hundred directions***" At times to find their way thru Puzzle Lake they stopped and observed the movement of Hyacinths. So impressed, she wrote an entire chapter in her book, **Cross Creek**, "Hyacinth Drift'.

This area is where relic salt water makes its way to the surface. In the last 900,000 years (7 times) Florida was mostly flooded by oceans. The valley itself was most recently flooded up to 10,000 years ago, before that, 120,000 years ago. Relic sea water mixed with fresh water during those times, entering the upper aquifer, where it seeps out in places such as this today.

On an island some Duck hunters has just returned; we talked for a while and they mentioned Econolockhatchee River and how it meandered to the west (36 miles) almost to Orlando. They said, "*See those Cypress Trees, it's in there somewhere*". Well that seemed easy enough, however was certainly not. I motored down dead end passages, one after another and talked to some folks in another boat who were also trying to find the entrance. I was determined, and after considerable searching, a little cursing and backtracking for a mile I found the obscure entrance to the Econ. Now this was about the most wildly meandering waterbody I've ever seen. I followed it west for a few miles, under huge Oaks festooned with Bromeliads. And on my return, saw an Otter.

Back in the river I passed under the SR 46 Bridge and was soon in Lake Harney, now I was on a chart of the river and no more questions as to the correct channel.

Decided to explore Deep Creek to Lake Ashby (east of Deltona), but after a couple miles it became clogged with Duck weed and limbs. This area (like so much of the St Johns valley) has remains from the lives of Native Americans. The pre-Colombian and Timucuans used Palm frond nets to capture fish and shellfish, as evidenced by huge shell middens. Later the mounds were used for living structures. They also fashioned bone fish hooks and years ago I found an excellent example in the Wakulla River. After the Timucuans vanished, the Seminoles used the same mounds. [In our era many of these mounds were used in the construction of roads.] Along this river (in the 1800's) lived a Seminole chief, King Philip and his son Coacoochee, known as Wild Cat. They called this stream, *Ocoska,* for Deep Creek. However, after the Seminole Indian wars ended these people were chased into the deepness of the Glades or shipped to Oklahoma. European settlers used the same mounds for their houses and (like the Indians) lived off the land. But where the 'primitive' Indians maintained a sustainable environment, the new settlers didn't know when to stop. As if in contempt, ambitious loggers built (in 1916) the town of Osceola over King Philip's village.

Naturalist Billy Bartram wrote of the Seminoles: "*They appear as blithe and free as birds in the air, and like them as volatile and active, tuneful and vociferous.*" He was impressed by their behavior; ***"Joy, contentment, love and friendship, without guile or affectation, seem inherent in them."***

I must interject my feelings about Native Americans. As a youngster I saw the movies portraying the Indians as the bad guys and it was only years later that I fully appreciated that they had lived in North America thousands years (at least 14,000) before Europeans arrived. Native Americans have been portrayed as the aggressors when they were just attempting to save their homeland. I feel deep regret over what my ancestors did to these people of the First Nations who were Native Floridians.

From here the river veers west toward Sanford and where there are houses, 'emergency no wake' signs are posted, however the river is back within its banks so I figured they just hadn't taken the signs down, so kept **Rose Bud** on-plane. I really needed gas, but the Marina Island Fishcamp was not open due to recent hurricane damage, so motored on. Thought I might buy gas at the Sanford Boat Works, but no. There, I saw so many 'no trespassing' and 'don't do this or that' that I didn't even pull in, I suspect that Yankees own the boat yard and marina. Around 2pm, at the city marina (in Sanford) I purchased 9 gallons of gas for $25. Lake Monroe was a little bumpy from the afternoon breeze, but I soon returned into the river. Was wishing I'd spent more time in the upper river, here it's too crowded and the shore lined with buildings.

Along the Wekiva River decided that I'd try to find a dry patch of land to camp for the nite, but first explored the Wekiva River all the way to the hiway 46 bridge. [Just above here is where Michelle and I camped, trying to find her a job in Sanford. Up river is where we canoed and she caught a baby Gator.] A couple miles back downriver I found a very small, somewhat dry spot to camp.

During the nite (after all the 747's had landed in Orlando) it was a pleasure to return to the natural sounds of the swamp: 'til complete darkness, the rustle of Squirrels bounding from limb to limb (sometimes noisily across Palm fronds); the evening croak and rasp of frogs and whine of mosquitoes, however they didn't seem to be too intent on bloodsucking, maybe most were males. I was exhausted from lack of sleep and a full day on the river; read for a while and by 6pm tried to sleep. During the nite Owls hooted and answered in some far off tree; occasionally a Limpkin would emit its blood curdling cry and frogs keep up there chorus most

138

of the nite. Got up to pee and it was only 9:30! I read and sometime after midnite managed some sound sleep.

By 5am I was wide awake; lay in the darkness for a while; finally got up; began packing and was on the Wekiva literally by first light. Back in the St Johns I was disappointed that Blue Springs State Park was closed (due to hurricane *Francis*) however the river was back in its banks and I didn't see any damage. Blue Springs is a pre-Columbian Indian ceremonial site and where many Manatees spend the winter.

After entering Lake Beresford I pulled over to Hontoon Island State Park. [When Michelle and I were visiting the Natural History Museum in Gainesville there was an 8 foot Owl totem from here. This is the largest, Native American artifact from Florida and here there is a replica. Living here was the Owl Clan and possible the Otter Clan. Prior to the Timucua tribes, the Stone Age Mayaca lived here and left shell middens over 15 feet high. Imagine a totally different environment in the Pleistocene, that ended 10,000 years ago: with Saber Toothed Cats, giant Wolves; 8 foot Beaver; Ground Sloths 15 feet tall; giant Bison; herds of Horses (later becoming extinct); Camels; huge Mammoths and Mastodons and even Rhinoceros. These Native Americans were hunter-gathers who trapped fish, hunted Deer, cultivated Squash and collected wild Grapes, Fern stems, Acorns and the tender shoot of the Sabal Palm (Swamp Cabbage). Later the Seminole lived on this high ground. They called these island mounds *hummocks*-from a word meaning 'home'. Like other Indian words that have slipped into our vocabulary under disguise, a *hummock* became *hammock*.]

At the marina I asked if going up Dead River (to Lake Woodruff) was possible and was told *'**probably, if it's not blocked by fallen trees or Hyacinth jams'**. Got off the main river; found Dead River (an ancient river channel) interesting and deep enough for David to ply in 'Fat Boat'. Once in the lake I searched for and finally found the Spring Garden Creek leading to Ponce de Leon Springs. At the spring there were also 'closed' signs along shore, however I found a spot where I could pull **Rose Bud** onshore. First I laid out my tent on a dock to dry then explored the area, including remains of a Spanish sugar mill. [Now there is a restaurant where you cook your own breakfast at your table.]

In the 1500's Europeans first arrived here and of course this area was inhabited by the Native Americans, however with no immunity to common

European diseases the original Americans died in epidemic numbers. By the early 1700's they were virtually extinct. Later, Creeks and other Indians moved into the area and became the Seminoles, who farmed corn; potatoes; watermelons and squash. The area was surveyed by the British in 1779; in 1821 the land was acquired from the Spanish and a sugar mill was constructed here and in the 1800's this was called Spring Garden Plantation. In 1835 the mill and Joseph Woodruff's farm were destroyed in skirmish between militia and Seminoles who held the land for two years.

Just before I left David's I realized I didn't have my current, boat registration sticker, so (back in the river) when I was stopped by a Marine Patrol officer I hugged the left side of the river and kept talking. He never noticed the missing sticker.

Back in Lake Woodruff I missed the channel to Lake Dexter and ran down another dead river. There I spotted several huge Gators and probably the largest one I've ever seen; he must have been 14 feet, if an inch and I'm in a 10 foot rubber boat. This is an area where few humans travel; foolishly I headed south for a few miles until stopped by a Hyacinth jam; after carefully checking my chart I realized my mistake, turned back north and apprehensively took a side creek to the northwest that took me into Lake Dexter. Now I was off my chart, but back into the St. Johns River with channel markers to follow. The disadvantage was that there were more boats to contend with, or rather their wakes.

Got more gas in Astor Park and headed across Lake George toward Silver Glen Springs; Lake George is just a wide place in the river; the (shallow bowl shaped) lake is 6 miles wide and 12 miles long, but averages only 6 feet deep; it is Florida's second largest lake and is sometimes visited by Dolphins, Sharks and Tarpon. Bartram commented: *"**Behold the little ocean of Lake George**"*. When Florida was under British rule the lake received its name from England's crazed King George III. For 60 years the east side of the lake has been used as a naval bombing range. It's frequently reported that a strong northeasterly can produce dangerously steep, 4 foot waves, but today the only waves were gentle wakes from boats, heading to and from Silver Glen Spring.

Thought David and Caroll or Bill Dillard might be at The Glen, but didn't see anyone I knew. Sure felt good to rinse off some of the slime that I had collected over the past 3 days. The Glen is different from local streams in that the run is so short and it's not a Manatee sanctuary. People have been visiting this spring for at least 8000 years, and of course the raised shoreline is an Indian shell midden.

Back into Lake George, about 2 miles south of the Salt Springs Run I found a spring creek. Tried to follow it to its source, but the mud was too deep and too many fallen trees. Was really surprised how high the banks are along here. Some are more than 40 feet above the lake (a Florida mountain) and all are topped with houses. Along shore there were vast schools of Mullet; one school ran for a hundred yards. On the lake there was a pontoon boat overflowing with 15 or more Hispanics cast netting for Mullet.

In Salt Springs Run I'd planned to camp where Freddie Shaw, Phil Land and I used to camp as teens, 50 years ago. It was on an Indian shell midden and we would branch out from there to catch snakes, to sell. One time Ross Allen's Reptile Institute (at Silver Springs) was overstocked with water snakes so I released them in the pond of the new Ocala High School. [By the way, Ocala comes from the Timucuan name *Ocali*, which implies many things: bucolic-fertile soil, green, fair land, abundant, even big hammock.] Along Salt Springs Run I recall going out one nite to capture a Gator with a pole with a rope noose on the end. After exploring up a narrow creek we came to an open area and there was a Gator much bigger than our boat. I mean its eyes seemed to be foot from each other. Evidently we were in a Gator wallow so this was probably a mother protecting her den, so we quickly decided to high tail it out of there. One nite there was an Armadillo scratching thru our camp and (for some obscure reason) I shot it with a speargun. There was a spring nearby and I recall shaving my newly grown beard. The spring is now dry and the area too wet to camp, so I set up camp on a shell midden across the river.

At dusk, sitting around the fire, it occurred to me how a fire is like a friend being with you, a warm companion. Just after dark I saw a light across the river, where we used to camp. The light wandered along shore until I could hear someone pushing a hidden boat back into the water. I suspect that they may have been illegally digging in an Indian mound.

Got up at a little after five am and took **Rose Bud** into Lake George. I'd seen a spot the day before (with overhanging Oak limbs) from which to view the sunrise. But I was a bit early. I floated offshore and stared at the stars. The most prominent view was the two morning 'stars': Venus and Jupiter. The water around me thrashed and splashed like thousands of Piranha, frenzy feeding. Millions of fingerling Mullet churned the water and occasionally leaped into the air. Later the air was becoming thicker, more humid. As sunrise approached a mist arose from the water, threatening to obscure the sun. As the dark gave way to faint light I moved to shore and selected an ideal spot to video the sunrise. The location was perfect; overhanging Oak limbs, festooned with moss with just enough space to view the sun. All I needed now was the sun, but it was not to be. Clouds along the coast rose higher and higher and after almost 2 hours I finally gave up. Such is landscape photography.

Returned to my camping spot; warmed some oatmeal and read my book waiting for the sun to burn off the river mist. It was 8:30 before the warming rays filtered down to me, so I packed up and launched **Rose Bud** on our final leg of this journey.

Back into the river I passed the Ocklawaha River. This mile wide valley dates back almost 17,000 years ago and before the St. Johns was a major river it sliced thru Florida from its headwaters lakes and springs into a more ancient marine lagoon, then to the sea. The river cuts thru limestone beds (ancient sea bottom) millions of years old, exposing a tremendous variety of marine fossils. Some common fossils I have extracted from caves were: Sea Biscuits, many Corals; Sand Dollars; Sharks teeth and near Ocala found a prefect Blue Crab in a cave. Many of these fossils are found in Eocene beds, 40 million years old. In younger layers are Whales, Dolphins and Sea Cows.

As in Lake George, I continued to witness considerable hurricane damage. Many docks were damaged or destroyed and along shore thousands of trees uprooted. Would have explored some side creeks, but the sky had become cloudy and just felt like getting back. Passed the Burger King (at East Palatka) and that reawakened me to the fact that I'd traveled the primeval Florida, but was now back in the 21st century. Returned to David's paradise by noon and ended another noteworthy adventure.

A couple of photos along the **St Johns River**:

WAYCROSS GEORGIA

When I was in the second grade we lived in Waycross Georgia. There was a canal behind the house and in those days it was a convenient dump. One dreadful experience I still recall (with a cringe) was when I stepped on a broken bottle; I felt the glass cut though the tough sole of my foot, then deeper and deeper. I also recall catching a Catfish by hand, without getting punctured by the poison spines. Also the times a few of us boys would run naked thru the woods and over the pipes that crossed the canal.

Anyway, service stations would dump oil into the canal and occasional it would be detained by a fallen tree to form a huge oil slick. This particular day, into such a pool of oil I threw matches and when the crackling flames arose I'd throw a rock to put it out. Well this one time the flames would not go out and spread across the canal. I knew this was not good; so ran home, hoping no one would notice. To my alarm soon there were fire trucks and crowds of people streaming down to the canal. When Mom got home I was inside reading the paper; since I wasn't out among the action, she knew it must have something to do with me. Later I phoned my friend Bobby Vann, who lived across town and told him what I'd done. He said *"Sure"*.

I said if you don't believe me go outside and see. You could see the pall of smoke all across town.

The canal bank was pockmarked with holes; the oil had gotten into them and the fire re-erupted over a period of three days. I guess my Mom didn't tell on me. From that day forth I never liked matches.

Along the canal was a city park evidently frequented by late night couples who parked there and sometimes ended up in the back seat of their cars? There were rubber balloon looking things around. We boys knew what they were, but Becky didn't; we got her to blow one up and then tried to explain what they were. To this day she probably remembers that disgusting thought and dastardly trick.

I remember catching an especially wild feral Cat that got loose in the house and escaped being located for 3 days. Later the Cat hid in the woods, yet I was the only person the Cat would approach. For a long time I fed the Cat, then he failed to return.

Before approaching storms I'd climb the wild Cherry tree (next to the house) to experience the exhilaration of the wind swaying the tree; the rustling of the leaves and the excitement of the lighting and thunder. Since I considered myself invincible, the danger of being struck by lightning was completely ignored.

When we lived in Waycross there was a small pond just below a couple of houses. We would sneak onto the property and fish for Bream using dough balls as bait. The fish we caught were so small that Mom would fry them crisp and we would eat bones and all. One day we decided to skinny dip in the pond. All of a sudden we saw two cops (with guns) coming down the hill. In a panic we took off, but I was the only one to get over the fence and into the woods. However it turned out that they were there to shoot snakes, not to arrest four, 9 year old boys for skinny dipping.

Of all the relatives Mom's age I was the first born, so received an inordinate amount of attention. At 3 years of age it was bad enough for Brother David to come along and receive some of "my" attention. But, in Waycross Georgia, at 6 when Paul was born I was now just another kid. So, a short later, a friend and I planned to run away to Savannah Georgia. From there we would hop a ship and travel around the world. We packed a little food, put it in a handkerchief (like we had read that Tom Sawyer had done) then hiked along the railroad tracks until dark. We planned to spend the nite, then be on our way, although we were feeling a little lost and homesick. Late that nite my father somehow found us and we were glad to return home.

Whenever the church doors were open we were always there. At 7 years of age I guess I felt a need for money so devised a plan. Mom always gave us change to put in the collection plate. So the plan was for David to hold the collection plate while I thumped the bottom as if depositing the coins. Well David let go at the critical point and the collection plate crashed to the floor and the change nosily ran down the aisle to the dismay of my Mom.

KATHLEEN FLORIDA

When I was a kid (at the Barrett's farm) you could dig into the sand a foot or so and reach ground water. This one time I dug a deeper hole, then found a use by burying my brother David up to his neck. I don't know why he couldn't see the amusement. However to increase the significance of the experience Ronnie and I would put ants on him. For some reason my grandmother became alarmed and helped us dig David from his 'resting place'.

To the distress of my grandfather we would bend the limbs of the Oak trees so the Cows could eat the Moss; then we would jump on their backs; these were milk Cows; as a result they produced less milk, so he would become somewhat displeased. Later he bought a Brahma Bull that I shot with my slingshot. For some obscure reason the Bull chased me; I dashed for the gate; as I scrambled over the top, the gate toppled over; I kept running and the Bull got into the yard. My Grandfather really enjoyed my visits!

It seems that I've always had a propensity for mischief.

Speaking of the Oaks, these were wonderful, giant Live Oaks with limbs that overlapped. I would climb from tree to tree, jumping from limb to limb, like a Squirrel. Somehow I didn't consider the consequences if I had fallen, however most of my life I felt absolutely invincible.

One Christmas, Ronnie and I took my newly received bow and arrow across Ross Creek and over near the Bay Head. Having a new challenge I would shoot at most anything, even a Mocking Bird (the State bird). Of course I missed and the arrow sailed into the brush. While crawling around to find the arrow I found myself very close to a Diamondback Rattlesnake with my only arrow lying next to the snake. As a matter of fact it was a HUGE rattlesnake; I was only a foot away and if it hadn't been cold he may have bitten me. I yelled to Ronnie *"**There's a 10 foot rattlesnake here**!"* Immediately he took off running, so much for helping your cousin. I carefully picked up the arrow and shot the rattler in the side; realizing this wasn't a fatal blow and since I only had one arrow I cautiously pulled the arrow from the snake and shot it through the head. Ronnie return; we drug the snake from the brush; slung it over my shoulder and started back; the snake was so big that its head and tail almost drug the ground. Mom had pictures taken and we were featured in the Lakeland newspaper.

While visiting Ronnie (who lived near our Barrett grandparents) we made a Bola (like the ones the Argentinean cowboys use). Pokin' around Ross Creek we sent the Bola sailing around the legs of a big Great Blue Heron. After carrying the bird into grandmother's yard we were "messin' with it and to this day I clearly remember what happen. The Heron's head went round and round, then plink, he embedded his beak in Ronnie's forehead; luckily missing his eyes.

As a kid I was always busy, come to think of it I've always been extraordinarily active. Most of the time (in the woods) I'd run rather than walk. At my grandparents I had a Lone Ranger hut in the woods. [For years I thought he was the Long Ranger] One day I was running to my hut; my leg became impaled on a broken, glass, 5 gallon jug, I hobbled back to the house with no small loss of blood. My grandfather was stoic, but as he loaded me into the car said, *"**Boy, I don't think you'll live to be a teenager**."* The Doc sewed it up with 26 stitches and Mom said I didn't even whimper. By the time we returned, Granddad Barrett had custom made me a pair of crutches.

I had other stitches: several when we lived in Waycross. Some cars of the era (early 50's) had chrome visors over the headlights. Walking to the store, somehow I raked my arm across one and (before the blood flowed) still recall seeing things inside my arm I didn't want to see. Don't recall how many stitches, but my brothers and I were in a pillow fight; the bandage was knocked off and the Doctor couldn't find 2 of the stitches. Then I was hit between the eyes with a heavy, wooden swing and had a few stitches. Oh yes, when I was a toddler I fell off the bed; hit the bridge of my nose and had some stitches there.

The only time I wet my bed was when visiting my Grandparents in Kathleen. I was on a sleeping pad (in the living room) and to this day vividly remember the dream. While walking thru the woods I came to log; had an urge to pee; was streaming over the log, until I immediately felt warmth in my PJs.

At the Barrett's a joyful memory was making ice cream. This was a joint effort beginning with crushing the blocks of ice; adding rock salt and taking turns hand cranking the ingredients. My favorite was Strawberry, since this area was known for its delicious Strawberries that we picked fresh from the bushes.

In the backyard (after the ice cream) we would jump from the huge Oak Trees onto our bag swings. These swings were made of crocus sacks (we pronounced it 'croker') filled with Spanish Moss we had pulled from the trees. We delighted in having as many kids as possible attempting to jump onto on a bag at the same time, frequently losing at least one kid.

David and I were camping near Grandmother Barrett's. In the coals of the fire I had placed a can of stew to heat; the plan was to take it out before the can swelled too much, but with my foot as I pushed a log aside the can exploded. Fortunately no metal hit anyone; however we had to explain to Mom why we were covered in Beef stew.

Around the time I began elementary school we were living in Lakeland where I recall a Fig tree behind the house; as usual I was running; stepped on broken glass, gashing my foot. The neighbor bandaged my foot saying the cut wasn't too bad, however next day Mom took me to our Doctor who said I should have had stiches.

I also recall finding paint in the storage shed and needing a use, so painted my brother David. At the time it seemed a reasonable action, but after the scolding from Mom and watching a crying David being bathed in kerosene I had second thoughts.

MOUNT WASHINGTON, NEW HAMPSHIRE
A WINDY PLACE

The courageous do not live long, but the fearful do not live at all.

After some typical maritime weather, there was supposed to be a 'rain window' in the morning, so I will be able to climb Mt. Washington. This is the highest mountain in the Northeast (at 6288'); has the world's highest recorded wind speed, from the summit wind speeds of 231 mph have been recorded and temperature reaching 40-50 below zero. At the Visitor's Center I noted that 137 people have died in these mountains, deaths from: heart attacks; avalanches; to rock falls. In mid-September one guy died of hypothermia in a snowstorm.

I was a little apprehensive about the climb; I hadn't been at altitude for a while and haven't really done much hiking lately. It's a 4000 foot vertical climb in 4.1 miles, so the climb is 1000 feet/mile. To someone not familiar with mountains this doesn't sound so terribly high, however imagine yourself on Daytona Beach and before you sits a wall ¾'s of mile into the sky.

Got on the Tuckerman Ravine Trailhead (at the Appalachian Mountain Club) at 7am and started up and I mean UP. I was told there weren't any switchbacks, just a continuous climb. This turned out to be like being on stairs and stepping up for 4 miles, however the Sun was shining and it looked good for photos at the peak. After a mile or so I got off onto the Lion's Head Trail; began scrambling over rocks at an even steeper angle. Many of these rocks were so large and I'd have to jump from one to another; the trail continued up and up, so steep that in a couple places wooden ladders were provided. Every time it seemed the climb was going to level out, up again. Just below Lion's Head I came out above the tree line, this was at an elevation around 5000 feet and the horizon was filled with views of mountain tops peeping above the clouds.

I continued to climb, as valley clouds rushed up the hillside. For some reason when I got to Tuckerman Trail I thought the trail leveled out to the summit. NOT!!! For the next half mile a huge rock field opened before me; there wasn't a trail, you just jumped from rock to rock at a precipitously steep angle. This was brutal climbing. I was really tired and my feet were killing me.

After 4 ½ hours I finally reached the summit; amid tourist cars; a cog railway and shuttle vans. Really wanted to lie down and rest, but the Sun was partially out, so I got some photos and then lay down for a while to read.

I seriously considered taking the shuttle down. I was in pain and knew climbing down would be murder on my knees. But to take the shuttle would (somehow) be dishonest; the goal I set was to conquer Mt Washington; so I started down and immediately my knees turned to mush. I took a different route back down and didn't know what to expect. Then I came to a sheer cliff, with several cascading waterfalls.

I thought when I got to the cliff base the trail would level out, NOT! I was going slower and slower, at times stepping down sideways to reduce the shock on my knees and feet. I figure you need to add a mile to this trail due to maneuvering around rocks, matter of fact I have stepped on, around and over more rocks on this trip than in my entire life.

Finally got to the shelters and talked with the caretaker, she said the most popular season is winter, for skiers and ice climbers. In a cabin here she will stay until November, alone. I've talked with several young women who do this and most are young and attractive. I can't help wondering if they are escaping something.

I was quite disappointed to see that it was still 2.4 miles back to my truck. I hurt from one end to the other and now added to the other pains the constant shock was hurting my neck and giving me a headache. I stopped a couple times, rested and read. Hiking the last mile and a half I was taking baby steps and trying to ignore the pain. I really wanted down and if a shuttle was near, I'd happily jump on it. By the time I got near the Visitor's Center I was exhausted. I should have been able to get down in 3 or so hours, but this took 4 hours.

Drove into Gorham where Burger King advertised 2 Whoppers for $3. I couldn't resist. Got back to Maybellene feeling better, but as I got out of Sammie, suddenly chills began. I rushed inside, got under blankets for an hour until the chills subsided. I didn't think I was that tired, I wonder if this reaction is normal for someone in their late 60's? This was probably the most brutal, difficult hike I've ever made, at that time. Not the distance or elevation change, but the rock scrambling. My body just ain't as forgiving as it used to be. At the time I was surprised that my legs didn't hurt, but the next morning I had trouble standing; it was 3 days before the pain in my legs subsided. One of these days a personal challenge such as this is going to kill me.

HIGH SPRINGS FLORIDA

When I was in High School three of us boys bought a 'car' (**Mamie's Revolt**) for $9.99, we lost a penny on the way to the sale. To Mom's chagrin we sawed off the top; Mike was a hemophiliac and she was concerned that he'd end up bleeding to death in our car. The brakes barely worked so we had a rock on a chain, so to slow down I'd gear down, then throw out the rock. Since she frequently died, an advantage was that we'd cut off the fenders, so we would walk on the tires to get her down the road where Mom would find us and tow us home. Of course we had no insurance or tag, however the police seemed to just ignore us. **Mamie** met her demise near Blue Springs when a crowd of us kids were driving thru the woods; hit fence, then were surrounded by angry Wasps. I stayed perfectly still and was not bitten, not so for most of the passengers. She wouldn't start, therefore rusted away in those woods, all alone.

After returning from the Air Force Judy and I rented a house (well more like a fishing cabin) on the Santa Fe River at Poe Springs. This was truly a Barry abode: located just above Snake Island; with a huge Oak Tree horizontal almost across the river; a lantern suspended from the porch to view fish at nite and catch Butter Catfish; a zip line across the river; a floating dock I built and attached to the tree; fossil Mammoth; Horse and Manatee bones in the river; and up and down the river-springs; caves and animals galore. A truly wondrous experience.

One day while walking around Poe Springs (from an Oak Tree) a baby Raccoon fell in front of me. We decided to keep her as a pet and named her 'Connie the Coon'. During the summer we would sleep on the front porch, which extended over the river; this porch was cooler, although a bit crowded for both of us on the Army cot. However it was certainly too crowded, late at nite, with Connie climbing over us.

I had captured a Red Shouldered Hawk with the intention of training it to hunt. The Hawk ate better than us, with a daily allowance of beef heart. As the 'coon grew she became bolder and would rush at the Hawk who would then lie on its back; open its wings and extend its powerful talons. That coon wasn't stupid, it never got closer. One of the hazards of training a Hawk is that they didn't always stay where you wanted them; this one delighted in walking up my arm (off the arm protector); onto my shoulder, leaving bloody punctures in my skin. I'm not sure the Hawk did this on purpose, but later the Hawk got after Connie who dove under some lumber where she died.

Judy had been raised in California and it took some adjustments to accustom her to the Florida animals, especially the large insects. Here we have huge roaches called Palmetto Bugs and when upset extrude a horrible odor. Judy did not like them and evidently they knew this. One nite one crawled across her face and she *lost it* for a while. For some reason she never befriended a Palmetto Bug.

During this time we had a Cat, Sammie, who would sleep on the bed with us. One morning I awoke to find the Cat under Judy. I rolled her over and the Cat was as flat as a pancake. I exclaimed to Judy, "*You've squashed the cat, Sammie is dead!*" However there was movement and Sammie squirmed; stretched and amazingly came back to the world of the living.

After we moved back to High Springs I continued to spearfish in the Santa Fe River. On day I was at Dunnigan's Dam (now just some shoals) and saw a Florida Fish and Game enforcement officer approaching; I hid my speargun among the rocks; as he closed in I recognized him as a guy I'd gone to High School with, although that didn't deter his intent to bust me; Woody knew what I was doing and rode around searching for my speargun, but finally gave up. Whew!

Later I worked for Game and Fish in Lake City and one day an enforcement officer came to our office, saw me, and said, "*Aren't you the same Barry that has been illegally spearfishing on the Santa Fe?*" I had to admit that it was me, but replied that I'd retired.

In High School I recall when Bobby and I put my boat in the Ichetucknee River with the goal of boating up the Santa Fe River back to High Springs. We had Bobby's 3 HP outboard motor; with the camping gear and extra gas we were really slow; going upstream was even slower and when we got the shoals at Dunnigan's Dam we barely moved forward. We paddled like crazy; barely made any headway, but finally made it thru the whitewater.

DEER CROSSING SANTA FE RIVER

While in High School in High Springs I decided to take a shop class. My project was to build a crossbow. Not wanted to build a conventional crossbow (actually not knowing anything about crossbows) I decided to use a car spring as the bow and an eighth inch cable as a 'string'. The real problem was a trigger mechanism and a way to cock the bow. Following completion we bunched up outside; fired an arrow (actually at the time I did know it was called a 'bolt') the bolt zipped out of sight and was never found.

At home I decided to target practice in the back yard, but when the bolts struck the Hickory Nut tree they disintegrated. Obviously this was a powerful machine. To get an idea of its range I fired across the street into the school yard and the bolt went straight through a window.

I differ from my 5 siblings is numerous ways: I've never abused drugs or alcohol; smoked cigarettes; have always been extremely active; never gained excessive weigh; always traveled and have been extremely curious. Liberal; skeptical; logical; tolerant characteristics permeate my brain, resulting in a necessity to observe evidence before I am able to understand and accept. I'm certainly not prone to believe something based on hearsay or faith without supporting evidence. In order to understand many concepts I'd first start at the molecular level and work up; also I am personally distraught by being wrong, so attempt to know before I make claims of validity; I encourage discussion as a method of learning and am frustrated that few conservatives are capable of objective discussion. Later in life I discovered that this innate curiosity was leading me into a study of science.

Too many people find it easier and more comforting to believe in dogma, thus preventing them from even seeking evidence. I have always been skeptical of authority and dogmatic pontifications; it takes no effort to believe in dogma even though most dogma, especially current conservative 'truths' are predominantly erroneous. What really frustrates me is the arrogant assertion of their dogmatic beliefs, even though they have never made any effort to research or understand the issue.

Since these people are reluctant to accept that which lies outside their personal experience most are, inexplicably prone to believe in conspiracy stories and false hoaxes, such as: humans didn't land on the Moon; Death Panels; alien encounters; living Dinosaurs etc. Take for example, global Climate Change: A few years ago I was spending the winter (in my motor home) at a friend's in The Florida Keys. Chris was a very intelligent and conservative person who brought up the subject of Global Warming. I replied to his query that 'of course this is a confirmed phenomenon, this is science'. To continue my discussion I contacted two leading scientists (people Chris would frequently hear on FOX entertainment media) who replied to me, stating that conservative media had misrepresented their positions. I stated to Chris that almost every climate scientists agree, therefore it is by definition, science.

Later I heard a more logical argument: This was a Republican congressman who was conservative on almost all issues except he accepted Climate Change as human caused and a scientific reality. Unfortunately (in this country) frequently it is not reason or evidence that sways public opinion, it is money and the Koch brothers are at the forefront of spreading money to yield bewildering ignorance. Anyway, a moneyed campaign was mounted to defeat this fellow Republican; he was defeated and a marginally qualified replacement was elected. Before leaving office, this congressman presented the following argument before Congress: '*So your child has a serious illness; you approach 100 Doctors for diagnosis and treatment; 97 Doctors discover the same cause and propose a certain treatment; however 3 Doctors propose an alternative treatment. <u>Which treatment would you select for your child?</u>*'

This is exactly the situation with Global Warming; more than 97% of climate scientists accept this as valid science. What is scary and disappointing is that millions of ignorant Americans would arrogantly defend the 3 alternative paths above, not resulting from evidence, but blind faith in misdirected, industry driven dogma, perpetuated by conservative entertainment media such as FOX and Rush Limbaugh.

Something I've recently seen relative to the eventual acceptance of science by the American public is that even on conservative media I hear more talk about how global warming is actually happening. Most people forget that just a few years ago this same media fervently denied this fact. As more evidence becomes obvious the fact that Climate Change is human caused will become fully accepted.

Tragically this misinformation (portraying Climate Change as a hoax) was originally generated by oil companies; has delayed action to address Climate Change and future generations will indict this generation for its colossal ignorance and failure to take positive steps to diminish its tragic impacts.

Due to dogmatic misinformation, most Americans don't understand science and conservatives fear science, unfortunately frequently relying on urban legends. The Founding Fathers of America trusted science and until recently we excelled thru science. Science is a tentative, self-correcting discipline that relies on majority consensus, largely thru peer acceptance of testable evidence. Unlike religion, science (in most cases) doesn't state something as an unwavering fact. It says that: under these conditions; based on this evidence, there is a high probability that this is true. With valid, contrary evidence, this consensus can change.

I recall that an Arkansas Federal judge (when addressing the issue of teaching religion in schools in the guise of Creationism) searched for a definition of science. His response was, **science is what scientists do.** The issue of human caused Climate Change is undeniably science, therefore should not be debated thru conservative dogma or public media.

Current conservative dogma, especially by the Tea Party, tragically has become anti-science in a world that sees science as being essential to progress and improvement to the lives of its citizens. These efforts will certainly lead to America becoming a second rate country.

MY MT. WHITNEY CHALLENGE

Life is a great adventure or it is nothing. Helen Keller

Seeds for this adventure were sewn on Guadalupe Mountain (in Texas) where I met people who had a goal of climbing the tallest peaks in all of the states. Mt Whitney (being the highest peak in the lower 48 states) became my paramount challenge.

So in my usual cavalier style I decided to climb Mount Whitney, since I had just climbed Guadalupe Mountain (at 8749 feet) I thought *"What's a few more 1000 feet up?"* Later I discovered that there is a significant difference between a mountain more than 1 mile high and one almost 3 miles high. Having recently seen the IMAX movie 'Everest' I had heard of altitude sickness and casually considered the consequences, but never considered that I couldn't climb any mountain in America, this is from a guy raised in Florida at an elevation of less than 100 feet.

In July of 1999 I arrived in Pine Mountain Club (California) an alpine village, not really a club. The plan was to spend a couple of months there helping Bryan build a house. Bryan and Catherine had recently moved to California from Tallahassee. Their lot is at 5700 feet where I experienced some of altitude sickness: headaches and difficulty sleeping. But after a couple of weeks I had acclimated to <u>that</u> elevation.

In late August Linda and I took a trip into Sequoia and Kings Canyon National Parks. After a little more backpacking in areas that a Florida boy would call <u>very up</u>, I felt ready for Mt. Whitney; then discovered that I must have a permit, something I hadn't expected. However, I agree with the objective of not overstressing the environment by restricting the crowding, therefore maximizing the wilderness experience.

When I returned to Bryan's I called, however there were no permits available until after October 15th. Well, I was to be in Yosemite that week, then would be heading for Death Valley. While in Kings Canyon, I talked with a guy from San Francisco who said he climbed Whitney in mid-October and almost froze to death. However there was hope, in Sequoia National Park I talked with a guy from San Diego who said that you could go to the Ranger Station in Lone Pine and probably get a permit when people with reservations cancel are just don't show up. My other thought was that I just go; climb the mountain and not get caught; it's not like you're stealing the crown jewels.

So, the second week of September, with extreme confidence, I headed north. It was hot in Owens Valley and I didn't appreciate how cold it would become just a few miles to the west of Lone Pine and a couple miles up. I stopped in the welcome station in Lone Pine where I was told that people with day-use permits left a 3:00 AM and made the 22 mile trek in 15 to 17 hours. I wasn't in a hurry; wanted to take video, so what I needed was an overnite permit. At the Ranger Station, just 5 minutes before I arrived, two guys had gotten the last overnite permits.

The Ranger explained that they don't track no-shows, however they issue permits to 8 to 10 people a day who don't have reservations. He said they held a lottery at exactly 7:00 AM. The woman said you take a ticket with a number, which I mistakenly read that was 'first come first serve'. They recommended that I camp at Whitney Portal (at 8000 feet) to begin my acclimation to the elevation. Looking from Lone Pine toward the mountains they resemble the Grand Teton Mountains: stark; treeless; vertical spikes and appeared absolutely unclimbable; certainly nothing like the subdued mountains in the east.

Mt. Whitney was named after the State geologist. It's interesting that he and John Muir had a substantial difference of opinion concerning the formation of Yosemite Valley. Whitney was a Harvard professor and at the time Muir was a sheepherder. Whitney felt that a cataclysmic event dropped the bottom from Yosemite Valley, whereas Muir, thru observation, contended the valley was formed by glaciers. Muir was correct to the embarrassment of Whitney.

Speaking of geology, in 1872 the 'noble earthquake' in Yosemite of which Muir wrote, was centered below Mt Whitney around Lone Pine. It was claimed to be a magnitude 10 earthquake that destroyed 95% of the buildings and killed a bunch of people. A magnitude 7 quake is considered severe, a 10 is eight times more devastating.

At Bryan's the week before leaving for Whitney I had twisted my knee while moving house beams. Disregarding my age I assumed that my knee would be healed after a couple days rest; a problem was that was my good knee, the other knee was my 'toboggan knee' suffered in a crash in these Sierra Mountains.

In the campground they were cautions about the 'Bear problem'. Each site has metal boxes for food or anything with an odor that might attract Bears: toothpaste, suntan lotion, deodorant, smelly socks, etc. I didn't see any Bears, whereas in the Smoky Mountains you would see at least a couple of Bears in the campground.

Looking from the campground there appeared to be no sensible way to the summit that mountain; the side walls were shear and to the west the only place for a trail was almost as steep.

MT WHITNEY THRU ALABAMA HILLS

I crashed around 8:00 PM and cars heading to the trailhead woke me around 3:00 AM. It is kind of amazing that this sleepy looking town of Lone Pine (population around 2000) comes alive at 1 to 2 am for people making a day-hike of Mt. Whitney.

In the morning I arrived at the Ranger Station at 5:30 AM and found no one before me, so felt confident I could get a permit. Little after 6:00 AM two guys from Round Rock Texas arrived, also expecting to be assured of a permit. Actually Geoffrey had an overnite permit for Monday, but his friend didn't have a permit at all.

By 7:00 AM there were 10 people waiting, however, since I was there first I <u>assumed</u> I should have first shot at a permit. Not! Precisely as 7 am the Forest Ranger came out holding a box with numbered slips of paper. I drew number 16 which put me out of contention. Geoffrey drew number one. Now, if his friend didn't get a permit I could use Geoffrey's permit. My luck held; he gave me his permit so I immediately headed for the mountain.

Between Lone Pine and the Sierra Nevada Mountains are the Alabama Hills. The granite rock here is the same strata as along the crest trail thousands of feet higher, this difference resulted from a block fault that has raised the west side of this chain of mountains. There were hundreds of movies; TV segments and commercials filmed here. Movies from: Hop a Long Cassidy; Roy Rogers; Humphrey Bogart; Khyber Pass; Bonanza segments, to John Wayne movies. In my younger days I'm sure I've seen these hills and mountains in numerous films.

MAYBELLENE IN ALABAMA HILLS BEFORE MT WHITNEY

I arrived at the trailhead at 7:15 filled with exhilaration. From here the trail covers over 6000 vertical feet to the summit. Soon I began passing other hikers although I wasn't really in a hurry. I found out later that some were already suffering from altitude sickness. At first the trail was a somewhat steep, steady climb, but just above Lone Pine Lake the trail switchbacked straight up the cliff. After a while I dropped into lovely, lush meadow and at the other end was Outpost Camp where a waterfall released the river into the valley; from that point, amazingly the trail became even steeper!

It was here I met a woman in her 50's or 60's who said she intended to spend a leisurely week getting to the summit; she said she had her books; enough food; a water filter and was there to enjoy the wilderness. I don't think she realized that above Trail Camp there isn't a flat place to stop or camp.

After catching my breath and I was again on the trail above Outpost Camp; here the trail crossed bare rock and the trees tenaciously hung onto the vertical walls; many trees were damaged by fallen rocks and the dead ones looked as if they would lay there for thousands of years, their trunks being as hard as metal.

I met an Asian woman who had planned to climb to the summit, but in the nite her tent blew over and "*I heard something outside my tent*". She wasn't the first to say that the wind was howling at Trail Camp.

Three guys passed me almost jogging, they had ropes, but I don't know what they're planning. One reminded me of Gary, my vertical climbing partner in Florida. After a while the trail dropped into another valley exposing another lovely lake: Mirror Lake. Almost immediately the trail resumed its skyward climb across bare rock; much of the trail was rock steps and after thousands of steps plus the weight of my backpack, pain arose in my left knee. Then I descended into another small meadow where I took off my boots, soaked my aching feet in the COLD stream and lay back on the grass soaking up the sun. I told a guy that I was probably acclimated to the altitude because I'd been almost 6000 feet for over a month. He said, "*No you're not acclimated*." Unfortunately I didn't believe him. Then I heard a loud high pitched bark, but at first couldn't locate the source. Finally a spied a Marmot (also called Whistle Pigs) on a rock, I guess we were infringing on his territory.

As when I exited valleys and meadows below, the passage up looked absolutely impossible. I finally located the trail that began swithbacking, almost vertically up the face of a cliff to the north. When I looked up and up and up I could see people (tiny people) on the trail high above. By the time I crested that cliff I was awfully tired, my legs and both knees ached and I found it difficult to get enough oxygen. I was now at 12,000 feet, twice as high as I've ever climb, before scaling Guadalupe Mountain.

At Trail Camp the wind was ferocious and I could see people trying to right their crumpled tents. That's when I ran into two guys from San Diego who had gotten permits just before me. They had decided not to go over the next hill where most people camped and set up their tent out of the wind behind some big rocks. That sounded good to me, I was exhausted! However there was no way to stake a tent to the ground, so I tided the corners to rocks and put rocks inside the tent. The cold wind was gusting to at least 40-50 mph, sometimes throwing up small stones. Even with rocks inside, some gusts almost collapsed my tent.

Below us was Consultation Lake where whitecaps were forming and across the lake you could see snow banks left from the previous year's snow. Walking over the hill I could see tents upside down and the temperature was 10-15° colder, I was pleased to be in a protected area.

While talking to Ken and Stan a Chipmunk scurried up to us evidently looking for a handout. I discovered that Ken flies hang gliders and frequently kayaks. We hiked down to the lake and through a filter they pumped water for me. You're not supposed to drink any local water due to the probable contamination by animals and humans. You could see Horse poop along the lower trail and the solar toilet was 'out of order'. The primary concern is *Giardia*, a protozoan that can be fatal. Most of the weight I had carried was water; however I drank most of it on the way up. As we were well above the treeline there's no concern for Bears, but Marmots getting into our food was a constant problem. I use my Bear-proof Container, but the guys tied their food out from some rocks. They cooked dinner, while I had nuts and berries. They had more than they could eat so offered me some hot food, a welcome treat. At sunset the temperature dropped rapidly, so I climbed into my sleeping bag, wearing all my clothes. The wind blew most of the nite, but was not as fierce as in late afternoon.

At 5:30 AM I was up taking video of 'the stars': Venus and Jupiter. The elevation at Pine Mountain Club is 6000 feet where the stars are unbelievably clear, but here they looked as if you could reach up and touch them, they just clearly stood out without twinkling. What an exhilarating experience!

In the morning I loaned Ken and Stan my Bear container and at 6:30 began hiking for the summit. Looking from the valley it seemed absolutely impossible to scale the upper wall of the cliff before me. I could see only two people on the '99 switchbacks'. After a ways the trail was icy and very treacherous. While catching my breath a crowd of about 10 people passed me. They had guides and the two older Japanese looked like they couldn't go another step, they were panting and their faces ashen; one problem was that they carried too much weight in camera equipment. Every time I felt the trail couldn't go any steeper, it would! In places the trail was cut into solid granite and the switchbacks passing only a few feet above the trail below.

I just walked like a zombie, one short step at a time. My nose was running trying to adjust to the excessive volume of dry air; my throat was dry; my knees hurt; a headache was beginning; when I stopped a chill set in immediately and my right foot hurt; I was really having fun now! After resting, every time I resumed climbing I would have to gulp air for a while to get enough oxygen into my system. However I focused on ignoring the negative, the view was simply magnificent! Snow along the trail; water flowing under the rocks; more and more green lakes; glacial moraine; Chipmunks; Rock Rabbits (Picas); specks of people and tents below and the exhilarating thrill the goal.

To my relief one of the guides said there wouldn't be any more switchbacks, just a steady climb to the crest. Upon reaching the crest of the mountain chain my first sight was that of a young woman coughing; she had come up in the west side and said it was really cold in the shadows. By the way, this crest is at 13,500 feet and is the John Muir Trail to Yosemite. It had taken me 3 hours to climb the 2 ½ miles from Trail Camp.

Here was another absolutely spectacular view! To the west I could see the lake where the Kern River originates; snow on the north face of Hitchcock Mountains; the chain of mountains that make up the Pacific Continental

Divide and below, the edge of the treeline. The trees (many over 100 feet tall) appear as green specs and above the treeline: stark, rugged brownish rock rising to the crest; to the east was Trail Camp (near Lake Consultation); from this vantage point you could barely make out the colorful tents below; down the valley was Lone Pine Lake which looked too close, in actuality the lake was many hours away and beyond was Death Valley.

After a while Ken and Stan showed up, together we headed for the summit 2 miles to the north. The trail was cut from the west face of Mount Muir, from this point the trail proceeded down although I <u>really did not want to go down</u>, because that meant <u>up</u> on the way out. They set a pace faster than I wanted and I was low on water. As my headache intensified I recalled being told you need lots of water to thwart altitude sickness. [Keep in mind that Ken and Stan were in their 20's and I was 58.]

After a while, as we passed several vertical pinnacles, the trail narrowed to just a few feet where the openings between was a vertical drop of thousands of feet to the valley floor. For a time we were in the shade and it became much colder as a frigid wind screamed through these crevices. We came to an area of loose rock where the trail was more or less horizontal, yet alarmingly narrow. At this point we were at 14,000 feet and in view of the summit although it was partially obscured by clouds. By the time we got to the base of the summit I was tired and my headache progressed into nausea. The last several hundred feet was through a field of immense boulders and no clear trails were evident, so you just scrambled through the rocks, up and up, at a very steep angle.

On the peak of Mt Whitney (at 14,505 feet) blasts of frosty wind subdued the excitement of finally reaching the top. We took photos of each other and a Marmot who was looking for handouts. Unfortunately Stan didn't operate my video camera correctly and the narrative was lost. It was my fault since I wasn't clear about the instructions; another symptom of altitude sickness is loss of mental function. I could tell I wasn't thinking clearly, but by now my heart was pounding and barfing was a real possibility.

Stan started down and I told him I was going to wait and see if the clouds cleared, so I could take better video. We couldn't find Ken; he wasn't feeling too well either. Now I was freezing! I scrunched up behind some large rocks; drank my last swallow of water and ate some trail mix. The rocks felt like solid ice even though I'd put a canteen behind my back. By this time I was shivering violently, the wind chill had to be near zero. I had to move, so I got up and quickly took some video.

From the summit you could see the desert below where the temperature was in the nineties and just beyond was Death Valley where the elevation is 282 feet below Sea Level and probably over 100 degrees. It's amazing that in only 10 linear miles the temperature can be over 60° colder.

Talking about a small world, there were two guys, one came up from the west side and the other came up from the east side and they ran into each other here at the summit of all places. They had been neighbors, years earlier in LA. Then a woman began seen a classical song, but soon ran of oxygen. Only in California!

A little after noon I begin the long trek down. Now that I had experience the summit I could give advice to people coming up. For example, *"It's such and such distance; It's very cold along the crest; Watch for rock cairns in the boulder field and the view is worth the extreme effort"*.

I warmed some, but deep down I remained chilled. Then the worst part of the trail, the slog back up to the crest of a mountain chain. Some people were stopped along the trail panting. I had to breathe harder, but my cardiovascular system is in pretty good shape, so I wasn't in distress.

I kept thinking that a few more feet down and my headache will abate, but so far no such luck. Back up to the crest trail I rested for a few minutes; people congratulate each other and talked about what a fantastic experience they just had, whereas I just wanted to get down to where it's warmer! I looked to the specks of tents and people spots far below and wished I could be transport down, where was Scotty when you need him?

There was no choice, I had to put one foot in front of the other and get down the hard way. I took my time and talked with just about everyone I met. By the time I reached the area of the trail that had been covered by ice, now water was flowing, confirming that this morning was indeed below freezing. It took me an agonizing 4 hours to reach my tent.

165

I had hoped that Stan and Ken would be there with water, but evidently they had gone on down. My original plan was to pack on down to Outpost Camp or on to Lone Pine Lake for the nite, but by now I was really feeling terrible. Trying to warm up I crashed in my sleeping bag. I tried rapid breathing to get more oxygen into my brain hoping to dissipate my headache, but that didn't do any good. I was just plain miserable! Then I thought, ***"If I die up here my only ID is a permit with some guys name on it from Texas. I could see them calling his wife and telling her that her husband had died on Mt. Whitney."***

I really wanted a drink, but just couldn't make the effort to get up. The wind picked up, but not as severe as the day before; around dust some dark clouds came by and it snowed a little bit. Here at this altitude you can get snow on any day of the year. I had left my boots outside the tent so, sometime in the nite, I struggled to put on my boots; took a pee then got back into my sleeping bag. Finally I slept. Wind rattled the tent, sometimes sounding like an animal. I awoke hoping it was almost daylite; however it was only 2:00 AM.

I drug myself out of the tent at 5:30 am and began packing. I desperately needed water and had been debating whether to get it from the lake; the river or beg another hiker for water. In the end I climbed down to the lake and drank and drank, figuring if I got sick it would be a few days later, then I could get treatment.

The problem was that from the lake I took a short-cut down to the meadow, following the river and crossing a boulder zone, where the continuous pounding on my knees really accelerated the damage to my left leg. But rather than stopping I just set a slower pace.

I talked to many people on the way down. It really didn't hit me until several people asked ***"Did you summit*?"** then I began thinking of the many people who don't make it. Some make it the first 2 or 3 miles; some to Trail Camp and even a few to the Crest Trail, then turn back. It never occurred to me that I couldn't make it to the summit; only a grave physical injury would have stopped me.

I talked at length with two women from New Jersey; women who had the adventurous spirit to the point where they would attempt to climb Mt.

Whitney excite me and one of these women was particularly appealing. However they had left late and I'm not sure they made it.

As I descended I met more and more people I knew would not make it to the summit. Some left too late; some were just not physically fit; some set a pace too slow and some lacked the internal drive to overcome the obstacles. One woman asked me if she really needed a tent. Thunderstorms were forecast and a wet sleeping bag at that altitude could spell disaster.

Two guys came down the trail almost running and later I discovered they were coming down from 220 miles along the Crest Trail all the way from Yosemite Park. They were definitely physically fit; however I was in serious pain. I tried to land on my right knee to protect the other knee. Any slight twisting on my left knee produced excruciating pain. Also my calves and shoulders were hurting, so I adjusted the straps on my backpack taking the pressure off my shoulders, but then my lower back began to ache. To my relief, finally my headache had dissipated.

Every 10 minutes or so I'd stop and talk to people on their way up. One lone woman left at 7:30 and expected to make the summit that day, she didn't have a flashlight, so I explained that it was a 15 to 17 hour trek; I explained that it would be well after dark before she could return to the trailhead; finally she realized the futility of her hike and turned back.

Later I met an older couple who were overweight and in poor health. They ask if they were half way up, so I replied "***No, less than quarter of the way. You haven't really started up yet.***" Whitney is for a select group, it's not politically correct to say it but most people just can't do it, especially overweight American couch potatoes.

In Outpost Camp I ran into Geoffrey and his friend. They had planned to pack in on the 15th, but had gone to Yosemite and through misinformation got on a trail that didn't get them back until 2:00 AM, so they were finally on their way up to Trail Camp. Geoffrey had also thought of me getting in trouble; his wife being notified and they joked about his wife celebrating his demise and then returning home, completely healthy. I thanked them for the permit and they gave me some treated water. Geoffrey and his wife had come here the previous July, but didn't make it past Trail Camp. He also said that in July the waterfall into Outpost Camp was a roaring torrent.

Steady switchbacks were fine for me, even if they were down precipitous cliffs, however what produced anguish were the rocks steps. Now I was hobbling, trying to land on my right leg, but that constant shock was beginning to cause pain in my right 'toboggan knee' so I concentrated on the beauty of the area in anticipation of soon reaching Lone Pine Lake.

The people coming down had a new attitude, camaraderie. We had summited. Several times people would say *'congratulations'*. Now I saw this as more of an achievement than I had anticipated. Between May and October a number of people summit each day, yet compared to the billions of people in this world, very few have or could summit this mountain. It's similar to some of the beautiful caves I've visited, only a handful of people in the world will ever share these experiences, these memories will forever be my personal treasures.

Finally I reached Lone Pine Lake and took some video. Having always been drawn to water I sure wish I could've camped here. From the eastern edge of the lake you can see down to the Whitney Portal area and the Owens Valley beyond. Chipmunk and Squirrels jumped from rock to rock and the clear water was inviting, yet quite frigid. A contradiction was the sound of military jets flying over and the sound echoing back and forth among the canyon walls. Edwards Air Force base lies just to the south where new aircraft are tested and further west is the infamous Area 51. Flying over the valley I saw several of the new jet fighters, including the F-22 **Raptor.** Whenever one flew over I was reminded of Pete Collins, just a good old Florida boy from Live Oak, who flew the SR-71 **Blackbird.** He told me many stories about experiences in this area and the Kern River, as well as flying a secret plane to Mach 3 to 80,000 feet. He also visited Area 51 on numerous occasions, but never met the aliens. When I see how clear the stars are a 12,000, I think of his experience of seeing stars from the edge of space.

It didn't look that far down to The Portal, but the trail went on and on, across the river on logs cut with a flat side up; across small streams falling from the cliffs to the valley and among thickening growths of Fir trees. The air was warmer, so I stripped back to a T shirt. To protect them from the high altitude sun, many of the people climbing up look like desert travelers, with large brimmed hats and white cloths around the back. Eventually I reached a point that I had enough; this was beautiful, I climbed the mountain; I had a great time, but I was in pain and just wanted DOWN. Finally I could see cars, at first they were colored spots; then toy cars; then they grew to an inch; 2 inches, a foot; then I could see people below, then the trailhead. I made it! I cheated death again. I dropped my backpack on a Bear-proof container and limped to the overflow parking lot for my truck. It was a relief to remove the backpack, but my knees wanted to stop moving.

When I return I'll hike slower to better acclimate and have more water; camp a nite at Whitney Portal; a nite at Outpost Camp; leisurely get the Trail Camp and spend two nites; then climb to the summit and return to either Trail Camp or down to Lone Pine Lake for the nite.

This was consummate adventure, now to Alaska for Mt. McKinley.

ADVENTURES AT SALT SPRINGS

When we lived in Ocala a couple of High School friends and I would make frequent trips to Salt Springs, in the Ocala National Forest. Near Lake George we would camp on some Indian middens and catch snakes to sell. One time we captured quite a few Water Snakes; Ross Allen's Reptile Institute was overstocked, so I released them in the pond at the new High School.

Speaking of releasing things at school, I had a goal to find the cave no one had ever found and would search out sink holes all across the area looking for 'my unexplored cave'. Sometimes we would bring Bats home, so I decided it would be interesting to release a few during Friday Assembly at school. So here we were in the Auditorium, with girls by the hundreds screaming, *"They're going to get into my hair!"*

Later, back at Salt Springs, we decided to catch a Gator. We had a pole with a noose and went way up into a slough from The Spring Run, into a place that widened where we saw the glowing red eyes of a big Gator, a really big Gator! It was much larger than my boat and we were probably in a Gator 'waller' with an irate mother Gator who seemed actively protective of her young. Quickly we exited left!

Salt Springs was one of the few places in Florida where you could legally spearfish in fresh water. With a permit you could spear rough fish such as

Suckers and salt water Mullet, so we called the Large Mouthed Bass, Large Mouth Mullet. There was a gigantic Bass that we called Ol' Iron Sides; no one seemed to be able to get him and more than one spear had bounced off his opercular plates. I just had to have that Bass, so saved my money and bought a more powerful speargun.

The spearfishing technique was to stick your head under the Lily Pads until your eyes adjusted to the darkness, then swim back into the darkness where the big Bass (that is, the Mullet) hid during the day. Well I was hanging there looking back into the darkened area and without looking, reached for what I thought was a floating limb. As I grabbed 'it' the Gator and I realized something was terribly wrong. It startled me as much as the Gator and we sped off in different directions.

Don't recall if I ever got Ol' Iron Sides.

In the winter on 2013 I was near the head spring with 15 or 20 Manatees when one rubbed the bottom on The Shanty and disrespectfully passed gas. Another one rose before me and seemed to smile.

MANATEE AT SALT SPRINGS

BACKPACKING AND HIKING

Back in the early 70's it seemed that everyone was hiking the Appalachian Trail so we (or maybe that was just me) decided to join them, with the thought of someday hiking the entire 2200 miles. So Judy, Michelle (age about 11) and I packed for 5 days on the AT. We drove to North Georgia and as we began removing our gear from the car Michelle says she is not going. We asked, *"What are you going to do*?" She replied, *"Wait here on the car for 5 days until you return."*

Somehow we convinced Michelle that she will enjoy the experience and she agreed to accompany us. Soon our enthusiasm from the trail was diminished; we expected a mountain experience with great vistas and all we were seeing was Rhododendron bushes. Also, in places, the trail itself was a foot deep due to heavy use.

The second day out we came to a clearing (actually a treeless Bald) were two young people from West Palm Beach Florida were parked. That was it! This was not the wild experience we expected, after struggling up and down over mountains the last thing we desired to see was a car parked only a few feet from the trail.

Then it began to rain and rain and rain. Searching for a road, we came down from the trail and became lost. We camped and all I can recall is that we had a freeze dried Blackberry pie that was so sweet that Judy could not eat it and Michelle and I (who both have a sweet tooth) could not finish.

Next day we found a road and hailed down a couple of mountain folk who were Bear hunting. They said, *"Jump in the back and don't mind the cans."* Well the bed of the truck was a foot deep in beer cans. Somehow they got us back and that ended our Appalachian Trail episode.

Another time we were camping at Smokemont (in The Great Smoky Mountains National Park) and hiked on a short section of the Appalachian Trail. Still searching for vistas we took a side trail to a Bald and again Michelle said she was not going. We walked a short distance down the trail hoping Michelle would join us and came across a log ripped apart by a Bear. We called Michelle; she viewed the log and decided to go along with us.

A lesson in not following advice. While working for the Department of Environmental Regulation three of us who had backpacked together relayed some stories of our trips. Later, three neophytes wanted to accompany us into Linville Gorge in North Carolina. Based on my experience I gave them advice: put some rocks in your backpack; walk around some each day to become accustomed to the weight; when loading your pack don't bring cans and bring light-weight tents. Evidently this advice went in one ear and out the other.

We arrived at the Cabin Trail to begin our descent and I noticed they struggled to mount their backpacks. I had told them to expect fallen trees over the trail, so with their heavy packs; they were struggling over and under tree trunks. By the time we got to the Linville River their legs were quivering and they were totally exhausted. As they removed the contents of their backpacks I could see lots of cans, including beer; I asked about food and they replied that they would catch fish. Then they set up a huge canvas tent and some guys hiking thru asked them if they live there. As usually happens, in the afternoon it began to rain, wetting some of their gear and they couldn't get a fire started. Of course they didn't catch any fish, so the next day packed out. Rip, Doug and I stayed a couple of nites then hiked up Cold Mountain.

This is Linville Gorge:

HAWKSBILL FROM WISEMANS VIEW

Cold Mountain was made famous with the book and movie and I've hiked to the summit 5 or 6 times. I recall one time with Michelle; Rip and his two boys. The weather forecast was free of rain, however in the Blue Ridge Mountains a forecast is worthless so it poured on us. One the way up several items became soaked including our toilet paper, Oh the horror. During the nite the temperature began to rapidly drop and we were not adequately prepared, so Michelle and I lit candles in our tent and huddled together for warmth. Next day the rain continued and I recall Michelle with a plastic garbage bag over her, with her eyes peering out a hole. The highlight of the trip was around dusk; with the sky clearing and Rip and I sitting on the peak (entranced by the view) drinking a small bottle of wine.

THE BOWL IN THE GUADALUPE MOUNTAINS

After my first trip west (in 1999 I'd climbed the highest peak in Texas (Guadalupe) at 8749 feet.) I set a goal to visit The Bowl, in the Guadalupe Mountains National Park. The Bowl is a depression in the mountains, with trees left over from the last Ice Age. Amazingly here in the dry, Chihuahuan Desert of Texas are trees that also occur in Canada. Around 260 million years ago this was the largest coral reef on earth, leaving marine fossils and a legacy of oil in the surrounding basins.

Now it was a couple years later; I was camping in Guadalupe and had planned to hike up on Friday, but there were clouds in the morning and a strong wind was blowing, so I decided to go for it the next day. The wind was still howling, but the temperature was mild so unfortunately didn't take a coat. I was apprehensive because I hadn't been hiking lately and was still tired from the short hike the day before. The elevation at the campground was 5700 feet and The Bowl around 8000 feet.

As I switchbacked up the mountain the fierce wind retarded my progress and the higher I hiked the colder it became. More than once I looked back at the sound of a jet plane, only to discover it was just a mighty gust of wind. It had been blowing for the past 5 days (up to 60 mph), the longest duration and windiest place I'd ever been.

Along the trail are pockets of calcite crystals, formed after this rock had been uplifted, about 60 million years ago. This area is the best preserved Permian aged, fossil reef in the world. It's called the El Capitan Reef and was formed 260 million years ago, when this part of the earth was near the equator. To the east had been a sea, and that area is now called the Delaware Basin. The next basin over (which was also a sea) is the Midland Basin, where for years oil has been pumped.

By the time I reached the ridge, the wind was ferocious and downright cold, I was freezing. Once down into the trees of The Bowl the wind was somewhat blocked, but the shade didn't allow me to warm. Some of the trees species are: Aspen; Ponderosa Pine; Douglas Fir; Oak and Pinion Pine. After 4 hours I was near the eastern edge of the mountains, but I had to climb up to get into Bear Canyon.

Amazingly the settlers below had installed a pipe to the top of the mountain; built a large metal reservoir; pumped water from the springs below and used the water to raise crops. However, from the edge it was straight down to the valley and they had to frequently travel up that canyon. What a chore, that's when 'men were men'.

At the edge, the wind was gusting to at least 50 mph. It was difficult to remain standing and the trees thrashed about like they were having a demonic fit. I hurried down into the canyon, out of the full blast of the wind. While I lunched, gusts roared through the bushes. On down the canyon the air warmed, but the gusting wind continued to rattle the trees and pockets of air roared down the canyon like freight trains.

The trail was so steep that my knees began to ache. Back into the valley the wind direction shifted to a point in front of me and when the wind gusted I'd brace myself, but when it suddenly stopped I'd almost fall down. After 7 hours and 9 miles I finally returned to the campground, somewhat tired.

MY FIRST MEXICAN MISADVENTURE

I was RVing outside Patagonian Arizona and on Friday evening felt an urge for a 'happy hour' just to socialize with people, rather than rocks and trees. What I had in mind was something like Applebee's or Bennigan's. I asked a woman who worked for the Border Patrol where I might go, she said, "**Nogales U.S. is dead, everyone goes over to Nogales Mexico. Go to the Lipstick.**" She said it was a tittie bar (which wasn't what I was looking for), but that they'll be Americans there you can socialize with. She also said she had been kicked out of that bar, something about messing with a married man, maybe not a good sigh.

So I parked on the U.S. side (for $4.00) and walked over to Mexico. Some impressions of Nogales Mexico: there were few traffic signs and even fewer lights; driving is a lot like a group of oozing amoeba, you just keep going, driving much too fast and merge with the flow usually announcing your intentions with a horn blast, amazingly I saw only one collision. Of course trashiness is expected throughout Mexico. The street vendors were along every sidewalk although they weren't as persistent as some Mexican towns. There were steep hills above town topped by multicolored, living hovels appearing to be abandoned adobe relics, but for the washed clothes on the line and fences. In front of an auto parts store I saw someone working on their car, in the street that was on in incline of at least 30°; with a rock behind a tire; a flimsy jack and was <u>under</u> the car, certainly not an OSHA approved situation. The commercial billboards were Americanized; the people (especially women) didn't at all appear Mexican or Spanish. What was depressing and frustrating that was that when you line up to the border station to return to Arizona, there were beggars and peddlers and even groups of Indians with a dime store spears, playing flutes accepting coins from returning Americans.

I'd been looking all over for the **Lipstick**, then a local guy asked if he could help, then said he never heard of the **Lipstick**. He asked me if I wanted women and I said "*No*". He said he'd take me to a good place to have a drink and meet some Americans. We walked quite a ways; closer to the edge of town and I became somewhat apprehensive. We cross the railroad tracks (a bad sign) and when he signaled to a friend, then a red light went off in my head. Am I in some kind of scam or robbery! I checked around for an escape outlet; put my billfold on my front pocket and hesitantly followed him, a few paces back. He said where I needed to go is what I understood him to say as **Sherry's**. After a while we came to **Cherry's** and he said there was a $3 cover, but you get a free drink. He obviously wanted a tip for his 'services', which meant I was freed from probable criminal action. I pulling out a dollar, however he said how about $2, which I gave him.

The entrance was so dark I couldn't even see the people collecting the cover charge; from $10 he gave me back $5 Before I entered I knew this was definitely NOT my kind of place. The music was at a decibel level that permanently damages hearing and it was so dark that I stopped, allowing my eyes to adjust. The women stood out because UV lights illuminated what little clothes they <u>temporarily</u> wore. A woman was dancing on the bar with the smallest possible G string and nothing else. I looked for

Americans but didn't see any, like I was an Owl and can actually see in the dark.

After I bought a beer a guy near the bar called me over. He spoke passable English and said he was sitting with two Americans. He seemed to know everybody and was always doing high- 5s and banging beer bottles in a salute. The girls were voluptuous while slithered and contorted across the bar where guys slowly put money in various places. (Quite like my brother Paul in Key West) But these girls wore less to nothing.

A guy came by several times asking if I wanted a 'table dance'. Of course this shouldn't be called a table <u>dance,</u> they are very erotic lap dances as close to sexual intercourse as you could do in a chair. Then a particularly attractive woman approached with one of those bras that made her breast look like two firm Grapefruits and asked if I wanted a table dance. When I said 'No' she said "**Porque, no me gasta.**" that I understood to mean; Why, don't you like me? There was a time in my life that I may have taken her up, but that time was lost in foggy memories.

The friendly guy (something like Jose) explained that for $15 you could take any of the girls in the back room then pointed to the several rooms along the wall. Later he said something about $20 for woman and it comes with a rubber. Then he said something about him being a gigolo and <u>had</u> 4 married women, this and many other things he said confirmed that he was quite a bull shitter. I was going to have one more beer then leave so, of course at the critical moment Jose asked, "***You going to buy <u>me</u> a beer?***" I really had had enough, as well as feeling anxious.

In a way I sincerely felt sorry for these women. One was an Indian with a dark complexion and I visualized her coming to the 'big city' from some tribal 'tepee' looking for a job and ending up prostituting herself for money. When Jose went to the bathroom I hurriedly split.

After crossing back into Arizona I asked a customs guy about the **Lipstick**, he said "***Oh yes, it's just down the street from Cherry's.***" This was certainly another experience, one I'll not ever repeat.

THE CHARACTER

After another week of exploring the area around Patagonia (population less than 1000), for the next 'happy hour' I found a local watering hole, the Longhorn Saloon. The décor was a dusty, western clutter. Of course this included the required huge, suspended wagon wheel; old rifles; a diorama with a howling Coyote; bow and Wal-Mart arrows; a stuffed Moose (with enormous rack) and a stuffed Javalina (a pig like animal). I almost retreated when I realized <u>everyone</u> was smoking. But the Mexican waiter was very outgoing and I was determined to partake of a little *local color*. Well it wasn't long before the *king of local color* came by; his name was Joker; 84 years old; had only one leg and an exceptionally weathered face.

Soon after a trio of 'cowboys' arrived all wearing 10 gallon hats with brims so broad that it could shade the cowboy <u>and</u> his horse. That last guy was the size of a Buffalo and had to duck down to clear the doorsill. They said they weren't here for beer, they wanted real drinks and ***"lots of them"***. I had the impression that they had been out on the range too long or had already had some 'real drinks'. I also noticed an artist looking girl who years ago would be called a hippie who was flirting for drinks from the tourists from Michigan.

Well, the Joker was born in the current ghost town of Duquesne and lived in Patagonia almost all his life. He worked the mines, mostly the trench near World (something) Mine, in Flux Canyon. Leaving before daylight he would walk the 4 miles up to work the mine and walk down after dark. I can attest that this trek is not just <u>up</u>; in places it is a rock scramble, just the walk would exhaust most humans. For a while he and two guys lived in a nearby mine, later he and another guy staked a claim in another area, but it didn't pan out. Joker said he carried 15 tons of ore down the mountain. Each trip he would put 200 pounds on his Mule and he carried 100 pounds in a pack, this man was something else or I was falling for a tall tale. You'd think he'd be too tired, but he sired 11 children, always boy/girl. One of his sons just died of liver cancer and a son from Auburndale Florida was currently visiting. His wife also had liver cancer, I think they had 'a drink or two' in their lives, however his real compulsion seemed to be cigarettes. When he came in, he had said he needed a cigarette before he could begin drinking. He probably lost his leg mostly due to his atrocious vices. We talked for a couple hours and I forgot to ask him how he got his nickname. Joker was the kind of real character you'd meet in Wakulla County Florida.

PS: Later at Tonto National Monument (Salado Indian Cliff Dwellings) I met a Ranger who was raising Patagonia and knew, **The Joker**.

DRIPPING SPRINGS ADVENTURE

In 2008 (at the Grand Canyon) I arrived at Hermit's Rest trailhead at 7am and read the warning. A woman who ran the Boston Marathon (in 2004, in less than 3 hours) died here. She was on a day hike; didn't carefully read her map (the distance was twice what she thought); didn't take enough water and died of dehydration. I had a gallon of water (half with Gator Aide) and before the day ended discovered that this wasn't enough either.

The first part of the trail was steeply down, very steeply. I spied some Mountain Lion tracks, hopefully not a hungry Mountain Lion. Since the distance to Dripping Falls was only another 3 miles I cut off north to Santa Maria spring, which was really disappointing since the 'spring' was a pipe feeding a 'cattle trough'. There I met a couple of people who work at the Park (for Xanterra) and a group of Pennsylvania hikers who are heading down into the canyon for a week.

Back up to the Dripping Springs trailhead I hiked out of the wash and again started up. This narrow trail was not for the faint hearted, in many places along the edge there was a vertical drop of hundreds of feet.

Now it was getting hot and the trail alternated between short, level places to steeply up and up.

Finally I reached Dripping Springs which is just as it sounds, a little water dripping into a small pool, from a fern festooned overhang. In the coolness of the overhang I rested for an hour before starting back.

I set a slow pace because I knew the real challenge would be the rock wall back up to Hermits Rest. Looking from here the climb out really looked absolutely impossible. This was the worst kind of hike: easier going down; then when you are tired, an exceptionally difficult climb out.

Some clouds formed, but none over me and even before getting back into the valley I knew I was running out of water and energy. When I'd stop I become dizzy, I don't recall this ever happening before, even on the 40 mile backpack (a year and a half ago) down to Thunder Spring and the Colorado River. It appeared that my heart was pumping large quantities of blood and when I'd stop, excessive blood overloaded my brain. Anyway, I arrived in the valley and lay under a Juniper tree for an hour, hoping some clouds would come my way. Finally I had to leave and get onto the switchback trail up. Frequently I'd stop and sit under a tree feeling much more exhausted that normal, I can't believe my body had fallen apart in 2 years (although I shouldn't expect young energy in a 66 year old). On I trudged, stopping more and more frequently and becoming more concerned with the dizzy spells. A couple of times I really wasn't sure I could make it all the way out, it was brutally hot and I was totally exhausted. I'd come around a corner, looked up and it seemed the rock wall was getting higher.

Finally I made it to the rim and treated myself to an ice cream bar and a coke. Now I realize that I'm going to have to be more careful in challenging this 'not so young' body. This trip was only 8 miles and on the 12 mile hike on Bright Angel trail (3 year previous) I was not nearly so exhausted.

At the Grand Canyon I attended what will now be the best Ranger program so far. The subject was Mountain Lions given by a woman barely 5 feet tall who surely has ADD. Her bouncing around the stage reminded me of a Mick Jagger concert and made me tired. She talked about how rare it was to have seen a Mountain Lion. She has searched for 12 years and just this year got a glimpse of one. She also stated that only 1% of Grand Canyon visitors actually descend into the Canyon.

That caused me to think of being in the 1% of people who have done particular things: I'm of the 1% who has seen a Panther in the wild; been to the bottom of the Grand Canyon: has caught Gators by hand; in Belize, scuba dove 240 feet; stung by a Turkey Fish in Australia; sailed solo to

Central America; been in a rubber boat bumped by a Whale; explored caves inaccessible to most everyone; bitten by a Shark; had an encounter with a Wolverine; sky dived; bitten by a Dolphin; took ocean liner from Australia; to New Zealand; Tonga; Hawaii; Vancouver to San Francisco; bitten by Kingfisher; driven Black Bear Pass in Colorado; hiked to the top of Mt Whitney; stung by a Scorpion; shot the rapids on the Kenai River in Alaska; shocked by an Electric Eel and bitten by a Piranha; surrounded by a herd of Bison at Yellowstone; backpacked for hundreds of miles and hiked over a thousand miles; located (barefoot) Howler Monkeys in a Guatemalan jungle; found a human body on a beach in Baja; caught Rattlesnakes by hand; stung by a Sting Ray; dove in underwater caves alone; found perfect Mammoth teeth; backpacked 40 miles into the Grand Canyon at age 64; been in a rainstorm of 25 inches in one nite; been shocked by lightening; fallen out of a moving car; in my late 60's climbed several 14,000' mountains, including the highest mountains in several States; driven from one side of a hurricane to the other; in my 70's, hiked on a ledge inches wide on a cliff face in Colorado; had a pet Hawk and Raccoon; drag raced in California; sunk a sailboat in the Bahamas; driven a truck up a mountain above 13,000 feet; climbed a vertical rope into and out of a 310 foot deep sinkhole; had a Bear charge me; rode in a hot air balloon and a blimp; surfaced in a lake (in California), in an electrical storm with a scuba tank on my back; slashed with a machete; flown in the first 747 in service; stuck in the jungles of Belize; in the Blue Ridge Mountains, drove thru The Storm of the Century; made a submarine; in my 70's, rappelled in a 150 foot waterfall; and on and on. I guess I'll never stop seeking adventure and excitement.

LEWIS AND CLARK CROSSING THE BITTERROOT MOUNTAINS OF MONTANA

Today, in 2007, I walked in the footsteps of History.

In 1805 when Lewis and Clark reached the headwaters of the mighty Missouri River they expected to look to the west and see a great plain (as they had just passed to the east) with rivers extending to the Pacific

Ocean. They were at Lemhi Pass (near Salmon); peering over the Continental Divide and instead: the optimistic dream was shattered when they saw "**immence ranges of high mountains still to the West of us**." After trading with the Shoshone for horses, they still expected to canoe down the Salmon River to the Pacific. This too was not to be. After exploring (west of present-day North Fork) they could see the turbulent river was not navigable (Lewis called this, **The River of No Return)**, so (on horseback) they headed north (over Lost Creek Pass); thru the Bitterroot Valley, no doubt dreading passing over the fortress of snowcapped mountain peaks. At Traveler's Rest (just outside the town of Lolo) they met 3 Nez Perce boys who had just crossed the Bitterroots in 5 days. It will take the Lewis and Clark group 11 grueling days to make a trip they described as a "**verry bad passage over hills & thro' Steep hollows**". Undaunted then they headed west along Lolo Creek, into the Bitterroot Mountains. It was September and an early snow had covered the old Indian trail. [This trail had been used for thousands of years by the Nez Perce heading east to hunt Buffalo and west by the Salish to gather Salmon. The undergrowth along Lolo Creek was too thick to pass, so the trail followed the ridgeline over the mountains. Tragically, 77 years later, this was the same trail used by the Nez Perce (led by Chief Joseph) being pursued by US troops.]

Clark recorded this statement concerning their westward passage: "**I have been wet and as cold in every part as I ever was in my life.....men all wet cold and hungary...to describe the road of this day would be a repetition of yesterday except the Snow which made it much wors to proceed.**"

In late July of the following year (with Nez Perce guides) they retraced this trek over the mountains. A final comment was: "**leaveing these tremendious mountains behind us, in passing of which we have experienced cold and hunger of which I shall ever remember.**"

Back at Traveler's Rest the group separated and Lewis headed north to the area east of Glacier National Park.

Bear Grass along Lewis and Clark Trail

At Howard Creek I began my hike along this trail; the trail immediately rose steeply to the ridge, then along the steep mountain slopes.

For the first couple of hours the trail was easy to follow, as it led me steeply up and down the ridges. Then it began reaching for the sky and became extremely steep and difficult to locate. If it had not been for tree blazes, the trail would have been impossible to follow. It was beginning to get hot and I'd stop to rest and reread Da Vinci Code. Now I was higher than any nearby mountains and to the southeast I could see clouds and hoped they would move into this, then I slipped on some loose rock and twisted my lower back.

Around 2 pm the trail started precipitously down, I assumed to Lolo Hot Springs. At a logging road was a sign, but I didn't see a trail. Twice I walked thru the heavy brush and finally decided to follow the road down, however the road soon leveled out and began heading the wrong direction. Now it was dreadfully hot; with no shade so I returned up to the sign being determined to get on down the mountain. After a ways I could see a faint trail, but no signs. In places this trail would head up and I desperately wanted to go down. Now I was almost out of water and the breeze felt like the opening of an oven. Below I could see a logging road, but not the hiway. Finally I reached the road and started down. Now I was really overheating and still there was no shade. After about 45 minutes I found a shady spot and lay down. Now I was completely out of water; there was not a cloud in the sky and the temperature had to be 100 plus. [It was 107 in Missoula, the hottest temperature ever recorded.] Finally I reached the hiway. While in the coolness of the trees I'd figured that I'd just hike down the hiway back to Tonya, but I was really tired and along the asphalt the temperature had to be more than 120 degrees. It was a grueling 40 minutes before a guy picked me up; I struggled into Tonya; gulped lots of water and ran the AC wide open. An hour or so later clouds rolled in!

YELLOWSTONE NATIONAL PARK

THE WORLD'S FIRST NATIONAL PARK
LOCATED INSIDE THE WORLD'S LARGEST VOLCANO

BACKPACKING HEART LAKE

To receive a backpacking permit I had to sign an understanding that hiking alone is dangerous and not recommended.

I started on the trail at 7:15 am with the understanding that the trail was relatively level for the first 4 ½ miles. Well it sure was humpy for being 'level'. Most of the time I hiked thru a Spruce/Fir forest that had been burned in the great fire of 1988. The new trees were typically Lodgepole Pine and were about 8-10 feet tall. In places the trail was covered with small slivers of volcanic glass (obsidian), relics of volcanic eruptions. The first mile I felt like I could hike forever, but then that back pain grabbed me. Since (in my past years of backpacking) I've never had this particular pain I wonder if it has to do with my busted shoulder I received in Mexico? It's a deep, vertical pain up the left side of my back and no matter how I adjust my pack the pain increased with every mile.

Finally I reached the first thermal features. This boiling, fuming water was accompanied by a violent hiss and some steam.

A short distance further east I could look down on Heart Lake; appearing deceptively close, but was still 3 miles away. The trail descended steeply down to Witch Creek where I left my backpack and explored up among more thermals, hot springs and geysers. Surprisingly this broiling creek supported a luxuriant growth of flowers.

I rested a bit and read my new book. Shortly after continuing down toward the lake I meet 2 men and a young woman who said they were Rangers and were going to a cabin (by the lake) for a few days, now that sounds interesting. It's unclear what they were to do there, but I'm sure they would have a good time. One guy said he had been seasonally working here for 18 years.

After 4 ½ hours I reached Heart Lake; stretched out in the coarse sand and read my book. Then half a mile along the west shore I dropped my backpack and explored another geyser area. Up until 1984 there was a mighty geyser (Rustic) that was the destination of most hikers, however it is now dormant and the silent pool supports an appealing growth of geyserite. I thought these geyserite deposits were calcium based, but they are composed of silica. The pool remains sizzling hot and supports the growth of some yellow, extremophile bacteria.

I read that there was an active geyser in the area, but didn't know which hot spring, so I found a shady spot and settled in for a wait. After a half hour a pool just in front of me began to gurgle; erupted and the steam enveloped me. Quite a spectacle.

Returned to the trail to discover what I dreaded and should come to expect, the trail didn't follow the lakeshore, but rose steeply up the side of Sheridan Mountain. Up and up I climbed. I was told there was cold, fresh water up here, but all the streambeds were dry. Just as I found one with a trickle of water, a pack train showed up and muddied the stream. I think its fine that some people have their gear and bodies carried by animal, but the horse poop along all the trails is not to my liking.

The trail continued steeply up and down, now I was REALLY tired of going up, but whoever made the trail had not listened to me. I'd crest a hill and just hope this was the last one, but NO there would be another, even higher. Finally I could see the south end of the lake and a cove and just hoped this was the designated campsite. I stopped just over the last hill; picked some berries and continued to read. With ripe berries in the area I was sure I'd be able to get photos of some Bears.

Hiked on down to the cove and was delighted to find the camping area, now it was 4pm and had been a long day. It was 11 miles to the camp and I figured I'd hiked/backpacked for about 13 miles today.

While exploring around the lake I saw what didn't really appear to be ducks. I stared at the spots and could only come to the conclusion that they were young Beavers, here is full daylight, diving (like ducks) in the lake.

I kept hearing about how devastating the Lake Trout were to these lakes, but didn't understand why. Well, later I discovered that someone illegally released the eastern Trout here, probably because they grow so large; however the problem is that the animals who feed on fish are adapted to the smaller Cut Throat Trout. For example a Bald Eagle can't pick up a large Lake Trout. Also the Lake Trout eat the Cut Throat fry and have decimated their numbers. The Park has removed 100's of thousands of Lake Trout and rules require fishermen to kill all Lake Trout they catch. In Heart Lake the record Lake Trout caught weighed 43 pounds.

While poking around the area near my tent I found a tree where a Bear had clawed the trunk. This was a big Bear and the highest marks were 10 feet up! Lost the sun around 7pm; explored the area some more and got into my tent around 8pm.

That nite I slept very well, partially because my ground pad held air _most_ of the nite. At daybreak I could hear Coyotes yapping nearby and later some Wolves howling. Later I found that the Delta Wolfpack was in this area and was composed of 16 Wolves.

Was up at first light to witness a breathtaking sunrise peaking over the Absaroka Mountains and the sun beams unfolding across the lake. Absaroka is the name the Crow Indians called themselves.

A short time later there was a slight breeze and across the lake I could see the Columbine fire heating up. It's amazing how these fires lay down at nite and just a little heat from the Sun and a hint of a breeze they build back up into a raging forest fire. At sunrise there was not a trace of smoke and in just a few minutes towering smoke rose from the mountains. From my travels during the past few years it appears that sooner or later the entire West will burn.

As with every place I've camped the first chore (when leaving) is to climb UP.

I exited some trees and faced a huge Bull Elk just in front of me. When he looked up and saw me there was no startle or inclination to dash away, definitely not a good sign! This was near Fall rut and I was not at all sure he wasn't going to consider me an intruder contesting his territory. Like Elephants, they go a little crazy; can become extremely aggressive and actually kill visitors. But I was relieved to see him return to grazing and consider me just another lowly animal passing thru his area.

So now it was time to bite the bullet and head up from the lake. This is a steep climb of 500 vertical feet and now the day was already becoming warm. I shouldn't complain, since the high temps were in the low 80's and not 100, like in the south, Janice said its 107 degrees near Birmingham. The lake is at 7400 feet and is actually quite pleasant, if you didn't have to lug a huge pack on your back.

After reaching the summit I found a shady, grassy spot and rested, there I talked with couple of girls who were day-hiking to the lake.

Now only 4 ½ miles to go. I kept thinking, I've had my fun and got some photos, if there was a bus I'd jump right on it. But no, I had to 'pay' for this adventure, my last backing trip of the year. When I was about 2 miles away from Tonya I could hear thunder and see dark clouds approaching from the west. I would welcome the coolness, but just didn't want to deal with rain or lightening. After another mile a humid cold wind blew and it looked like

I'd be doused, but made it back with a few sprinkles and the rain didn't begin until I was heading back to camp.

MIAMI FLORIDA

This was after we returned from Australia. I was on my way home from work; saw an 8 foot Boa Constrictor crossing the road; caught the snake and tried to maintain control, however at one point the snake wrapped around my neck, making driving an issue. Arriving at home I attempted to remove the Snake, but he was entangled under the seat. I began removing the seat; several neighborhood kids came around and I cautioned Michelle to not get near the Snake. Controlling an independent 2 year old is impossible; Michelle pointed toward the Boa; the Snake struck and enveloped her hand; as Judy arrived I was trying to work the curved teeth back so they wouldn't rip her hand; exited Judy yanked Michelle's hand from the mouth of the snake, resulting in scratches and blood. Judy was now concerned about disease; I told her that it's better to be bitten by a Snake than a Dog or Cat because Snakes don't have Mammal diseased; unconvinced Judy call Haas the local Snake expert who confirmed what I said, however Judy would not allow me to keep the Snake at home.

While in High School I visited my aunt in Miami and was spearfishing in The Keys. Under the Bahia Honda Bridge I shot at a fish and missed. The current was ripping through The Cut, so I wrapped my legs around some 'rocks' so I could cock my gun. Unknown to me the coral rock was covered with Fire Coral and it set my legs on fire. I remember another time Fire Coral got me. Our Marine Biology class had traveled from Tallahassee to The Keys to continue our studies. At low tide, while snorkeling out to Rodriquez Key my chest lit up from the stings of Fire Coral.

When we lived in Miami some friends got us tickets to ride on the Goodyear Blimp. [I understand that the name Blimp came from England where they were called 'Bloody Limps"] I thought Blimps gently rose vertically from the ground, but soon discovered they 'gun' the engines and go up at a steep angle. After gaining altitude we flew over the stadium where the Dolphins and Jets were playing football.

I was snorkeling from a beach in The Keys catching tropical fish for our aquarium; I'd located a barrel with several immature French Angel Fish; was concentrating on netting the fish and as I surfaced a Cigarette type boat zoomed past me only a few feet away and I could see the surprised expression on their faces. I suspect that I also had 'an' expression.

Another time when I was out capturing fish, Judy was sun bathing on the beach while wearing a two piece bathing suit with a plastic ring holding the top. As luck would have it, just as a group of hiway workers dropped by she raised up; the ring snapped and they got an eye full.

At home we had two aquariums: one with tropical fish and the other with invertebrates, including an Octopus. We had gone to visit my family in Ocala and when we returned all the tropical fish were gone. What could possibly have happened? After some searching we saw a slimy trail to and from the Octopus tank. Our buddy, the Octopus, had crawled out of his tank; eaten the fish and returned to his tank. It is a known fact that the Octopus is the one of the most intelligent invertebrates or was he just cunning?

THE SUBWAY

For years I'd heard about The Subway (at Zion National Park, in Utah), but just never got around to it, mostly because I was usually in Zion in the Spring and the water is too cold. Well this time I was determined and secured a permit (for $10) to hike the 9 mile trail to The Subway (Oh yes, I was then told that this is not really a trail, but bushwhacking). I'd seen the dramatic pictures of The Subway, but heard you must have climbing gear to get into all The Subway area. Previously I didn't realize that you could come in from the lower end of the valley and not have to rappel and swim.

No one could tell me the best time to take photos, so I left early and was on the Left Fork trail by 7 am. After a half mile of a sane, relatively level trail I came to an almost vertical cliff into a deep canyon. Here the 'trail' is covered with loose rock; has numerous switchbacks and was extremely steep. Finally got to the valley floor and saw huge broken trees and mangled brush from a recent flashflood. [This time of the year the normal flow is less than 10 cu.ft./sec. During a flashflood a month ago the flow shot up to over 6000 cu.ft./sec, not a place I'd want to be. By the way I'd been attempting to photograph a flashflood; the previous year (in Northern Utah) I saw rain approaching a canyon; rushed to the area and could see a small flash flood coming down a creek bed. People envision this as flowing water, however a flashflood is nothing like water, it's more like molasses filled with rocks, trees and thunders like a freight train.]

As usual I made the false assumption that once arriving at the creek it would then be an easy jaunt along the creek bank. **Not so!** The bank was covered by bushes; rocks and trees. The first problem was discovering the best side of the creek and then finding a 'trail'; then I'd come to a rock dam and have to climb steeply up the rocky cliff and back down to the creek. Soon I was REALLY tired of this; I must have leaped across the creek 400 times and managed to keep my boots dry. After a couple miles I came to some Dinosaur tracks in some flat rock that had been a muddy swamp 100 million years before present (mybp).

On I pressed, setting a furious pace because the sun was now up and incorrectly assumed that I was missing the best light for photos. Presently came upon a guy, Terje (a landscape photographer from Norway) who had stopped to photograph a series of waterfalls, but I pressed on, not even stopping to drink. This was an extremely arduous trek and I was really sick of climbing up and down the cliffs; under logs and thru bushes. After 2 hours I arrived at The Subway and all my frustrations subsided, the view was awesome, even though the light was not what I wanted. I walked thru the tunnel to where you'd have to swim and the unclimbable waterfall.

The Subway, Zion National Park

Since it was still too dark to take photos I hiked back down the canyon to where Terje had stopped for photos. He is from Oslo and 2 years ago decided to take off; take only landscape photos; sell them on the Internet and mostly lives in rental vehicles. He has traveled to: Africa; South American; Australia; Thailand (more than once) and just returned from Hawaii. His pictures sell from a few hundred dollars to thousands. He is one of the few photographers who would wait for hours or days for the perfect photo, regrettably my attention span limits me to waiting only minutes or an hour or so. At first he limited himself to photographing concerts and sold one photo for $11,000 that was featured on the cover of Rolling Stone magazine.

After talking with Terje I began thinking about how FOX entertainment media had helped create an American public as the most ignorant of any developed country in the world. Compared to people from other countries Americans know little about: world affairs; history; geography or even an objective understanding of politics in this country.

Since I consider most people as sheep (needing to be told what to do) FOX and other conservative media has filled that niche. For America it's tragic for this media to preach a dogmatic, cynical point to view based on their agenda, rather than facts. And (as with most repetitive dogma) the recipients believe that they have received the truth.

Few Americans have the opportunity to discuss varied subjects with people from other parts of the world. In the past 15 years I've met these people and have been astounded at how informed they are; who (to a person) consider GW Bush as one of the worst things to ever have happen to this country and most know much more about American politics than the 30% plus of the really ignorant Americans. I was amazed by Terje's understanding of what has happened in this country during the past 8 years (under Bush) and his vehement disapproval. He has seen the decline of the American experiment; diminished respect for America in Europe; rampant cynicism and disrespect for government in America; the rise of the EU, China and India and is (like informed Americans) concerned for its future.

Ignorance in America is absolutely appalling: In the most powerful nation on Earth, 1 adult in 5 believes the sun revolves around the Earth; two-thirds of young adults are unable to find Iraq on a map; two-thirds of U.S. voters cannot name the three branches of government; 75% don't accept evolution as factual (only in Pakistan do more people share this belief); almost half believe the earth was created 6000 years ago; half don't accept the scientific facts confirming global climate warming; 40% feel that humans have been abducted by aliens and the math skills of 15-year-olds in the United States are ranked 24th out of the 29 developed countries.

I rambled on back to The Subway and took a few photos. Soon a guy (who arrived at the trailhead the same time as me) arrived; he had taken more than 3 hours to get to The Subway. He is originally from Slovakia and now lives in San Francisco. He swam across the pools and unsuccessfully tried to climb up the waterfall, returning quite chilled. There was a cool breeze in the canyon and I was chilled even being dry. The day before he had hiked 12 miles up the Virgin River (in the Narrows), then climbed Angels Landing (just that would tire a normal person).

I told the guys about The Wave and now that's their goal. Terje swam up to the falls for some pictures, but (for a Florida boy) that water was too cold.

On my way up I'd had way too much time climbing up cliffs, so on my return I just sloshed down the creek, sometimes in thigh deep water. Even though it was rocky, traveling was much easier that clambering up those cliffs. Several small groups came by and I pointed out the Dinosaur racks, none of them had seen the tracks or even some people who had been along this trail several times. I guess since I spend so much time outdoors that I look in the right places to see animals and things few other people see.

Part way down the canyon I waited and waited for Terje; later a group that had come down canyon from above The Subway (though the pools) said that someone had loaned Terje and Jerry a rope and they were heading above the falls. [When you come down the canyon you must swim several pools (one about 100 feet long) and down several waterfall shoots and must have a 70 foot rope.]

It was 1 ½ hours before they arrived. The young people (they had met) were overly concerned about the dark clouds that had rolled in, so fearing a flash flood, they set an almost running pace. I really didn't want to go that fast, especially since we must climb that awesome cliff to get out of the canyon. Met a guy from Japan who has been visiting the US for a few years and commented how America had so much more varied terrain than Japan and (since it is a volcanic island) no fossils.

When we arrived at the cliff it appeared too formidable to climb, it was barely light when I came down, now it looked like a vertical wall. Again I wanted to go slow, but the macho in me caused me to keep up with the 20-30 year olds. They were astonished that I could keep up, but I was really huffing a puffing, I'm not sure 65 year old guys should be stressing their body like this. When we arrived at the cliff top my head was swimming and I felt faint.

In 4 cars we caravanned to Springdale for pizza and beer. Even though we had 4 pitchers of beer, it is so weak (3.2%) that there was no buzz. The young couple (we met in the canyon) are rock climbers and the highlight of their 3 month trip was climbing Devils Tower in South Dakota. In Kentucky they had sold everything; bought a 5th wheel RV and journeyed west. Soon, pulling the trailed became a chore (in The Rockys) so they are now in rental car and sleep in a tent.

8TH STREET ELEMENTARY SCHOOL

This school building was constructed in 1914 and is the oldest continually used school in Florida; used as the Ocala High School until 1925; when I lived in Ocala it was a Junior High School (Middle School) and now it is just an Elementary School.

In the 1950's, even at 8th Street School, some kids had switchblade knives. I recall a couple of bullies who would brandish their switchblades at students, eventually they pulled out their knives in front of me so I decided to accept the challenge. Next day I slid a machete into the leg my jeans, so when confronted by the bullies I withdrew the machete calling their bluff never to again see their switchblades.

Then there was Bill who had a Cushman scooter. One adventure was Halloween when we traveled around town soaping car windows. So, for maximum effect we rode past cars, with a soap bar in hand, streaking cars. We were on Mericamp Road and as I soaped a window I hit a rear view mirror that almost removed my hand.

Later there was a dance at the 8th Street cafeteria so we drove the Cushman into and around the crowd in the cafeteria and got out before being absconded.

I also recall recess in the patio between classrooms and the cafeteria where guys would gather in small groups to tell stories and of course girls would be in other groups, usually giggling. I was fascinated to hear these older guys telling me about sex, however, later I discovered that EVERYTHING they told me was totally false.

During that innocent period it was forbidden to use the word sex, so in magazines it was written, s_x. Photos of partly clad women had a black bar over their eyes, Oh how things have changed. Now on prime time TV we see nudity that would have gotten the person in jail for indecent exposure.

I've always hear stories of kids walking to school thru rain and snow. Well, in Ocala we never had snow, however every day I did walk the mile to and from school, as well as for lunch. I recall that, along the way, I usually kicked a tin can along the street.

In my class was a very precocious girl who was much taller than others. Even in Jr. High she was sexually suggestive. I recall a time when she asked a boy if that was a knife in his pocket and reached down and grabbed 'it'. I wonder what happened to her in later life?

Another with a questionable future was a rather dull kid, I guess the current politically correct term would be: intellectually challenge. We were tasked with presenting a biographical sketch of famous people and this kid had Sir Francis Bacon. So (feeling proud of this drawing) he held up his sketch of a pig and showed the class the location of future bacon.

I don't recall the name of the science teacher, but I recall some gory war stories he would tell. I also remember that the classroom was in the lower level and after school I'd bring in pond water so I could view the 'bugs' under a microscope.

Since I had ADD (Attention Deficit Disorder), for years what I called a 'short attention span', I had extreme difficulty focusing on subjects that didn't hold an interest to me. One tactic I'd use was to draw a battleship with guns pointing to the sky; draw airplanes above; then draw a line from the guns to the sky to see how many planes I shot down.

I also recall when I'd place myself in stories I had created in my mind. One story took place in medieval times; I had built a steam powered tank, so was invincible against lance carrying knights. Another involved the tank in the American west against attacking Indians.

During this period it was our understanding that the Indians were the bad guys who were always attacking poor settlers and the Calvary. Too bad that our in our education system we didn't show respect for the noble Native Americas. Those 'poor settlers' were stealing the land where the Native Americans (or as in Canada, First Nations) had lived in North America for thousands of years, maybe as long as 14,000 years.

I had a pet Hog Nosed Snake, so one day I took him to school in my shirt. They are known as being docile, however while in the cafeteria (actually this was called a Cafetorium) this sucker bit me.

While in Middle School I became interested in rockets and space travel. I read everything I could find about the subject and was amazed that the knowledge was there to travel to the Moon. In High School I wrote stories about space travel and was condescendingly told by more than one teacher that it would be 50 years before we would be in space. They scoffed at talk of weightlessness, escape velocity and G forces. That was in 1956 and 13 years later we earthlings landed on the Moon. I think it is notable that the first human on the Moon was an agnostic. Hopefully in the future we will concentrate more on being good humans of planet Earth, rather than guilt ridden, god fearing sinners.

GRAND CANYON NATIONAL PARK, ARIZONA

No one can predict to what heights you can soar. Even you will not know until you spread your wings.

The Kaibab trail was built in 1924 because the person who had constructed the Bright Angel trail was charging a passage fee. It's about 7 miles to the Colorado River and I thought that going down should be a 'piece of cake', wrong again. I suspect that I'm too optimistic, always assuming the best outcome. However it is 4800 vertical feet back up to the rim with no water or shade along the trail. The Park Service doesn't recommend this hike from May to September, due to the heat. Temperatures at the river are 20-30 degrees hotter than the rim and most of the year gets into the 90's or 100's at the bottom.

Took the shuttle to the South Kaibab trailhead (at 7200' near Yaki Point) and started on the trail at 7:30 am. In the summer they recommend that you begin hiking before dawn, but felt it had been cool enough to not be a problem. The Park brochure says that (most of the year) failure to arrive at the campground by 10am could result in ill health or death and fatalities are not uncommon.

I felt strong, like I could backpack forever. Passed down the switchbacks (called The Chimney) cut into a sheer cliff face.

down The Chimney

From Ooh Aah Point are unparalleled panoramic views of the Grand Canyon. A view few visitors see.

Passed Ooh Aah Point then down a 300' cliff composed of Coconino Sandstone 275 million years old. After a mile and a half I arrived at Cedar Ridge, there I hiked out to a point and got a neat photo of a Western Scrub Jay and a Ground Squirrel looking over the rim. At this point I'd descended 10 million years in geologic time and with each step had traversed 100,000 years.

Barry at Ooh Aah Point

The trail continued mostly along a ridgeline. A couple of times I talked with a Ranger who was struggling down the trail, I didn't ask what his problem was, but it appeared to be Parkinson's. He said he would go down a ways and hang out in the shade until 3 pm before continuing down to Phantom Ranch. I was told that (in the past) 8 people have died of dehydration on this trail.

Now it was becoming hot and I found a shaded overhang, to have lunch. There were about 15 people around there and I was the only American, they were either German or French.

We saw a Condor fly over, those birds are enormous. [Close to extinction; eggs were collected by the San Diego Zoo; several were raised there without visual human contact and released in the Grand Canyon where they have successfully reproduced. Notice that all the Condors have numbers on their wings.]

Where I had stopped is called Skeleton Point and was the first view of the Colorado River. The name is because several Mules have gone over the edge here and their bones are below. From here you can also see Cheops Pyramid and here the trail drops steeply down in some awesome switchbacks, called The Red and Whites. This is thru Redwall Limestone (evidence of another sea) about 340 million years old.

looking down the Red and Whites switchbacks

One reason I took this trail was because I knew the Bright Angel trail was filled with Mule poop and smelled of urine. However, a couple days before I discovered that Mules also have stunk up this trail. I do really not like this trail, it is more like a staircase 7 miles long and many of the steps are twice as high as regular stairs. It's a killer on my knees; also the Mule traffic has certainly torn up the trail.

Now it was really getting hot because you gain 4-5 degrees for every 1000 feet in elevation drop. Fortunately the trail was not as steep (across the Tonto Platform), then I came to what they call The Tipoff, and that's what it does. You can see the river below and it was WAY down, 3900 feet down! From that point you can see where the actual river canyon drops another 1600' to the Colorado River.

Silver Bridge at Phantom Ranch

[A month or so ago I had hiked (with Steve) to the legitimate headwaters of the Colorado, near Rocky Mountain National Park of Colorado. From there it meanders down for 1500 miles and what water that remains empties into the Sea of Cortez in Baja, Mexico. The Grand Canyon surrounds only 277 miles of that distance.]

In places the trail was cut into sheer cliff walls, then I look down toward the river to see that the trail becomes even steeper. Now I was getting really tired and changed my overly optimistic plan t (once I get to Phantom Ranch) to hike north, up the canyon. At that point all I wanted to do was lay down under a Cottonwood Tree and not move for a while.

Now I was out of the horizontal sedimentary rock; past The Great Unconformity (where 1.25 billion years of rock eroded away) into the dark metamorphic rock of Vishnu Schist 1.7 billion years old!

Soon I could see the tunnel just before the Black Bridge, first built by miners in 1921. Here I met 6 young guys going up who were utterly unprepared for the afternoon ascent up the Kaibab trail. Evidently they had hiked down Bright Angel Trail, and contrary to all the warnings were attempting to hike Kaibab the same day. To make it worse they had little water. One tall chubby guy had 2 small bottles of bottled water, whereas the Park Service recommends a liter per hour. Just as a black guy passed me he collapsed on the trail. I knew these boys were in trouble.

Passed thru the tunnel; over the bridge and was now on flat ground; however the dark dirt now radiated oven-like heat. Summer temperatures at Phantom Ranch reach 120 degrees in the shade; 137 in the sun and on the trail in this area Rangers recorded 150 degrees. To make matters more uncomfortable a line of Mules came by kicking up flour-like dust.

At this point I had descended 4800 feet, more elevation change than almost every mountain in the Eastern US.

Just down the trail are the remains of a pueblo built by the Ancient Puebloans. Just ahead I could see the Cottonwood trees, however, upon entering the trees I failed to see the campground. After a half mile I could see a bridge and the campground on the west bank of Bright Angel Creek. I had 'planned' to take not much over 4 hours to reach Phantom Ranch and it took 6 exhausting hours.

I had fixated on having a cold coke, but first I removed my shoes and soaked my feet in the stream. This water comes from Roaring Springs several miles up the canyon and the water gushes out at 40 degrees. Brenda and I had come down there from the North Rim in April of 2000, at that time there was deep snow on the rim, yet amazingly warm at the springs. Water for the North and South Rims originates from these springs and the South Rim uses 500,000 gallons per day.

After a short rest I hiked the quarter mile up to the canteen to discover they had no coke, only lemonade for $2.50 a glass. They are quite proud of the meals here: breakfast is $19; a steak dinner is $39 and a glass of wine-$4.50.

I hiked back to my campsite and lay down for a while. The temperature in the sun was 102 degrees. [When I got up next morning it was 34 degrees.]

Around 4 pm I walked back up to the Ranch for a Ranger talk. Talked with a Ranger who hikes the trail about 40 times/year and there are people who run from rim to rim (24 miles) in 3-4 hours. He said he had to get back up to the South Rim and the Ranger who was to give the evening program might not be back from a medical emergency on the Kaibab trail. I'm sure it was one or more of those foolish guys I had passed.

My original plan was to hike down and up Kaibab trail, but now heard that this is not recommended; the trail is without shade or water; is a leg-killing staircase and is brutal during the afternoon, so will take the Bright Angel Trail up to the South Rim.

From the Ranch I hiked back down to the river for photos, then returned to camp and rested. Finally the sun set behind the cliffs; temperature cooled and it became an idyllic setting with the Cottonwoods; bird sounds and the babbling stream, life was good!

I had been looking for Tarantulas and didn't see one until after dark, while going up for the evening program. To the astonishment of some hikers I scooped it up in my hand. This time of the year the males are on patrol searching for mates.

Since the Ranger didn't return, a Mule Skinner answered questions about Mules. They cost $500-$2500; are bought from a broker in Tennessee and at least one new Mule a year spooks on the trail to become Condor food. Although they have a breakaway system (to prevent all the Mules from being pulled over the side) a Mule he was riding was drug over the edge and was recovered, but the other Mules didn't survive. Amazingly there has never been a fatality involving tourists. The term Mule Skinner comes from when wagons were pulled by Mules; the driver used a whip and he was good if he could 'skin' a Mule with the whip.

Back at camp the ground was too hard to sleep on (without a ground pad), so I laid out my sleeping bag over some grass. Laying there looking up at the stars was awe-inspiring. Even though the elevation was only 2500 feet the sky was clear; the stars were unusually bright and the Milky Way showed itself between the trees. As I watched Shooting Stars caress the sky I thought of how many women in this world would love to be lying beside me here, yet they were only in my imagination.

I slept very well; around 5am was awake, so were many other people. You could see flickers of light as people prepared for an early departure and some were already heading down the trail. I wanted to wait until later for photos, but went ahead and packed up; gobble down a bagel with peanut butter and left at 5:45. By the time I arrived at the Silver Bridge the sky had lightened, but was not good for photos.

I followed a sandy trail along the Colorado for about a mile, this trail was blasted from sheer rock walls by the CCC in the 1930's. [Before the Glen Canyon Dam, every day the Colorado would carry 380,000 tons of sediment past this point, now it's only about 40,000 tons.] I was now back into the dark rocks of the Grand Canyon Supergroup, rocks 1.7 billion years old.

Arriving at Pipe Creek I headed up, thankfully at a pleasant steepness. This trail was much more scenic than Kaibab, with waterfalls; lush vegetation and the sound of a rushing creek; also the trail has few steps. On up the trial was a high spring (called Columbine) feeding Maidenhair ferns along the canyon wall. After a mile or so I came to the first switchback (called the Devil's Corkscrew), but I was fresh and it wasn't really an obstacle. I was in the sun for a while and at the top found a shady overhang and ate some trail mix. There I met a friendly group of 8 and we talked for a while. Just past that point was a nice waterfall. If it had been later in the day I'd have sat under it to cool off.

Soon the trail was back in shade and continued along a shelf; thru the Tapeats Narrows and above the creek from Indian Gardens. This is Tapeats Sandstone laid down when a desert covered the area.

After a little over 6 miles I approached Indian Gardens. In past summers, this is where the Havasupai would come down to farm. When this became a National Park the Native Americans were run off. This is certainly a typical story of the settling, or rape, of the west. Looking thur these Cottonwood trees I got my first glimpse of the shear walls beyond Indian Garden and began to wonder where the trail went from here. I knew there was a plateau to the west because I had come down to it a few years ago and assumed (again) that I'd soon be on a plateau. **Boy was I wrong!**

Finally I arrived under the trees of Indian Gardens with its myriad of springs and cool air. Again I met that friendly group and we talked. One of the wives (Linda) was uncommonly beautiful and gregarious and they were really having a grand time.

Indian Garden lies in shale (of the Tonto Group) that was deposited in a shallow, warm sea during Cambrian, 510 mybp.

I met another group that was going back up Kaibab and I tried to convince the leader that it is not a recommended route. They were ignorant of what lay ahead, so I told them that this trail was more interesting and 'a piece of cake' compared to Kaibab.

After a short rest I headed out, filled with optimism. It was only 4.6 more miles and I should be on the South Rim in a couple of hours. **Not!** I was astonished at what lay ahead. It was a box canyon with sheer walls rising thousands of feet, I could not see any possible way out. I asked a couple of people about the trail, but couldn't get a definitive answer except that there was no plateau and the trail was extremely steep.

impossible climb to South Rim

Hiked on up the riverbed (in the bottom of the Bright Angel Fault) and came to the first switchback. From there I still could not see a way to ascend those sheer walls. A couple thousand feet up I could see what appeared to be switchbacks, but the route there appeared to be absolutely impossible.

Now I was getting a little tired and not a little disappointed. I really was tired of eating dust from Mule trains and smelling their obnoxious discharges, and the switchback seemed endless. I'd greet everyone and frequently stop and talk with folks. I stopped one guy wearing a St Augustine T shirt, asked if he was from there, but (surprise) he was German and had visited last summer, commenting on hot how it was in Florida.

Now there was no respite, the trail was either steeply up or you must trudge up switchback that were sometimes only a few feet higher than the one below. My right foot was really hurting although I wasn't that tired; I just wanted to get to the South Rim.

Finally arrived at the 3-mile rest stop, where the Ground Squirrels were a constant pest, mostly because some idiots feed them.

While resting I could see a Condor soaring above and then he or she alighted in a cave where they were raising a chick. They only lay one egg (every second year) and don't build a nest, just deposit the egg on the rock. To the west of where I was is what they call The Battleship; is easily viewed from Bright Angel Point and is where a nest is located. Condors were first released here in 1996 and now there are 67 birds, including 2 chicks this year.

Got more water; continued my trek and soon spied a Gray Fox below the trail. I'll bet a thousand people could pass this point and never see that Fox.

Now, across a canyon, I could see the trail cut into the rock and still bearing steeply up. Just above was the switchback called Jacob's Ladder I'd seen from below and couldn't believe it was going up that cliff. On I labored, setting a slow pace. Above I could see even more vertical walls and no apparent way to transverse it.

After another hour I talked with people who said it wasn't far to the rim, of course 'far' is a relative term and they were hiking down, not up. Most people now were day hikers who only came down a mile or so and some to Indian Gardens and back. One woman asked if she could go down to the river and back up the Kaibab trail. Here it was after noon and this woman was so out of it she didn't even know what lay ahead. This is how people get into trouble and die.

[While in Silverton I knew a couple who would volunteer here to intercept hikers to determine if they were adequately prepared and if not, try to convince them not to proceed.]

On I slowly hiked with more than a little pain in my calves and my backpack seemed to be gaining weight. Next I came to the Mile and a Half rest stop and more water. Now I had a little adrenaline boost because I was so near the Rim, however it was further than expected. Passed thru the first tunnel and approaching the second tunnel took a photo of some Native American Pictographs.

Once on top all I wanted to do was get in Tonja and drive down to McDonalds for the burger and milk shake I'd been fantasizing about. Of course it was much further to the truck than I recalled.

So this ended an adventure that would have been more enjoyable if I'd been 30 years younger.

MESA ARCH

While camping along the Colorado River outside Moab Utah I'd heard about Mesa Arch and to photograph the arch you must be there just before sunrise.

There are two ways to reach Mesa Arch: the long way around on the paved road or the short cut; up along the Colorado, then up the Shafer Trail into Canyonlands National Park. I was up at 4:30 am planning to take the short cut; followed the paved road for 6 miles to the Potash mines; then a graded road for a short ways, then a rocky path along the Colorado River. At one point, at the Goosenecks, I drove above the river, hundreds of feet below. Then onto a road, I dare call this a road, being more like a trail over the least rough area of the canyon; then passed thru deep canyons, still in darkness.

[A few years earlier I'd been exploring this area and came to what appeared to be a dead end in a box canyon. Before me was an absolutely vertical wall and I was astonished to see snippets of a road high on the canyon wall. This was Shafer Trail built by uranium miners who had a feverish desire to reaching the plateau above.]

Since I was in a hurry I started up the switchback road going much too fast. This road is cut from (hopefully) solid rock into the cliff wall; is just wide enough for one vehicle; once up a ways there is an almost vertical drop from the road and the curves were unbelievably sharp. After a few heart stopping moments I made it to the plateau just as the sky began to brighten. It seemed that I had plenty of time to drive the 6 miles to the arch; however I didn't anticipate how curvy the road would be and arrived at the parking area just after the sun rose. Well that was a frustrating bummer. You must be at the arch <u>as</u> the sun rises because the sunlight shines on the red rock below and illuminates the underside of the arch, a sight I heard was enchanting.

A couple days later I again attempted to reach Mesa Arch at sunrise, so I took the long way around, past Dead Horse State Park, then into Canyonlands NP. This time I left with extra time to reach the arch, however as I reached the plateau the sky brightened, I began to think I'd be late so speeded along the paved road at 70 mph, squealing around the curves. Fortunately there was no other traffic; finally I arrived at the parking area well before sunrise only to see many more cars than expected; I rushed thru desert landscape and as I reached the arch a line of photographers completely blocked the view! I scrambled around attempting to find a clear spot to photograph the arch; however the effort was futile, foiled again. I learned that most of these folks were in a photography tour from San Francisco.

It was a week later before I had the enthusiasm to attempt to photograph Mesa Arch; I took the long way around; arrive before sunrise and only a couple of people were there, so finally was able to snap a couple of photos:

Mesa Arch in Canyonlands NP

HURRICANE FRANCES

(The Mountain Storm of the Century)

By early September 2004 Maybellene and I were traveling along the Blue Ridge Parkway, near Boone, North Carolina. This was Labor Day weekend and we found the Linville Falls campground almost full. We apprehensively listened to storm reports as hurricane **Frances** moved across Florida; thru Lakeland (where I was born); Tampa, then into the Gulf of Mexico. In the Gulf she was downgraded to a Tropical Storm and turned to the north. **Frances** limped into Apalachee Bay (south of Tallahassee) with surprisingly little rain and soon became a tropical depression.

Sunday at Linville was unexpectedly sunny and warm. I spent half the day lounging with a couple of school teachers from a nearby town. The Cherokee called the Linville River ***Eeseeoh,*** appropriately meaning "a river of many cliffs". Now Linville is named for explorer William Linville and his son, John, who were killed in the gorge by Cherokees in 1766. The geology is especially interesting to me: at the top of the falls is the Linville Fault with billion year old continental basement rock thrust over much younger limestone. This thrust occurred when Europe collided with North

American about 400 mybp. As this softer limestone eroded away the falls were at least 12 miles downstream from their present location.

On Labor Day Sammie (my Suzuki Samurai) and I went exploring; first to revisit Beech Mountain, but it was shrouded in clouds. On into Tennessee (near Bristol) the sky was clear and surprisingly warm. Returning to the Blue Ridge Mountains I found it clouded and (around Newland) beginning to lightly rain. Amazingly when I returned to the campground it had become a "ghost town". A couple from Polk County, Florida and I were the only remaining campers and they soon left. For some excitement, of course I stayed.

Tuesday brought drizzle; rain at times; was occasionally breezy and the forecast was for the full effects of **Frances** not to be felt until that night. In the evening the rain increased and there were a few gusts, but nothing over 30 mph. A persistent annoyance was Apples falling on Maybellene's 'head'. By the time I retired the tropical rain had begun. As Maybellene rocked in the gusty wind I awoke a few times and listened to the thrashing rain. This was certainly what I'd call an incessant "frog strangler". Even though I was raised in Florida I don't recall such a continuous deluge of rain. Later I heard estimates of 25 inches of rain in that 12 hour period!

Although I couldn't find any other leaks, around 6 am I felt water dripping in my ear. I got up and found the thundering sound of the rain replaced by a breeze in the trees and a faint sound that sounded like rushing water. Maybellene; Sammie and I were safely on a hill, however much of the campground was along the banks of the Linville River. First light gradually revealed that the lower part of the campground was inundated by an orange torrent of water. An ominous sign was a dead Great Blue Heron up the path from the flooded amphitheater.

Now it was time to see the falls and explore the mountains for exciting video. During the nite I repeatedly told myself, "***Barry, do not do anything stupid today. Do not drive off in deep water.***" Today I repeated – "***I will not take any chances today, I ain't as young and indestructible as I used to be. You recall how you sunk Linda's truck in hurricane Opal.***"

Sammie and I headed toward Linville Falls and were surprised that we couldn't even drive to the Visitor Center, although I tried until the water began leaking under the doors. A deluge of water was rushing down Dugger's Creek; across the road and into the parking lot, that was now a 'lake'. As I stepped out there was a loud crash as a tree tumbled into Dugger's Creek and scurried toward the river. I was determined to get to Linville Falls, even if I had to climb over the mountain. So (with camera safely in a plastic bag) I headed up the mountainside. I discovered that climbing over, under and thru Rhododendron bushes is almost as difficult as Mangroves. I scrambled higher and higher, panting like an "ole hound". I could hear the roar of the falls on Dugger's Creek; assumed the bridge was submerged, so I was intent on climbing above the creek. However I was drawn to the thunderous sound; so made my way to the creek for a 'look see' and discovered the rampaging stream had not quite covered the bridge. On the other side the "trail" continued, as a flowing stream of rain water.

At the Linville Falls Visitor's Center I was shocked to see it almost submerged by the rampaging river. The water was almost to the roof line, but what was most interesting was that the front of the building was like the bow of a boat, from front to back, this 'bow wave' dropped more than a foot. The previous Monday afternoon I'd been here; talking with the attendant and bought some post cards. Guess I should have purchased more cards and some books, because they are now history, under 8 feet of water. We had talked about how the river had flooded last Thursday, but it never crossed our minds that the river could actually flood the Visitor's Center. He also told me they unfortunately just purchased a state-of-the-art computerized cash register.

On up the mountain, a creek thundered across the trail, however this wasn't going to stop me. Struggled across several 'creeks' of rainwater; waded innumerable 'lakes'; slogged thru mud bogs and finally neared the Plunge Basin Overlook. Before arriving, the sound of the falls was deafening. Having preparing myself to somehow be disappointed in the view, I descended the steps, now cascading with water, rocks and limbs. Safely perched on the overlook I was astounded by the power and violence of the falls, blasting itself from the canyon walls. In the gorge below, a mighty surge of water burst out about 125 feet up the rock face, normally the Lower Falls is only 45 feet. I'd expected the falls to be surging from the rock face, but not the maelstrom before me. The majestic power held me in awe, I was mesmerized. Now I could easily see how canyons are formed and rocks pulverized by the force of water.

This is the falls that morning and a photo of normal flow.

LINVILLE FALLS FLOOD 2004

Normal flow over Linville Falls.

As I watched, this frenzied orange water dropped down into the plunge basin, then heaved up higher than the falls, to a height of 150 feet! I was spellbound, watching the soaring water reach for the heavens. Occasionally trees would only briefly be exposed before disappearing into this cataclysm of water. And the sound: as if you were <u>under</u> a speeding train or behind a 747 taking off. I've read that waterfalls produce a field of negative ions resulting in exhilaration, as during a thunderstorm. I can attest to this phenomenon; this experience was truly exhilarating and greatly surpassed my expectation.

<u>It's fascinating to consider that I may very well be the only living human to have witnessed Linville Falls in this violent condition.</u>

After a time I hiked down into the gorge where I hoped to view the falls from a different angle, however the river washed over the trail. Undeterred and somewhat concerned about the waves that frequently surged over my legs, I slogging my way along the river. Within a foot to my right was the vertical canyon wall, to my left a river 'out of control with standing waves several feet high. I'd been backpacking into Linville Gorge for the past 30 years and never had seen the river as anything but a clear running mountain stream, gently making its way around rocks and boulders. During that time the rocks 'controlled' the river, now the river was rampaging far above the (now insignificant) rocks. From a somewhat placid stream, the Linville was now, angry! I was soon awakened from my philosophical trance by waves washing over up to my knees. My imagination briefly saw a huge wave sucking me out into that ferocious river.

Moving back downriver I marveled at the tremendous standing waves as the river rushed down the mountainside at what seemed to be an impossible speed, oblivious to my presence. This reminded me of the mightily Colorado and rapids in the Grand Canyon. The climb back out of the canyon was much more difficult than the passage down, complicated by the cascade of water and debris streaming down the trail.

Back at the Visitor's Center I was surprised to see the water had subsided more than a foot since I first arrived. Then I slogged on and apprehensively crossed the bridge over Dugger's Creek; up the trail a ways, then clambered through the forest back down to Sammie.

At the campground I talked with Terry (the Park Ranger) and showed him the video I'd taken. My plan was to go to the Toe River, but (in Boone) I needed to mail a package to Catherine and purchase some blank video tapes. Sure wish I'd gone south to discover where the Parkway had been washed out and flooding along the Toe River.

Sammie and I took the back roads to Boone, did some business and drove back through Newland to check my email. While in Newland I heard estimates of 20 inches of rain having fallen in Avery County, an area at a lower elevation. The library was closed; so we returned to the Visitor's Center and found that I could now drive into the parking lot.

At the Visitor's Center the water was now only a foot and a half deep across the floor. The level had dropped about 6 feet in the past 5 hours. What really amazed me was the rushing river, just past the Visitor's Center. It appeared to be traveling at warp speed, with limbs and trees rushing past like screaming banshees. I should have attempted to measure the speed, but it had to be at least 30 mph.

I just had to see the bridge over the Linville River. My feet had been wet all morning, so I waded on thru the Visitor's Center to the bridge. What a sight! Water was boiling up and over the bridge. Some of the aluminum railing had broken loose and all the railings were festooned with limbs, logs, and even a trailer tire and rim. It appeared the river had risen more than 3 feet over the bridge, which means the river flooded over 22 feet above the normal river height!

Tentatively I crept out onto the bridge, without considering the risk. It seemed sound, but shuttered when trees crashed into it. I imagined that if it gave way I'd 'swim like hell' for the trees along shore, before the prospect of being ground into organic particles under the falls. At the far end of the bridge was a 5 foot muddy ditch where the tempest had eroded shore. At the other end water gushed from broken water lines.

The Visitor's Center was an absolute mess; door smashed (some hanging); mud everywhere; rock walls missing and amazingly the power was 'on'. Not only that, but the hand dryers were running and gave off a disconcerting electrical odor. I tried to turn them off, but they were determined to self-destruct. Downstream of the center the Rhododendron bushes were shrouded in leaflets and trash. Then I heard a 'phump' as the hand dryers expired.

At this point Terry drove up. As I waded toward him, I entered an area where the water was almost waist deep. While we watched, the water rapidly subsided. We marveled at the force and speed of the rampaging river. As Terry and I stood by the book store, a huge log floated up and perched itself over the stone wall that immediately collapsed. Terry tried to unlock the door to the bookstore, but debris prevented the key from being inserted all the way.

Of course this stands as only one of many adventures, but this was unique in its exposure. A personal reward is that I was able to share this experience (via video tape) with hundreds (if not thousands) of people, including the Governor of North Carolina. The next year I was again on the Parkway and several Rangers asked me if I was the one who took the video they had all seen. For the past 30 years Linville Falls has been a very special to me, and for the rest of my life I'll be able to visually relive this remarkable experience.

FLORIDA KEYS

On the Wakulla River Linda and I spent hundreds of hours converting a 48 foot cabin cruiser, *My Sharona,* into a home.

About every 10 years I get an urge for greener pastures, so we decided to move to the Florida Keys. A problem was that we had removed the 2 huge diesel engines, so propulsion became an issue. Since people told me I couldn't push a 48 foot ship with an outboard engine, I felt compelled to do just that; so attached a 75 HP Mercury outboard to the stern; filled barrels with gasoline and searched for crew to get *My Sharona* and our sailboat, *The Rose*, the hundreds of miles across the Gulf of Mexico. Linda and I convinced my brother Joe and a friend, Marjorie, to crew. Also Linda talked to a local character (Joe Walker) into accompanying us.

On our slow (very slow) passage across the Gulf we occasionally snagged a Crab trap for fresh food; were boarded by Customs and survived tempestuous weather off Venice. I'm certain we were a sight: with 2 boats on our deck; a straining outboard engine and plants hanging all over the boat. After a few hundred gallons of gas we finally approached the 7-mile bridge at Marathon, then saw Linda dive from *The Rose* into the ocean!

Soon we found out that the rudder had broken; was floating off, so she jumped overboard to retrieve it.

LINDA APPROACHING 7-MILE BRIDGE AT MARATHON

After this harrowing trip we had fixated on having pizza and beer at the Pizza Hut in Marathon, however since there was a church within a short distance, the Pizza Hut could not serve beer, that's un-American.

For a while we docked at a marina on Coco Plum (near Marathon) then moved nearby to be with some other boaters in an illegal, but less expensive docking area.

MY SHARONA IN MARATHON

NEWLY PAINTED ROSE IN MARATHON

Somehow we thought we could get by without an air conditioner; however when the water temperature climbed into the 80's, comfort became an issue, so I drove to Key West and bought an AC. But when the water temperature continued to increase I returned to the store for a larger capacity air conditioner.

One nite we could have lost our home. I had replaced our bed with a waterbed causing **Sharona** to heal to one side, but I figured that I'd move things around in the morning, so went to bed. As usual Linda arrived home late then I heard her exclaim: **"We're sinking!"** She had gone down into the galley finding several inches of sea water. I dashed over to a neighbor's boat; borrowed a water pump and after the flooding water receded discovered the seawater was coming in a thru-hull fitting for the bilge pump.

A year or so later State and Local officials boarded boats in Boot Key Harbor, a protected harbor used by boaters for hundreds of years. During the current era (in the 1990's) many sailboats anchored in Boot Key Harbor for the entire winter. Most of these people were Cruisers or full-time sailors and most had been coming there for years.

The origin of the current problem was that Yankees had moved to the Keys, typically just for the winter; their condos now lined Boot Key Harbor; they didn't want the water before them filled with sailboats, so blamed the sailors for pollution of the harbor, when in fact most of the nutrients came from a golf course; street runoff and these land-lubbers cleaning fish and throwing the guts into the harbor. Anyway, many of these 'foreign residents' complained to local governmental officials, so police officials surrounded the harbor and boarded (or as the sailors considered it, raided) the sailboats searching for any illegal items; they really didn't find much so this was really just about harassment, however to the boaters this was an illegal invasion of their <u>homes</u>.

Following the uproar I wrote a 'letter to the editor' to the local paper and describe why the sailors were so upset. I made the point that, to the sailors, this was no different than the officials (Marine Patrol; Coast Guard and Sheriff) blocking off the causeway to the exclusive area of Key Colony Beach and invading the resident's homes <u>without a warrant</u>. At the time I was working for the Florida Department of Environmental Regulation, so writing this letter was somewhat of a conflict.

Next day I get a call from a guy in Key West who has a TV program called ***The World According to*** …. (I don't recall his name, but it wasn't Garp) asking me to be on his TV call-in show. Always interested in stirring things up I agreed, however I also invited the President of the Boot Key Harbor Association. She and I drove down to Key West and at the time for the TV show to begin the host hadn't arrived. They ran some commercials, then asked if we wanted to host the program, I said "***Certainly***". Having never done anything like this before I was extremely nervous, however we answered the questions without faltering. Midway in the show was a commercial break and when we resumed I was less apprehensive and more confident so began with "***This is the World According to Barry***". Fortunately most of the callers were in support of the sailors, so I could relate. After the TV show the station gave me a VHS tape of the program, so ended my only TV appearance.

A few days later a hugely attended meeting was held to allow the sailors to address their concerns. It was my impression that most of the regulatory officials were sorry they had succumbed to the complaints of those few residents and invaded the sailor's 'homes'.

We were in a race in The Keys and as we approached the 7-mile bridge the wind died, so we bumped thru the old bridge moved only by the current. In a later race we lead 20 or so boats to a point where we started downwind; we didn't have a spinnaker, so boats with spinnakers passed us.

In 2001 I was spending the winter in Chris and Kathy's yard (in Maybellene) and David and Caroll came down for a visit. As usual we had some harrowing rides (at nite) in David's boat. He was an avid NASCAR fan; Dale Earnhardt died in a crash; we were diving at John Pennekamp Coral Reef Park, where there is a huge Christ statue on the bottom; I swam down, put an Earnhardt hat on the head of the statue; took a photo and was going to send it to NASCAR but never did.

After almost 3 years in The Keys we, or rather I, decided to move to Belize where I'd build a tree house for us. All this sounded rational at the time; however it turned out to be a colossal mistake.

I had traveled to Belize with a High School friend and scoped out a location for our residence. I discovered a small fishing village called Placentia (in southern Belize) that seemed ideal.

I knew the outboard engine wouldn't survive in the open ocean so installed a small, Perkins diesel engine; cut a hole in *Sharona*'s stern and installed a shaft and propeller.

I was so confident that the trip would be successful that I quit my job with the State environmental agency and took off for Belize with both boats; scads of building materials; hundreds of gallons of diesel fuel and a local guy for our only crewmember. Just making it to Dry Tortugas National Park (70 miles west of Key West) was an adventure in itself and when we arrive found the water to be unusually cold and the weather quite windy. Finally we left Tortugas heading for Yucatan Mexico with a weather forecast of calm winds. After 40 miles the wind produced a following sea that broke a rudder bending the propeller. The already apprehensive crew was now in hysterical mutiny, so we turned back toward Florida.

The trip back up to St Marks wasn't without trauma. Two episodes were: my Sister and her kids, Sara and Pete, accompanied us to Sarasota. We anchored for the nite in Florida Bay with Patty staying in *The Rose*. During the nite a rain shower blew thru and at first light *The Rose* was not within sight! We panicked as we searched the horizon for Patty, how would I explain this to our Mother. In the dinghy I took off in the direction that I thought the rain shower had passed and finally found Patty; still asleep, unaware to the situation. I could imagine her waking in the morning and just see ocean from horizon to horizon.

We had a water hose collapse, overheating the engine, so took *The Rose* into Marco Island for a new hose. We dropped Patty's kids off with a friend in Sarasota and continued our trek toward Tallahassee. *My Sharona* was so slow that as we motored along St Petersburg beach a guy walking along the beach was going faster than us.

Linda and I lived on *Sharona* for a couple of years; then my ex-wife Judy lived on her for a year; then I sold the boat to a guy who had travel to Mexico with me on *The Rose*. He and a friend were going to visit the Cayman Islands and I never heard of them again, so sold the boat to another guy who moved *Sharona* to the Ochlocknee River where she sank in a hurricane.

WOULD YOU LIKE TO GO ON AN ADVENTURE LITTLE LADY?

On the World Wide Web I contacted a woman from Oak Ridge Tennessee; we met on the Blue Ridge Parkway in the Fall of 2012; had a good time, so I said to her: "*Would you like to go on an adventure little lady*" She asked: "*What kind of adventure*? and I said a trip on my pontoon boat. I'm certain she expected a vessel more luxurious than reality, although a hint should have been the name: **The River Shanty**. I told her I wanted to start on the Chattahoochee River as close to Atlanta as possible and end up at Apalachicola on the Gulf of Mexico, a distance of 262 miles. This was in November and the weather in Florida had been consistently warm, sometimes with temps in the 80's, so she expected balmy weather on my 'yacht'. **The River Shanty** is an 18 foot pontoon boat to which I added an aluminum structure to support canvas sides and a plastic roof; the Galley is an ice chest; cooking is with a camp stove and the Sleeping Berth a blowup air mattress; however I did bring along a porta potty for her.

SueAnn met me near Tallahassee; to drive the trailer back, my cousin Richard accompanied us into Georgia where the weather had deteriorated to a cold drizzle and a temperature in the 40's. Richard expected us to turn around, but I have this problem of not backtracking and dragging along women having second thoughts. Thankfully she didn't yet know about 'Barry Trips'.

The first nite was nothing like the warm Florida sunshine as SueAnn expected; on shore we built a fire; tried to warm our bodies; later crawled into our sleeping bag and tried to sleep. Soon we began to hear gunfire and later, gunfire and explosions and they were getting closer. We thought we had passed Fort Benning, but evidently hadn't and war games were heading our way. After a while the gunfire and small explosions became giant explosions and now were much closer. About the time I got up to move us downstream the explosions terminated, to our great relief.

The morning temp was 25 degrees; ice was everywhere and surely SueAnn began to think she had made terrible mistake.

The next day's weather was just as crummy and both of us remained bundled.

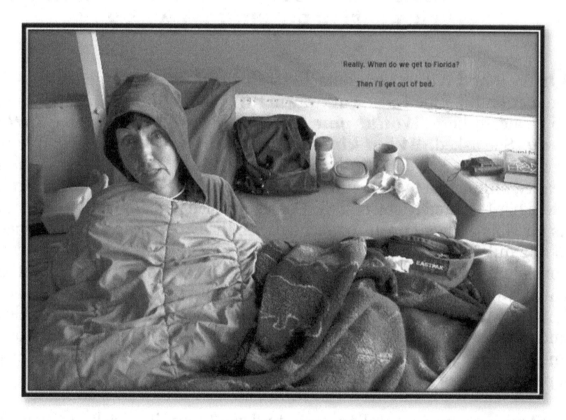

That nite the air mattress deflated, so I got up several times to re-inflate it. Around midmorning I needed to nap so asked SueAnn to steer; just as I got into my sleeping, bang; crash, bump, we rammed shore and as I looked up a rotten tree was falling, in slow motion, right on top of **The Shanty**.

SueAnn assumed I'd come up screaming, like her ex-husband would have done, yet I bounded out and exclaimed: "***Where is my camera?***"

The further south we traveled the better the weather; we passed thru several locks; reached the Apalachicola River; spent the night on Lake Seminole and passed Fort Gadsden, or rather the remains. Four countries have occupied 2 forts on this site; the British built the first structure to recruit free-Black (ex-slaves) and Indians to fight against the rebellious United States. Later, Blacks under the leadership of an Indian, Garcon, occupied the fort. It became a free-haven for run-a-way slaves and free blacks. Left in the hands of the Native Americans and black allies, the British evacuated the river in 1815, then the post became known to U.S. authorities as the Negro Fort on the Apalachicola. In 1816 it was destroyed by the U.S. Navy with one of the deadliest cannon shots in American history. The first shot fired by a gunboat hit the ammo dump resulting in the 'Negro Fort' being blown to bits, killing or wounding 270 of the 320 men, women and children in the fort.

Sue along Apalachicola River

Overall we had a somewhat enjoyable experience, certainly memorable. However before arriving in Apalachicola SueAnn made reservations in a hotel.

A CASE FOR SERENDIPITY

My Grandson Jason and I were camping at Mesa Verde National Park in Colorado taking the tour of the cliff dwellings. I heard a woman speak who seemed to have a southern accent so asked her where she was from. She replied, *"Ocala Florida"*. I asked her name and discovered she had been in my High School class; her father had been the Governor and her name was Julie Bryant. What a small world. Julie invited us over for dinner at their camp where we reminisced about experiences in Ocala. She was surprised to learn that a lifetime ago it was me who had driven 'donuts' in their front yard.

Speaking of a small world, Judy; Michelle and I moved to Australia from St Augustine Beach. While in Florida I'd purchased a pair of really nice sandals with car treads for soles (the rage at the time) and ran into a couple who had just moved to Australia and had made those sandals. Later I met a woman from Lakeland Florida, where I was born. I've heard that 1 of 5 people you know will know someone you know or someone that person knows.

I was hiking in the mountains of Idaho; had stopped to rest and a guy approached and asked: *"Hey, aren't you Barry McAlister?"* We had been in same year at Santa Fe High School near High Springs. The world is certainly becoming smaller and smaller.

DELICATE ARCH

Arches National Park near Moab Utah is a wonderland of stone arches; spires and windows. About 300 mybp this area had the world's largest sand dunes, now turned into sandstone thousands of feet deep. Delicate Arch is the most recognized symbol of the Park and is even on the Utah license plates. I'd previously visited the arch and even have video of the eclipsing Moon thru the arch.

A goal of thousands of people is to view the arch at sunset; Janice was visiting, so Delicate Arch for sunset became our objective. The trail is less than 2 miles, however is a steady climb over red sandstone, then steeply between some rocks. Although Janice struggled a bit we made it to the arch well before sunset, where many people sat among the rocks. I took photos of Janice before the arch; produced comments from some people, but I ignored them since the sun was still well above the horizon.

In order to get the sun's rays on the arch I climbed down a steep wall to a ledge. That's the La Sal Mountains behind the arch.

Janice in Delicate Arch

AN UNCOMFORTABLE
SITUATION ON: 02:20:2000

While camping in the Coronado National Forest (near Chiricahua National Monument) I met fellow campers: Brenda and Bill. We shared tales around their campfire; drank a little wine and I explained that I was searching for a woman to accompany me to Alaska for the summer. Brenda said she has a High School friend who is relocating to Prescott Arizona who may be interested in joining me for a trip to Alaska.

Next day we began exploring a huge, abandoned mine (The Hilltop) up the mountain from our camp. At the first cave-in Bill chickened out and we thought returned to the entrance. Shortly, Brenda said her friend Sharon probably wouldn't have gone further into the mine and I failed to pick up on the significance of that statement. Later Brenda said *"I've always wanted to go to Alaska"*. I thought that was 'cool', remaining oblivious to her hidden meaning.

She continued to hint and I remained slow in picking up on her meaning. Later she became more direct, 'She wanted to go to Alaska, <u>with me</u>'. I began to sweat. Not that I thought we would be incompatible, but it was so sudden and from her description I had zeroed in on Sharon. Brenda had obviously made up her mind and I needed time to grasp the consequences of this developing situation. I said to her, if we did this we would have a clear understanding that no commitments would be made beyond the trip to Alaska. She agreed. Then I asked, what about Bill? She said she was looking for a way to end her relationship with Bill. I replied that, I'd be real uncomfortable if you committed to go with me and it didn't work out. She said, *"I was going to break up anyway"*. Obviously she had thought about this and said she had the four wheel drive Toyota; was a good backpacker and could handle primitive conditions. At this Point I could see her logic and we did seem to be compatible in many ways.

On the way back to the entrance we began to talk again about the beginning of our relationship. I reiterated that I felt quite uncomfortable because of Bill and would be apprehensive about committing to Alaska while they still had an active relationship. She repeated, *"I've been looking for an excuse to end our relationship"*. <u>Just as she said that,</u> my light shone on Bill, sitting in the dark! I was really freaking out now, I felt like rolling back into the darkness of the mine; felt embarrassed and sorry for Bill since he heard it all. What would he do? But I kept up a conversation like nothing happened and he acted as if he hadn't heard us, however my stress level was now running at 98 percent!

Bill is a retired aerospace engineer; six years older than Brenda; they had met on a Sierra club backpacking outing and for a while actively did things together. Lately he had spent excessive time with his computer and computer games, now he would only rarely backpack and resisted a lot of hiking, something Brenda really enjoys. For the past eight years they have been traveling in a camp trailer and work-camped in Death Valley and Sequoia Parks. I had notice the testiness between them, but up until now had no reason to consider they were having problems. Now the poop had hit the fan; I was in the middle and had to make a decision.

On the return I told Brenda that I needed to go to Wilcox for gas; groceries and if she went, we could talk. At this point my feelings were becoming more and more receptive to the idea that Brenda and I travel to Alaska; a strong feeling of sympathy for Bill's disappointment and a concern that he might do something rash or might even kill himself.

Before we left I talked with Bill about rockets; astronomy and airplanes. He acted as if he wasn't aware of this monumental life change. Around 4:30pm Brenda and I began driving toward Wilcox, 35 miles away. We talked and I was more relieved that we had so much in common and appeared to be compatible. Her father had led them on travels and outdoor experiences; she was a successful competitive swimmer in early life; but married early at 18 into a less than rewarded marriage; raised 2 fine boys; eight years ago her husband died of cancer; she immediately met Bill, then entered into another compromising, sometimes frustrating relationship. In Wilcox we ate dinner at the Best Western where we learn more about each other; agreed to travel together after she moved Bill out of her mother's house in San Diego and we would meet in Phoenix in mid-March.

Returning to camp we went to our respective RVs. After a while I heard a knock on my door and there was Brenda prepared to spend the nite. She had talked to Bill, however evidently the gravity of the situation hadn't sunk in, because a short time after lights out, knock, knock. Oh no, it was Bill! He called out *"Is Brenda in there*?" Where else would she be, there are only two RVs in the middle of a forest. She replied, *"Let's talk about this tomorrow."* No answer. I insisted that she go over and talk with him.

He told her he would change, however Brenda laid it on the line, the die was cast. Bill was a person who had significant mood swings and she had no idea what his reaction would be in the morning.

Morning and confrontation time. During the nite the implications had finally sunk into Bill's head; he wanted to immediately pack up and leave for San Diego, so they did, without further trauma.

We met in Phoenix; took boat camping trips on Lake Powell; visited the Tetons and Yellowstone; backpacked to Havasupai; a trip to San Diego; Banff and Jasper in Canada, then on to Alaska. We had innumerable adventures; hiking, backpacking and exploring; Brenda was a good cook and very sexual, but I just couldn't develop a spark for her, although she was serious about a commitment from me. A huge problem was that she was 'dumb as rock'.

While at Skinny Dicks (south of Fairbanks Alaska) we were planning a trip to Prudhoe Bay. After Linda and I divorced she had traveled each year to meet me somewhere: Seattle; Silverton; LA and wanted to visit in Alaska and already purchased her ticket. I had this unrealistic idea that I pay Brenda's way to visit her Mother, while Linda visited. That made sense to me; however Brenda exploded, packed and departed south.

THE WAVE

I'd heard The Wave was an exceptional spectacle; the only such site on this globe, and tried twice to get a permit to visit this unique wonder. The Wave in a minute area of Vermillion Cliffs National Monument (in Arizona and southern Utah) and is so popular that Rangers only allow 20 people per day to visit. The Wave was featured in a German magazine, so many of the visitors are German. Matter of fact Germans are fascinated with the American Southwest, especially Utah, so if you want to know about out of the way locations, ask a German. Where I was camping I met a school teacher from Germany who published a book about such areas, rarely visited by Americans. She has been visiting the Southwest for the past 18 winters.

Just before reaching this area I'd been in Page Arizona; stepped on a screw; gouged a ½ inch chunk from my heel; bled like a stuck Pig, then pulled the tissue back with a band aid. I was planning some serious hiking and more than anything else this episode pissed me off.

Anyway, at Vermillion Cliffs, each day a lottery is held for the 10 people who don't have a preregistered permit and there is always a crowd desiring a permit. Twice I entered the lottery and they didn't pick my number, so this time I decided to camp there and stay as long as necessary to secure a permit. If you aren't selected the first day, on the second day you receive 2 numbers; 3 on the 3rd day etc. Several people were there for their 3rd or 4th try and half those were Germans. Well, when I arrived there were 60 people packed into the Ranger Station, so I wasn't optimistic that my number would come up, also I would have preferred to wait a day or so giving time for my heel to repair. Surprisingly the 3rd number drawn was mine!

Since the permit was for the following day I headed for the southern edge of the wilderness area, to Paw Hole. I really wanted to allow my heel to repair, but received a free permit to enter the area, so went for it. Thank goodness I had a 4 wheel drive vehicle; the 'road' proceeded steeply up in deep, soft sand and on the way I picked up a couple of Germans who were hiking in.

Hiking into the spine of the uplands I really didn't know what I was getting into, I assumed that once I hiked over the first ridge I'd be in a valley, not! I trudged over several, increasingly high ridges, or rather mountains by Florida standards. The real difficulty was the soft sand. My left knee was giving me trouble, I think because I walked on my toes of take the weight off my aching heel. Now I was really up into the sky and realized that the prettiest rocks were near where I started. When I finally got back to Tonja, my injured foot was really hurting and bloody.

Next day, as usual, I left early and on the way to the trailhead it began to rain, then pour. At first I thought, after all these years attempting to get a permit and now it rains all day. Fortunately, after a mile the rain stopped so I continued hiking; first steeply up; then across a great expanse of sandstone rock, thru a Cactus festooned landscape. After 7 miles, as I neared the site, I trudged thru deep sand and passed between some huge rock walls, then I was there and what a magnificent spectacle! Although I'd seen photos of this landscape I was overwhelmed by actually walking among these shapely, beautiful walls of sculpted stone and was relieved to see only one other person.

Barry in The Wave

Later I met Jason (an air traffic controller from Phoenix) who asked if I wanted to accompany him higher up to see some arches. He had come with his father who has Parkinson's and a knee replaced, yet had the guts to hike to The Wave. I was really tired, but couldn't resist another adventure, little did I know that Jason is in the early 30's and is an active rock climber. He set a terrific pace, straight up the side of the rocky mountain, so stupid Barry followed as if I too was 30, however I was in the ripe ol' age of 68.

We found some arches, including the double arch: Melody Arches. Later we came to an area strewn with Mogui Marbles that are small iron concretions, Mogui being what the Paiute Indians called themselves. Now, I didn't look forward to the 8 mile hike back to the trailhead.

Back at camp I talked with the German author and she told me about the Wahweep Hoodoos. At first I thought she was speaking German, then realized that these are nearby hoodoos.

Native American legend tells that these rock spires (Hoodoos) are bad people (Legend People) turned to stone by Coyote. A Paiute legend called them, '**To-when-a-ung-wa** and states that: '*There were many of them. They were many kinds: Birds; animals; Lizards; Deer and such* *things-but they looked like people. Because they were bad, Coyote turned them into stone. You can see them in that place now: standing in rows; some sitting down and others holding onto others. You can see their faces with paint on them just as they were before they became rocks.'*

So I had to find the Wahweep Hoodoos, however (in a really rough terrain) I walked a mile or so and didn't find them. Later I found that this trail is not recommended.

I waited a day to allow my heel to recover and drove a 'road' that is 'open to all vehicles' however discovered that it is a rigorous 4 wheelin' path that actually got my adrenaline flowing. From a creek bed, switchbacks wind straight up a cliff wall. That day I hiked 4 miles and my foot felt better, and didn't even bleed.

Later (from a Ranger) I received directions for a short-cut to the Hoodoos. Got up at 5am, so as to arrive at the Wahweep Hoodoos at sunrise. In the darkness I had to drive thru 4 barbed wire gates and walk a couple of miles down a sandy streambed, or as they call it here, a wash. Well the results were certainly worth the effort. Before me was another wonder of the world. Not surprisingly, most of the people there were Germans.

Wahweap Hoodoos

How these hoodoos are formed is when less resistant rock, below a layer of resistant rock erodes away to form a pedestal for the resilient rock on top. [Just look at the photo.] The Wahweep Hoodoos are unique because the pedestals are composed of white rock, topped by red rock.

Thinking back, when viewing photos of these inspiring sights you just can't understand the exhilaration of being there.

ROBINSON CRUSOE

I've always been an independent/self-reliant sort and as a kid naturally found the book, Robinson Crusoe, fascinating. I frequently imagined myself on an island where I'd have to survive using my own ingenuity and skillfulness. While at FSU (when attempting to avoid stressful situations) I'd fascinate about a benefactor who would give me all the money I needed to explore the world if I could live on a deserted island for 2 years. I could take a modest box of tools and equipment, so I'd drop off in my dreamworld to plan what I needed to place in the box: things like a saw; hammer; fish hooks; some seeds etc.

Later I upped the stakes by visualizing me surviving on an island while being hunted by another person, the ultimate survivor story. I'd have to devise methods of escape and hiding to prevent my demise. These activities lifted me from the stresses of the day into a land of fantasy and clarity.

I guess these somewhat macabre thoughts were influenced by my early interest in military combat. Always seeking adventure and excitement, I'd felt that being close to death in combat would be the ultimate exhilaration. In a way, combat is the ultimate adventure.

Recently I mentioned this to a friend and she said I'd probably get Post Traumatic Stress Syndrome because so many recent troops were suffering from PTSS. With absolute confidence I said there is no way that could happen to me. I know that I can handle the most stressful situations, largely because I'm invincible, or am I still living in a dreamland?

TALLAHASSEE FLORIDA

Almost all my life I have been entirely invincible. In my mind I felt that I would survive any emergency, adventure or peril. I was 40 years before an event occurred that shook my confidence. Judy and I lived in Tallahassee and had 5 Corvairs. 'We' were restoring a 1966 Corsa convertible and needed the other cars for parts. One was blocked up in the back yard and I climbed under to remove a clutch cable. As I wiggled under the car I saw Judy and our friend Kenna driving off. Just then the car came down on my chest. I remember thinking, ***"Damn, now I'm stuck and will have to wait for Judy to return***!" Then I realized that I couldn't breathe. If the car had fallen another half inch or if I had been on a hard surface, I would have been dead. I did a Hulk (the big green guy) maneuver and wrenched myself from under the car. Physically all I had was a bloody chest, however, emotionally this had a major impact on me. There really are situations that might kill me! From then on I have been a little more careful, although not by the standard norm.

I think the only time I have been seriously terror struck, mostly because I was not in control, was when a drunk pointed a gun to my head. Judy, Michelle and I were camping on Hurricane (Shell) Island, near Panama City. This island is across the inlet from St. Andrews State Park. Late that evening three guys came into the cove and began making obnoxious noises. They would howl, scream, and played music as loud as it would go. There were several people camping around the cove and many asked them to quiet down. They seem oblivious to reason, so I went over to where they had anchored. I waded out to their boat to ask them to be quiet. As I neared the boat one of the guys pulled a gun; pointed it at me and said, ***"You come any closer and I'll blow your head off!"*** That got my undivided attention! Feeling that the prudent action dictated leaving, I returned to my boat; went to the State Park and tried unsuccessfully to get the Sheriff's office to come out to the island. These clowns were gone when I returned. Unless this has happened to you just can't understand the profound, helpless terror of a gun being pointed at your head.

While attending FSU my aunt, Elise, allowed us live in an A frame house on a pond near the Ochlocknee River, however when we moved in the house wasn't finished. Judy and I had gotten up in the nite and since the toilet hadn't been installed, gone outside to take a leak. As she closed the door it locked, so there we are in the yard, nude, and no way to get back inside. A guy (we didn't yet know) had just moved in next door. So I knocked on his door (in my all together); borrowed a knife; jimmied the lock, then went back to bed.

Later I discovered that the renter was an archeology graduate student; he knew I had some knowledge of geology, so brought me a 'Chunky Stone' recently recovered from a Native American burial site, asking me what type of stone the artifact was made from. I said, "***See the coral polyps in the stone, this is Chert, agatized coral, commonly use to nap arrowheads***." These round (wheel like) stones were used in a game where they were pushed with a stick of spears thrown into the center hole. Years later I noticed this stone displayed in Fort Marcos at St Marks.

The 'locals' (the Houston's) who lived on the hill above us said the pond was bottomless and connected underground to the river, also that there were no fish in the pond. So I 'had' to wade across the pond and discovered it was tittie deep at the lowest point, so ended another urban legend.

That summer I worked as a Fishery Biologist for the Florida Game and Fish Commission. One of my jobs was advising people on the creation of farm, fishing ponds. To be eligible to have the State stock the pond with fish everything must be killed using Rotenone. [This is a chemical originally extracted by South American Indians by crushing the roots of certain plants and using the white liquid to catch fish. The chemical suffocates (not poisons) the fish.] Well I added rotenone to the pond and up came multitudes of: Bass, Catfish and Bream. The second urban legend bites the dust.

Later I used Rotenone to gather fish specimen for my collection, not surprisingly this technique was far from legal. The idea was to put a small amount in the water so only a few fish bellied up. While collecting in the bay behind Alligator Point hundreds of small fish began popping to the surface. I frantically rushed around scooping them up before someone discovered my illicit activities.

Eventually I had hundreds of fish species in jars, yet I don't recall what happened to them, I probably gave them to the Marine Biology Lab at Alligator Point.

Also while with Game and Fish, 4 boat loads of us were sampling (legally) with Rotenone along the Apalachicola River. We expected to turn up lots of Channel Catfish, so planned to cook lunch on a sand bar. However, all morning the only fish we found were Suckers. Somebody said they really tasted OK; but were bony, however I was skeptical. Well I believe that person lacked taste buds. Thank goodness there were potatoes to eat. Of course the next sample after 'lunch' Channel Cats turned up everywhere.

After working in Lake City I was transferred at Panama City, then DeFuniak Springs. At the bus station was a restaurant of sorts. After sampling I'd take a few Bass there, give them to the cook, who would prepare a special meal for me.

Linda had a white Cat she adored; there was an aggressive Dog living next door; arriving home we found the Cat on the porch, dead; Linda became distraught; we assumed the neighbor's Dog did the dirty deed; I buried the Cat in the backyard and erected a cross assuming this was the end of Linda's pet. Not so; Linda and Judy (my ex-wife, were best buddies); they dug up the Cat; Judy placed it in her freezer; after building a coffin Judy thawed, then washed the Cat. They returned to our house; conducted a ceremony then again buried the Cat. At the time this possibly made perfect sense, but to most people this seems a little unorthodox to say the least.

Judy and I were sailing to Key West; the seas off Marco Island were discolored with a reddish film (dinoflagellates?) and at dusk the wind died, so we anchored some 20 miles off-shore. In the nite I was awakened by a premonition or maybe an unusual sound; bounding onto the deck I could see a shrimp boat (with nets extended) heading directly for us. Quickly I turned on all lights (including the spreader lites) and prepared to be rammed. After blowing my air horn the shrimper veered off.

After we arrived in Key West I looked up an old High School friend, then discovered that Gene Roberts had married into a shrimping family and the current talk was about one of their boats that almost hit a sailboat. **Us!**

I have always found Hurricanes exciting and would head to the beach when one would approach. Back in the 60's Judy and I tried to intercept a hurricane south of Tallahassee. Interestingly on hiway 98 West there were many Box Turtles along the hiway sensing a storm and seeking high ground. At Carrabelle the authorities stopped us before the bridge; said they had lost the hurricane's eye; didn't know where the storm would strike, so we drove back to Dick's house on the Wakulla River. After raising from a nap the sun was shining; we thought we'd missed the storm, so began driving back toward town. However we had been in the eye and were now in the northeast corner, the most intense area of a hurricane, so we found a little excitement.

When we arrived back home we found that the most damage we saw all day was there, a tree had fallen onto the side of the A-frame house and across the top of our pickup truck.

Many years later and another wife, Hurricane Opal was approaching the coast. Although it was a severe storm we thought we could at least get near it for a little excitement. We reached Carrabelle, to a bar/restaurant where Linda sometimes played music, where we had a couple of beers. Within that time the Gulf had risen into the parking lot; we headed out before the water rose any higher; plowed along in the foot deep water; got off the road and ended up at an angle in a ditch. Nissans are good trucks, but have a real deficiency I didn't realize, the computer is under the passenger seat. When Linda opened the door the water rushed in and caused the computer to do strange things, including killing the engine. A guy in a Jeep pulled us to a higher place in the road; the truck wouldn't start so we hiked up to Mike Marshall's to spend the nite.

Next morning I looked into the carburetor and discovered it was filled with gas, I mean all the way to the bottom of the engine. The stupid computer had run the electric fuel pump all nite until the tank was emptied into the engine. We were fortunate not to have tried to start the engine or we might have been sent into orbit. We borrowed a tow dolly from Mike and got the truck back to Tallahassee. That little episode cost the insurance company $3000.

A few months later I had discovered some interesting springs in the woods east of town, also there is a hill (unusual for Florida) where you could look down on Tallahassee. So we packed up my daughter Michelle, my ex-wife Judy and Linda and headed out for a fun day.

Just the day before I'd driven thru this particular mud puddle and found it was safe, i.e. not too deep. But I had gone to the right and now I drove to the left which had been scowered out by mud boggers. <u>Down we went</u>. We kept the door closed, but the water seeped in; desperately we tried to disconnect the battery, but couldn't; so, death to another computer. Since we doubted the insurance company would pay for another computer I found a rebuilt one for about $300, much less the $1100 the dealer charged for the first one.

While living in Tallahassee a childhood friend moved to town with her husband. Patsy said something about not have much excitement and I told her that if they stick around with Judy and I there would be excitement. Later she probably regretted having voiced a desire for a <u>little</u> excitement.

We live near the Ochlocknee River and planned a cookout somewhere along Lake Talquin; so loaded burgers and fixin's and raced downriver in our boat. [The boat was one my father bought in Ocala at a Florida Game and Fish auction of confiscated boats and motors. My father being the perfectionist had me remove the paint with a blow torch and replace all the screws in this wooden boat, then repaint.]

After a few miles we entered Lake Talquin which was an area flooded by a dam and punctuated by rotting trees and stumps, some just below the surface. We weren't far into the lake when 'bam!'; the boat lifted into the air landing upside down. The three of us paddled around and for some outlandish reason fixated on retrieving the floating hamburger, then realized that Judy was not with us. I swam to the boat and could hear Judy inside, fortunately saying she was alright.

We could see only one other boat on the lake; they had heard noise; came to rescue us, however only had room for 3 people so I stayed with boat. I guess this was something like a Capitan going down with his ship, although this boat was floating. When the guy returned I asked him to tow the boat to shore which he did.

What had happened was that we had hit a slightly submerged stump that raked a groove in the bottom and when it hit the transom, off center, it flipped the boat. There was so much damage that I burned the boat and saved the brass screws.

Linda and I were sailing back from a few days at St. Joe (Cape San Blas). As we approached the bridge to St. George Island the gaggle of oyster tonggers were rubber necking Linda on the bow, quite nude. In summer we sailed in that condition much of the time.

A few miles past the bridge we anchored for the nite, well outside the Intracoastal Waterway. During the nite a ferocious electrical storm swept over us. Next morning I discovered that the wind had caused our anchor to drag and we spent the nite in the middle of the ICW. Fortunately no barges had come thru that nite and I didn't inform Linda of this 'particular perilous predicament'.

I met a guy who led what he called 'canoe clinics' on the Chattooga River, who said that if I could get at least 4 others I could go for free. I was working for the Florida environmental agency so it wasn't too difficult to find some guys eager for an adventure. I assembled a group of 6 guys, mostly attorneys and we borrowed another attorney's VW bus for transportation to north Georgia.

The Chattooga has some of the best (i.e. most exciting) whitewater in the eastern US; originates in the Blue Ridge Mountains; flows for 57 miles; dropping more than 2000 feet to the Tallulah River and slashes thru some of the oldest rocks in the east, 600-750 million years old.

In ABS plastic canoes we launched into Section 2 of the Chattooga. Having frequently canoed in Florida Rip and I were the only experienced canoeist, although compared to this river our experiences had been thru minor rapids. In another canoe was a mismatched pair, one guy over 200 pounds and another 120 pounds soakin' wet. More than once those guys crashed into shore, sending Al high up the bank. Soon we passed a group from Georgia State University trying to retrieve a canoe tangled under a tree where a guy almost drowned.

On down river we waited below some rapids and watched a couple get catawampus and impale their canoe around a rock. Finally they extracted the craft and we watched as the crumpled canoe went 'blink, blink' and returned to its original shape.

At the end of the day we hiked steeply up a mountain where we met the guide's girlfriend who brought our camping gear and food. As I was slipping into my sleeping bag I felt something wiggle; jumped out and discovered a Scorpion, not a good bedfellow.

Back on the river (into Section 3) we passed a narrow, rocky area of Class 4 rapids, where most of the 15 or so people had died since the movie *Deliverance*. Finally our other two canoes seemed to stay upright more often, although the mismatched crew still occasionally capsized. Rip and I never went over on purpose until I convinced him to go over a waterfall. Normal people portage their canoe around this waterfall, but I was eager for some excitement, that is, until we were just a few feet before the falls. At that point I was thinking '***Maybe this wasn't such a good idea!***' We plunged over the falls sinking deeply into the river and flipping over, fortunately without colliding with any rocks.

The last big rapid (Bull Sluice) is class 4+ so we didn't attempt that in a canoe, although I would have tried it if the guide had allowed. Our adventure ended at the beginning of Section 4 where canoes were prohibited due to Class 5+ rapids below. Only rafts and kayaks are allowed in this section, later I made this section in a raft.

Later Michelle and I and Rip and his boys backpacked several miles along the Chattooga River.

While living in Tallahassee, Judy and I planned a canoe trip down the Wacissa River to the Aucilla River, thru the Slave Canal. The Slave Canal wasn't actually an excavated canal, but a shallow area filled with rocks that slaves had moved to each side of the narrow passage and the entrance was notoriously difficult to locate. We came to Goose Pasture where the wide river began braiding through a swamp and since it was early decided to explore a route to the east. After a ways we came to a junction of the Aucilla River and assumed we had somehow passed thru the Slave Canal, wrong! We decided to paddle upstream because we 'assumed' we were near the take-out point. We passed a fisherman on the bank who observed us paddling upstream and asked, "***Do you know where you are?***" With confidence we answered "***The Aucilla River.***" Soon we came upon another fisherman who also asked if we knew where we were, now we began to consider that something was terribly wrong. He explained that indeed we were in the Aucilla River; however were in Half Mile Rise and just downstream from where we entered the river it again sank into the ground, in effect we were in a pond. This was becoming a notorious Barry Trip! Now it was almost dark so we began to hike out; at first the trail was easily followed then there were multiple paths, but far away we could hear some machinery, so assumed that was on the paved road. Anyway in another rise we found a Highway Patrolman who just finished fishing and agreed to take us to the takeout point to retrieve our car.

Years later SueAnn; my ex-wife Linda, her husband and I were canoeing in the Slave Canal when their canoe capsized under an overhanging log; I stopped to help and SueAnn flipped our canoe and my 2 expensive Nikon cameras; a telephoto lens and a video camera sank into the canal. Bummer. I guess since the trip was my idea, then this was another Barry Trip.

I can think of another definite Barry Trip. Judy and I were camping at Cape San Blas; we'd boated to the end of the peninsula; after exploring and not wanting to backtrack, I led Judy into some trees; then into shallow water; the water became deeper as I continued to tell her "***We'll be to the other side soon.***" Well now we were neck deep in a swamp and the bottom was getting muddier. Just before Judy began screaming at me we entered shallower water.

David was up to Tallahassee one weekend; we sailed from Shell Point and returned after dark. When the tide is low boats like ours, with a 4 foot draft, couldn't avoid striking bottom in the channel. So we were stuck in front of the beach (with a couple other boats) until the tide changed.

David swam over to another boat and smoked a little pot. Being impatient I had David stand in the water and pull a halyard (attached to the top of the mast) to heel over the boat. Finally we broke loose, so continued to drag David into the Marina. Well, the people in the slip next to us had just purchased a new sailboat and were having a party at their slip. We towed David thru the basin and to our boat slip where he climbed onto the dock in his 'birthday suit'. Half the crowd thought this was cool, the other were less than amused.

We were one of the unfortunates who bought a Chevy Vega in 1972; later the engine "warped" and was replaced by Chevrolet. After a while this engine also gave up the ghost. I had a Buick V-8, from a car Dick Dunham had given us that I was going to put into a boat, so I installed it into the Vega. It had the same weight and twice the horsepower of the original and would easily pull our boat.

One of the many experiences was when Michelle and I were heading to Cape San Blas to boat camp. In the Apalachicola National Forest a thunderstorm enveloped us, a real *frog strangler*. I hadn't hooked up the heater, so had to use a towel to clear the fog from the windshield. The road was covered in water; we could see only a few feet ahead and as I raised the towel, threw the car into reverse. After a bit of slipping and sliding I get back into forward gear and back along this 'river road'. At the next town (Hosford) we stopped to discover that the boat had almost a foot of water in it, even though the drain plug was out.

Speaking of that boat, it was an 18 foot Arrowglas with a 125 HP Mercury outboard. When camping on Hurricane Island and the waves in the channel were high I delighted in speeding over the waves and allow the boat to sail thru the air. Never understood why Judy didn't share my enjoyment of that experience.

After we purchased **The Rose** sold the Arrowglas boat to an elderly couple, who had no off-shore experience. A few weeks later the Marine Patrol called to say that my boat trailer had been parked at the lighthouse for several days. I explained that I'd sold the boat and trailer. Then someone reported the couple missing and a search began. What happened was: they couldn't get the engine started and did not drop the anchor, so were blown off-shore. Soon they were out of sight of land; had no food or water; the wife needed her medication; they didn't have a radio and drifted thru the nite and the next day. That nite they were chilled so tore up the newly replaced boat seats for cover. Late the next day they had given up all hope of rescue when they heard a helicopter and were finally rescued. Such is boating.

Of interest is the fact that when you travel around America you see signs for cities established in year, such and such. In the East, typically an old town was settled by Europeans in the 1700's and out west in the 1800's. Of course Native Americans occupied this continent for at least 14,000 years; however the St Marks area was first visited by Panfilo de Navarez in 1528 and Hernado de Soto in 1539 and settled soon afterwards. The fort, San Marcos, was built in 1679; was active under the flags of 5 Nations; Andrew Jackson hanged two British subjects here, causing an international stir; later Jackson (the bane of all Native Americans) executed a noted Creek prophet, Josiah Francis (Hillis Hadjo) who was the father of Milly Francis, the woman remembered today as the 'Creek Pocahontas', for her role in saving the life of an American soldier captured by her father's warriors, and the fort (now called San Marcos de Apalache) was also captured by Pirates and Seminoles.

Most of the time I was in college I would schedule classes so I'd be out early on Friday so we could get an early start on our weekend expeditions. All my life I have rarely spent a weekend at home, unless I was sick or had a project that must be accomplished we were out: boating, backpacking, diving; caving; exploring; sailing; camping; etc. Sometimes Judy and I would just drive and camp where we ended up, even if it was in a sleeping bag on a beach.

For some camping trips I'd also carry our friend's gear to the site; get set up and be ready to relax when they arrived, frequently assisted by Michelle. One trip I recall, Michelle and I had gone to Cape San Blas (with that cheap K-mart tent we used to crossing America); rain ad poured down all nite; everything was wet; drizzled all morning, so by the time Judy, Rip and Kathy arrived we had had enough. We rolled the tent, sleeping bags and gear into a ball, threw it in their trunk and returned home.

When we returned I threw away that tent and got a quality one. Later we were canoeing on the Chipola River and it rained so hard we had to constantly bail the canoe to keep from swamping. During the nite as rain fell in angry torrents fortunately the new tent kept us dry throughout that ordeal.

For a friend from Wakulla County I was delivering a sailboat to the Florida Keys. David Waller said the boat was seaworthy, however I guess that is a relative term. First nite I anchored north off Cedar Key; some seams in the wooden boat had opened, so I spent much of the nite bailing water. Next morning, as I entered a thunderstorm I saw a huge waterspout (tornado) entering the cloud bank; was unable to see where it headed and as I passed into the rainstorm, became somewhat concerned.

At Cedar Key I picked up my teenaged niece, Sara, and we sailed south. One thing I learned when first beginning to sail is that if you are going in a particular direction, either there is no wind or it is from the wrong direction to sail, so you must motor or tack back and forth, or give up. In some areas of the ocean a sailboat (without an engine) could drift for weeks. Well, for a short time we tried to sail, then started the engine. Motoring down the Intracoastal Waterway near St Petersburg an alternator belt broke, so I had to go ashore and find a replacement.

Around Venice we were again offshore into another electrical storm. I mean there was no delay between the flashes and thunder. Both of us were quite concerned since we had a large pole sticking into the sky and we didn't share the same interest as Benjamin Franklin.

That evening we tried to anchor off the Everglades (near Florida Point), but hoards of mosquitos descended upon us, so we re-anchored further offshore.

Finally we arrived at Big Pine Island and were astonished by the sight of a Key Deer with a huge set of antlers. He appeared bizarre being only the size of a large Dog with antlers shaped like a normal sized Buck.

While Judy was working at the Sheriffs Bureau (later to become the Florida Department of Criminal Law Enforcement) we borrowed a 20 man Navy raft from Dick Dunham and organized a rafting trip on the Ichetucknee River. We piled 15 or so people into the raft (most from the Bureau) with lots of beer and struck out down the river. On the way we picked up several tubers that were 'freezing' in the spring water and all this made a raucous party. I had modified three inner tubes for pregnant Judy: with a chair, beer holder and umbrella, so she drifted down the river in style.

At Shell Point the shallowest place in the channel is a water pipe to Live Oak Island, where your boat bumping over the pipe was not uncommon. So here I am sailing with a Sandy Young who was second in command at the State Environmental agency. We sailed 'til after dark; Sandy was on the bow as we navigated the channel; I told him about the pipe and warned him to hang on, however when we hit the pipe I could see him disappear over the bow with his foot caught in the forestay. I wasn't sure he hadn't broken his leg, but he was OK. However Sandy lost his wallet containing a couple hundred dollars. Even though the water visibility was just about zero I dove into the water (with an underwater light); quickly found his wallet, leaving another sailing story for each of us. A few years ago (at his breakfast table) Sandy suddenly died.

After Judy and I divorced, Diana (a woman half my age) and I generated some memorable experiences, bizarre behaviors and crazy adventures. One nite we were at my house; had a drink or two; got into my VW Superbeetle and drove nude thru the neighborhood. Another nite we ventured out to the nearby Wendy's for a burger. And another eventful nite drove naked into downtown Tallahassee; down Tennessee Street; pulled into Burger King and got a milkshakes from an astonished employee.

Another nite, while lying before a roaring fire snow began to fall. So (for some obscure reason) I chased Diana into the yard and we ran around like idiots in the few flakes of falling snow. Another nite we did this in a pouring rainstorm, I recall us falling down on the muddy ground and ending up in the bathtub.

All our adventures were not that decadent. We were along the Blue Ridge Parkway, heading for Mount Mitchell. The weather was socked in so we really didn't expect to see much, but as we reached the summit there was a clear, azure sky. For what seemed to be hundreds of miles we marveled at the individual mountain peaks rising from the low clouds. What a breathtaking spectacle.

Linda and I occasionally raced our sailboat with the St. Marks Yacht Club, but never seriously. Our perpetual goal was to maximize our fun and minimize the hassles. On one race we came in second as the serious racers hammered for the finish line. We had the pop-top up; Linda was trailing a fish on her line and both of us crossed the finish line, quite nude.

JERRY CHESNUT ASYC RACE START

While walking in downtown Tallahassee I saw a Purple Martin smash into the window of a jewelry store and fall to the pavement. I felt so sorry for the poor bird; picked up the quivering body; after a few moments he opens, one then the other eye and suddenly bit me and flew away. Now that's gratitude. For a moment I felt like if I could catch that cheeky bird I'd ring his feathery neck!

While canoeing, Michelle and I made a point of jumping from bridges into the river. I just assumed that she enjoyed the experience; however, years later, I discovered that she only jumped because I expect her to jump. She was at an age where we took many trips together; had many adventures and generally she followed me everywhere. Those were the happy years.

I do recall Michelle telling me she had gone off a rope swing into Cherokee Sink, so I was obligated to also jump. For the jump you must climb high into a Cypress tree to a small wooden platform. From there the sink seemed awfully small; I grabbed the rope and jumped; swung down near the water then climbed higher and higher; at the apex I felt weightless and now the sinkhole appeared <u>really</u> small, and it took forever to fall into the water, with a painful splash.

For those of you who live in the highlands and are not familiar with sinkholes, allow me to explain. Most, if not all, States have had areas once covered by an ocean or sea, especially Northcentral Florida and Kentucky; calcium is deposited in the bottom of this salt water; over millions of years this forms limestone; later trees grow above the limestone, leaves fall and decompose forming carbonic acid; this acid water flows down into the limestone and forms caves; many of the caves run horizontally beneath the ground; occasionally the roof of the cave collapses forming an opening to the surface, and 'wa la' a sinkhole is formed. If Florida the water table is close to ground level so the sinks are usually filled with water, well, unless someone's house falls in.

I was in my late 40's before I retired from bridge jumping. We were scalloping at Steinhatchee and I decided to jump from the highway bridge; the distance to the water was 33 feet; I landed on my butt and water pressure gave me an enema that pushed my prostate somewhere up into stomach. When I returned home the pain persisted, so I finally went to a Doctor, who wasn't my regular physician; he penetrated me; I didn't feel any increased pain so he said I'd be OK. However the pain continued so I visited my Doctor, who evidently had longer fingers and when he touched my prostate I yelled. He said the organ was swollen; there was nothing to do but wait until it healed itself. Many times in my life I've had to suffer for my acts of stupidity.

Richard and I were in his boat near the St. Marks lighthouse, near Tallahassee. There was a boat following us, evidently he thought we knew to stay in deep water. Off toward shore I noticed a canoe, then noticed shallow water. Just as I alerted Richard we hit bottom, suddenly stopping. The guy in the following boat also looked toward the canoe, then back to see us within a few feet of him. Fortunately he swerved just enough so that when his boat hit us and crashed up over our stern it was at an angle and barely missed cutting us into fish bait.

One weekend I invited my siblings to Shell Point, where I docked my sailboat; rented a house on a canal; a friend who lived at Marsh Harbor tried to crash our party, so that evening we decided to get back at him; after considerable alcohol we took off our clothes (except Jeff who was running for county judge); covered ourselves with whipped cream, not realizing how sticky it would become; stumbled onto my sailboat; motored over to Phagan's house and jumped into his hot tub. Next day we made such a scene that most of the locals suggested we not return.

That reminds me of another episode that could have had dreadful consequences. Judy and I were having dinner with some friends on the west side of Tallahassee. I suspect that wine was involved, but a suggestion was made to go skinny dipping at the River Sinks east of town. At the time this seemed rational: since we were going to skinny dip, for three couples to remove our clothes and jump into their VW bus. After the cold dip in the river we reconsidered our situation, we were to drive all the way across Tallahassee with no ID or clothes. What if the police stopped us? We couldn't agree on a sensible story, we weren't confident that it would do much good to explain that most of us had been responsible citizens and worked for the State Florida. Actually Judy currently worked for an organization that later became the Department of Criminal Law Enforcement. Fortunately we didn't have to explain this to the police.

One more experience in my Superbeetle. I hung around with BJ and Kathy, who also worked for the Florida Department of Environmental

Regulation. We were out doing something and heard on the radio that it was snowing in South Georgia, so we drove north. Somewhere in Georgia we heard it was snowing in Alabama, so naturally we headed west. Now it was 3 am in a southern Alabama town that 'rolled up the streets' at 9 pm. We were somewhat inebriated and evidently I did something that attracted the attention of the sleeping law. He pulled us over and I recall, for some irrational reason, me immediately telling him that this was Kathy in the back seat. I handed him my driver's license and as he stood there I decided we had had enough fun for the nite, so grabbed the license from his hand and exclaimed: *__I think we'll return to Tallahassee.__*" As I did a quick U turn I could see him still standing in the street with flashlight in hand attempting to make sense of what had just happened. Fortunately his brain didn't catch up with reality before we were safely out of town.

After almost 20 years of marriage I guess I was 'letting my hair down' and did many things that were foolish and irrational. One was driving my Superbeetle up the steps of a bank in downtown Tallahassee. Then there was the time we could have been arrested at the State Capitol. Some politician had decided to spruce up the Capitol so they installed colored, stripped awnings over the windows. BJ; Kathy and I were driving around; decided the Capitol now looked like a pizza place, so we drove up to the back door and knocked. An apprehensive guard came to the door asking what we were doing at this time of the night. We said we'd like to order a couple of pizzas to go. For some obscure reason he didn't seem to be amused.

In *The Rose* I was motoring into Shell Point Marina when the engine died (due to a blown head gasket) so I had no other option than to sail into my slip. I'd never attempted this before, so began with considerable apprehension. I was well aware of the momentum in a moving boat; dropped the sails midway across the basin and perfectly coasted into my boat slip. People on the dock said what a good job of sailing and that I must do it all the time. Actually I was scared 'sh..less'.

After that (just for the excitement) I'd sail into the marina and to my slip whenever there was ample wind. One time I was sailing into the marina; the wind was honkin' and at the critical moment to lower the mainsail, the halyard hung on the spreader; I could see sailors on the dock rushing to their boats as if they could protect them from my out-of-control vessel; quickly I shimmied up the mast; untangles the line and gently coasted into my slip.

247

While living in Tallahassee I sailed with some friends down to the Tampa area for Suncoast Race Week. A short time before this race a ship had collided with the Sunshine Skyway Bridge causing several cars and a bus to tumble into Tampa Bay. I hiked out on the bridge to take this photo of Randy passing between the remaining bridge pilings.

RANDY UNDER SUNSHINE SKYWAY BRIDGE

This was as much about racing sailboats as having decadent parties, so each nite we ended up in different Yacht Club, where the hedonism began. The evenings were a spectacle with a hundreds of sailboats rafted together, so to get to your boat you'd stumble across several other boats, while not stepping on anyone or spilling your drink.

At the Tampa Bay Yacht Club I met a friendly woman from Tallahassee. Later we sailed from Shell Point on my boat, where she, like so many women, was quick to de-robe. A few months later I received a call from the Sheriff's office saying that my phone number was in her address book and that her body had just been discovered in the forest. This was a real shocker to me; she was a troubled woman searching for acceptance and probably trusted someone to much for her own good.

THE NO NAME STORM

Michelle, Vice and I were sailing to Dry Tortugas, 70 miles west of Key West. After Key West we were sailing downwind (in a light SE breeze) with the Genoa out from the whisker pole. About 30 west of Key West (as darkness was falling) suddenly a violent gust from the west broke the Whisker Pole and caused the sails to flutter like banshees. Without putting on my life jacket I jumped on deck and lowered the sails. Waves instantly rocked the boat such that Michelle and Vice were feeling rather queasy. In rapidly decreasing wind and waves we motor-sailed on toward Tortugas. Just before sunrise (as we neared the islands) a tremendous squall hit us, with waves sweeping the deck; it became impossible to sail into the wind; Michelle and Vice were now seasick, yet within an hour the sea was again calm.

As the sun rose we sailed passed the fort and anchored. Fort Jefferson is the largest masonry structure in the Western Hemisphere, built with 16 million bricks; Ponce de Leon visited the islands in 1513 and later, Dr. Mudd (the physician who treated John Wilkes Booth) was imprisoned here.

Randy; Ed and Mark (from Shell Point) arrived around noon. Around 5 pm black clouds suddenly appeared so (in my dinghy) Randy and I motored out toward our boats. Within seconds a very intense squall swept over Tortugas; some people in dinghies couldn't fight the wind and returned to shore and the bay became pandemonium as sailboats drug anchors and drifted toward the fort; a 35 foot boat was heading directly for the rusty metal pilings of an old coal dock; another had drug across the anchor line of another boat and the two of them crashed into the dock and one boat (a 40 foot Morgan) stayed tied to the dock rather than re-anchor. It was some time after the squall before the boats resituated into the bay.

There was a group of biology students who had been camping outside the fort, so for their protection they were allowed to set up camp inside the fort. Randy and I had an idea that since the students had ice and we had rum, we would party with members of the opposite sex. It was late in the evening before we realized they hadn't envisioned the same partying as we.

In my dinghy, as we headed toward our sailboats; another squall hit; we tried to buck the wind and waves, but capsized and were blown back to shore. An observer said he could see us (with rum in hand) diligently looking forward as the rapidly building waves swept across our stern, until we sank. Randy and I spent the remaining nite on the cement floor of the dock house, with our heads on cork life preservers. In the morning I found someone who would take us to our anchored boats.

During the next nite and most of the next day one intense squall after another punished us. Michelle and Vice were allowed to remain in the fort and in the morning (after quite a search) I found them relatively dry in room lined with wood.

Dry Tortugas

Next day only a couple of squalls passed thru, then we sailed north and Randy back to Key West. We could see extensive damage along the Gulf coast especially around Sarasota. This intense Low became known as the **No Name Storm**. It didn't quite develop into a Hurricane, but to us, it was as close and you can get.

WAKULLA AND ST MARKS RIVERS

(NEAR TALLAHASSEE)

During the late 60's (while at FSU) Judy and I spent most weekends at Richard's on the Wakulla River. [The head spring of the Wakulla is one of the largest and deepest springs in the world and releases over a billion gallons of crystal clear water.] Hurricane Agnes had blown salt water into the river, even up past the lower bridge; thus killing the Eel Grass and when the wind remained strong from the south the river would flood the parking lot. We were still constructing the 'River House'; had a huge

251

tent set up in the parking lot; one weekend the wind continued to blow from the south; we had been accustomed to sleeping on a water bed, so during the nite, as my sleeping bag began to gently rock I wasn't alarmed. However later we leapt from our bed as water flowed into the tent. Water had risen into the parking lot; flowed under our air mattresses; floated us and when it reached the front door, flooded inside. I recall another time, camping there when the morning temperature in the tent was 14 degrees! Seriously cold for Florida.

In the photo is cousin Jeff's pride and joy, The Wakulla Queen.

Linda and I bought a 48 foot boat for $1 and lived on it in the Wakulla River. We had built a rickety walkway out to **My Sharona** and one afternoon as I was passing I saw a huge snake. I mean it was so large at first I thought it must be an Anaconda, but it was the largest Cottonmouth Moccasin I'd ever seem. The Snake had inflated itself on the surface and appeared to be 8 inches wide and more than 5 feet long. I ran to my cousin's to get a gun, but couldn't find one. Normally I don't kill any Snakes; however this was where we bathed in the river, sometimes at nite.

Returning with a shovel I could see that the Snake had caught a Bream and was maneuvering the fish to orient it headfirst to swallow. I whacked him over the head, then laid him on the ground to show Linda the big Snake. Well she came home late, as usual; it was dark and I'd forgotten about the Snake until I hear a blood curdling scream that most of Wakulla County also heard. Of course she accused me of putting the Snake there to scare her, but this time I was not guilty.

A short time later a guy was swimming at the head springs, in an area he wasn't supposed to go, and a rutting Gator got him. This made quite a scene when the tourist noted a Gator with a man in its mouth. Being accustomed to Disney-like experiences, at first they thought it was just part of the show, although that wasn't the intention of the dead fellow. After this, while bathing, we keep a watchful eye out for Gators.

Another time David, Donna and I had been on the river and had a <u>little</u> Rum (Cuba Libre). I had an impulse to catch a big Gator. Since you can't pull a big Gator into the boat I was going to jump on his back. A foolish thing to do, but at the time somehow it made foggy sense.

Just below Shell Island Fish Camp we spotted one about 6 or 7 feet long; motored closer; I was just about to jump when, fortunately, the prop became ensnarled in a Crab trap and the angry Gator got away. Then I had to get into the water, with that angry Gator around and clear the prop.

The Wakulla River had been flowing heavily, which scowered out the bottom. Richard and I thought the current might turn up some fossils or arrowheads, so made a dive near Olin Park. There we found remains of an old wooden boat about 18-20 feet long. It appeared to be a sailboat with a center-board, but all that remained was the bottom and some ribs. We thought it would be proper to add to our 'underwater museum' in front of Richard's house.

We brought down my Hooka and some inner tubes; placed the tubes around the hull; pumped them full; lifted the boat and towed it to Richard's. Task accomplished, or so we thought.

A few days later a Marine Patrol Officer came down to the river with a 3 page statement (warrant) from the county judge saying we had removed a

State Historical Artifact and had used a dredge to remove 'said vessel' from the bottom of the <u>Waters of The State</u>. The officer wanted to arrest us, but we explained that the Hooka was not a dredge (only an air compressor) and the remains could barely be recognized as a boat. It's against Florida law to remove anything from the 'waters of the State', even logs. Somehow we convinced him we shouldn't be arrested.

The State Archeologist persisted and we heard that he offered the 'boat' to Wakulla Springs Park, but they didn't want it. Probably out of spite they towed it up river and it was never seen again, the remains probably fell apart somewhere along the river.

That reminds me of another boat tale. For several weekends I'd seen divers in the river, just beside the fort in St. Marks and they appeared to be surveying something. So one day I stopped to inquire. They matter-of-factly said they were surveying an ancient wooden ship, *"**Here look on this drawing where we found magnetic anomalies**"*. I looked at their sketch and said, *"**I'm sorry but that isn't a ship; it's the dock that was along the fort and blew down in a hurricane a few years ago**"*. They looked dejected and I never saw them there again.

This was not one of the smartest things I ever did. After Judy and I divorced Diana and I were sailing from Shell Point; into the Gulf of Mexico, to the Wakulla River. It was a cold winter day; we left port with a huge supply of Pina Coladas and sailed into a wind increasing in strength. Halfway there the waves were white capping and occasionally sweeping the bow. For some obscure reason (maybe the alcohol) I climbed onto the pitching bow to take a photo of Diana steering *The Rose*. If I had been swept overboard there is no way she could have gotten back to retrieve me and hypothermia would not be my friend. However, after taking a wave across the bow, the worse that happened was being soaked by the frigid water, however that likely sobered me somewhat allowing me crawl back into the cockpit.

SHEREE IN DANGER

At my Cousin Richard's river house we were soaking in his bathtub when he unexpectedly arrived and was somewhat astonished to see two naked sailors in his bathtub.

On the Wakulla River I would make "tunnels" in the Eel grass. I had a network of about half a mile of trails from Richard's dock and when the current was slack they were like caves and sometimes at nite I would scuba dive thru them. One nite I ran right smack into a Gator, who was as startled as me. But one time I was diving in mid river, at low water; heard a boat; hugged the bottom and with 'some apprehension', watched the propeller spinning past within inches of me.

On the Wakulla River we (well, mostly me) would catch Gators, mostly just to have something exciting to do. Someone, usually Richard, would maneuver the boat near them and I would reach over; grab them behind the neck and drag them into the boat. In the bottom of the boat we would lay them on their back; scratch their bellies so they would go to 'sleep', although we were known to cook up a few tails.

The Gator I was able to pull into the boat rarely exceeded 5 feet because it's almost impossible to hang on to a larger Alligator.

It wasn't until I was 50 years old that one got me. We had chased the Gator near shore; I jumped from the boat in knee deep mud; struggling through the mud I grabbed the Gator with my left hand and immediately he came around and imbedded his teeth in my right arm. Just as quickly he let go and I loaded him into the boat. Mostly I was concerned with infection, but a little Rum in the holes took care of that. As I was climbing into the boat, Linda and Richard allowed the hard fought Gator to escape over the side.

I recall two Gator stories in that area of the river. [Note: Female Gators must protect their young from all predators including papa.] I was snorkeling in mid-river; from our nightly trips I knew there was Gator nest nearby; she was a big Gator, more than 8 feet; a Gator swam toward me, so I moved away; then twice she rushed at me, fortunately a burst of speed for only a few feet, but that really got my attention, so moved on downstream at a hastened pace.

After flowing underground at Natural Bridge, the St Marks River flows thru the fishing village of St Marks, then joins the Wakulla at the fort. Just up river is where Linda and I kept **My Sharona** after returning from The Keys. We lived on her for a couple years and then my ex-wife Judy lived there for a while. That was when Judy and Linda were best friends, a dangerous situation for me, I'm certain they embellished stories about me.

Some nites you can ride down the Wakulla River and not see any Gators and other nites they are everywhere. Their eyes glow red in a light beam and the redder the eyes the larger the Gator. I had a friend, Barry Curley, who had a dive shop and taught scuba diving; he wanted me to take a group of neophytes down the river to the open area at Olin Park; I dumped off the divers; they were swimming thru thick Eel grass and were surely apprehensive; a woman surfaced near me and exclaimed: *"Get that light out of my eyes!"* I said: *"I'm not shining the light on you, I'm shining on that Gator right behind you."* She lets out a scream; dropped her weight belt; lost a fin and almost walked on water getting to my boat.

One time we had a couch on the dock and a woman friend was there when we returned from Gator huntin'. She asked what we had been doing and I replied *"Catching Gators."* She didn't believe me so, with a small Gator behind my back, I sat down beside her and laid it in her lap. She screamed, jumped up and fell off the dock.

Some friends were at the river house and I suggested we go Gator huntin'. Their daughter, Susan, suggested we do it naked and it didn't take a second suggestion to have us acquiesce. For a while, when we suggested Gator huntin' it was done in our all-together. Of course eventually someone removed our clothes from the dock and I had to go to house to retrieve them.

Michelle; her friend and I were camping on an island at the mouth of the St Marks River and they set up a tent down the beach from me. In the morning, when I went over to see them I could see where a huge Gator had come from the river; turned around at their tent and returned to the river. It was fortunate they didn't hear the Gator outside their tent.

THE NARROWS OF ZION NATIONAL PARK

"There will always be those who feel more comfortable not venturing from the warmth of the hearth, but to look out the window and wonder what's beyond the horizon" **and there are those who** *"see life not as a flickering candle, but as a torch that can illuminate an undiscovered world."*

This is another adventure I've been wanting to experience, but was usually at Zion in the Spring when the water was too deep and cold. The distance from the canyon entrance to Sinawava is 17 miles and many people do it in one day taking 10 to 12 hours, thank goodness that I didn't decide to make the trek in one day.

About 50 million years before present The Virgin River began cutting through this Navajo sandstone. The river cut deep, rather than wide because the sandstone is a less resilient rock. Just last week I was where the river gushed from a cliff along the Virgin River Rim at Cascade Falls, the water having originating from Navajo Lake and flowing underground.

The Outdoor Center in Springdale (Utah) rents special shoes; parkas; and long walking sticks, essential to some people, however, as usual, I was going to start off quite unprepared. I watched their movie on The

Narrows; watching people in cold, neck-deep water, falling over rocks and being stuck in rain and a flash flood. I'm not sure the purpose of the movie was to prepare you for the trip or convince you that you shouldn't attempt the trip. They also say you should be prepared to spend days in the canyon waiting for a flashflood to subside. I tried to get some clear information on the height of the river flow and water temperature, but I heard temperatures from 58 to 66 and hoped for the 66 degrees. I did pack more warm clothes than I'd originally planned, although to save weight I didn't take my tent.

At 6:30 am we met at the Zion Outdoor Center. A guy who seemed to be the owner asked everyone where they were from and commented on whether that area's pro football team had won or lost, like I was really interested. It struck me that this guy seems to have a shallow life that centers on watching football, life is too short to watch TV; go shopping and play golf. On the van there was a group of 5 guys from Indiana and Steve, from New Jersey.

The van began traveling uphill and we climbed higher and higher. I began to think it might be much colder at the trailhead and I was right. The ride up to the trailhead took an hour and a half; passing thru mountains at 7000 feet then down to 6000' at the Chamberlain Ranch. And it WAS cold, both the air and water.

The first 3 miles is across private land and you have to avoid cattle and cow patties. At first Steve and I hiked together and (wouldn't you know it) he was the one on a limited budget and we could have shuttled ourselves and saved $50!

We hiked several miles before we actually entered The Narrows. After a few stream crossings my feet became numb, although a plus was that it wasn't traumatic stepping back into the river. You must cross the river at least every hundred yards and I stopped frequently to take photos; explore several side canyons, however most side canyons were soon blocked by rockfalls.

About 150 mybp much of what is now western North America was covered by immense sand dunes and some of the sand came all the way from the Appalachian Mountains when those mountains were to the west. Whereas sand in the Sahara Desert is 200-300 feet deep, this desert was up to

258

3000 feet deep. Later water and minerals from: seas; swamps and rivers percolated into the rock cementing it into sandstone.

After 8 1/2 miles the campsites began. There are 12 in all and are little more that sandy spots along the river bank.

The Ranger told me about some waterfalls and how I'm to go up and around (to the south side), but failed to tell me about other obstacles. One was a climb down along a rock face that you can't manage with a backpack, so I left my pack on a log; slid down the rock and pushed the pack loose (with a long stick) so it fell to my feet. Then there was a place where a flashflood had piled up logs across the canyon where I had to wind myself thru that maze and jump several feet down onto a sandy spot.

Finally I came to Deep Creek and explored up-canyon for half a mile. Prior to this I hadn't seen any signs of Deer, but here there were Deer tracks, as well as a Mountain Lion.

Barry at mouth of Deep Creek

looking down Virgin River from mouth of Deep Creek

This creek adds 2/3rd of the flow to the Virgin River, so whereas I had been in mostly ankle deep water, the river was now almost knee deep, with much deeper holes.

I really wasn't tired for the first 8 miles and the only problem was the pain in my damaged shoulder. But now I was tired and really wanted to find campsite 10. I stopped to talked with the Indiana 'boys' (actually they looked as if in their late 40's, whereas I was 66) who were to be at campsite 9.

After 9 hours I arrived at my campsite. I wasn't that tired until I lay around for a while, then soreness possessed me. A few clouds rolled in; I didn't have my tent, but was under a rock ledge, so felt protected. Soon the Sun only shone on a smidgen of the opposite canyon wall, so I began to read my book. Soon after I was asleep and later awoke to a surprisingly bright canyon. The Moon had risen and was almost full. I just lay there watching the Stars, but there was a menacing face looking down on me, appearing to be an Indian in the rock wall. During the nite I became concerned that if the river rose it would wash away my boots, but didn't feel like getting up to move them.

In the morning I was awake before first light, as usual. For the $10 permit fee you also get a poop bag, so as not to contaminate the river even though upstream there are 800 piles of cow poop. I decided to leave early and just slowly mosey down the river.

For some reason many people had chosen to frequently get out of the river and take steep trails around rocky areas. I guess if I didn't have a heavy backpack I'd follow some of those trails, but that takes too much effort, so I normally waded in the river. I did follow a side trail a ways until I was forced to get my feet wet. Fortunately the temperature was not nearly as cold as the day before. At this point I'd probably come down 1000 feet, half the total drop of 2000 feet. The Virgin River drops in elevation more than almost any river in the US, about 8000 feet from Navajo Lake to Lake Mead near Las Vegas.

After a mile or two I came to Big Springs, a really delightful place with several waterfalls gushing from the canyon wall thru lush Maidenhair ferns. The bummer was that it was still too dark to take decent photos.

Then I entered the most difficult section of the canyon; there were deep holes (up to waist deep); a bottom covered with rounded lava rocks that easily rolling out from under your feet; with water depth generally to my upper thighs and several places where I was forced to climb high on the cliff to get around huge rock dams. I'm amazed that I didn't fall, although I came close several times. I really didn't like this section, although the towering walls were scenic.

However, at the lower end of this section, I finally became entirely wet. I was walking close to the canyon wall (for support) in a sandy area and the bank suddenly collapsed, sending me into the river. Fortunately I'd just put my cameras in plastic bags, but now my sweater was wet causing me to quickly chill.

I came to a spot where a huge section of the canyon wall is precariously hanging together. When that falls (today or a thousand years from now) the canyon will be blocked and a lake will form.

Now I was in what is called Wall Street. Here the canyon is narrow with cliffs that rise 2000 feet above my head, that's more than a quarter mile!

After another mile the river bottom was much easier for walking; sand interspaced between the rocks; not as deep and occasionally areas with sand almost all the way across. There was one interesting log and debris dam where the river flowed under and you could walk all the way across the river.

Now I was within 3 miles of the Temple of Sinawava and tourist (coming up canyon) appeared, first a couple from England; then a small group; then the multitudes. The first couple I met was from London, it's usually Europeans who push themselves further than American tourists.

The canyon remained narrow and the river covered the entire width, so it was just a few inches deep. People who come up river for only a mile or two certainly have no idea how difficult the section above became.

Finally I came to Orderville Canyon; dropped my pack and explored up canyon a ways. I'd talked to some folks who only went a short distance because they said there was a waist deep pool. Actually it was not even crotch deep, then you must climb high up into a waterfall, then up canyon.

Along the walls was seeping water and ferns were prolific, this must be the lower strata of the Navajo sandstone (with the Kayenta Formation below) and is where the water flows out at Weeping Rock. After a ways there was a rockfall and a pool deeper than waist deep. I was not really warm, so turned around. A few years ago I hiked way up this canyon; up a steep waterfall and finally to a place where I could get down, but was quite sure I would not be able to get back up without ropes.

On down the canyon I hiked; greeting everyone I'd meet and still concerned that some people can walk within inches of me and not make eye contact or say hello or even acknowledge that I'm here. I characterize them as big city, Californians.

Passed an area where the lower cliff walls were eroded much like the Subway, then past a high but fleeting waterfall and (after 5 hours) arrived at the end of the 1 mile walkway from the last shuttle stop at the Temple of Sinawava. This was an adventure and goal I'm glad I accomplished, however will not return.

MY LONGEST DAY

In a magazine (the previous year) I saw a photograph of the beautiful waterfall near Upper Red Castle Lake (in Northern Utah), so set that as my objective. However the hike would be 22 miles and stupid me figured I could do it in one day, not the smartest thing I've ever done, but it was a personal goal and a new challenge.

Was up at 6:00 am; arrived at China Meadows at 7:00 AM and signed in at the trailhead. Although there were no signs indicating the trail to Red Castle Lake I assumed it was the trial directly behind the sign, Wrong! After 100 yards I realized that this was not the correct trail, it was heading east and I wanted to go south. There is nothing worse than starting off on the wrong trail, as in my Kings Peak adventure. I found another trailhead; it too was unmarked, but seemed to bear south. What really pissed me off is that (in this National Forest) there is a management company charging $2.00 for parking, yet can't even provide a cotton pickin' sign indicating the trailhead. It really disturbs me that concessionaires can now operate public lands and charge for facilities constructed with public money or in many cases years ago by the CCC.

Shortly I entered the High Uintas Wilderness and almost immediately what do I hear? Elk; Bear; Mammoth, no, bawling Cows. It's not in my list of preferred wilderness experiences to step around Cow paddies, horseshit is bad enough.

There were a few short humps, but mostly the trail began as a steady climb along Smiths Fork. Evidently in the Spring many areas are boggy, so the Forest Service constructed several wooden walkways.

After 4-5 miles I was quite tired and really tired of hopping over rocks; by then I was barely lifting my feet and when I'd stump my boot on a rock, pain would shoot up all the way up my leg. Now the trail was becoming steeper and rockier, so what do I see, Sheep, hundreds of Sheep. Finally I passed that obnoxious noise and proceeded up. Came to a bridge, providing my first glimpse of Red Castle Mountain. Of course the sky was now overcast with a spattering of rain. I'd hiked about 8 miles and ready, really needed a rest, so stopped for a short 15 minute break. Up until this point the trail had not climb steeply, however 100 feet further were the first series of switchbacks. Now I was really moving slowly, I had planned to arrive at Red Castle Lake by noon, now that time had passed. As the trail briefly leveled out it began to sleet, then rain.

After about 9 miles I came to a trail junction without a sign indicating Red Castle. That was stupid since that's the destination of most people. I headed down toward a bridge in a small valley and could see a trail veering off to the right toward Red Castle Mountain. This trail climbed steeply up the mountainside and was extremely rocky. Now I'd been hiking over 6 hours and several times considered turning back. I knew the hike back was going to be torturous and now thought that I might not get back this day.

After 7 hours I finally passed Red Castle Mountain and now could see the waterfall. I suspected there would be little flow this time of year, but the flow was less than thrilling, however I had made it and I was still standing.

It was 2:30 PM and I figured it would be 10:00 PM before I could get back, another optimistic assumption.

After a photo I started down and took a trail that I believed passed by Lower Red Castle Lake. From the lake I had to climb steeply back up to the trail junction. Now I was really exhausted and taking baby steps, barely lifting my feet off the ground, because raising my feet over the abundant rocks was excruciatingly painful to my legs.

After the switchbacks I could hear an Elk bugling, then dreaded getting back along the herd of Sheep. When I arrived near the Sheep a dog came bounding up to me. I was concerned because he didn't look well and I wasn't sure he didn't have rabies or wouldn't bite me. It was forever before I passed all those noisy Sheep. Now darkness was approaching, so locating the trail became more difficult.

I was trying to hike an hour and take a 20 minute rest, but my body was having trouble regulating my temperature. While walking my forehead would create 250° of heat, however when resting I'd cool down and began to shiver; this was not good. I first recall this happening in 2003 (near Silverton Colorado) when I was on that near fatal backpacking trip in the snow, however the shivering didn't begin on that backpacking trip until after I had gotten back to Sammie.

Came to a meadow where two Bull Moose were grazing, but it was too dark to get a good photo. Slowly trudging down; I'd set goals of reaching a certain landmark ahead then rest, but the distance was always further and before reaching that point I'd have to lie down, curl up on the ground and rest. I had this idea that if I elevated my legs on a rock or a log, the built up lactic acid would drain from my legs, but this didn't seem to prevent the fatigue. Now it's dark and fortunately the full Moon rose above the mountains. Along the trail I could see the light tinted rocks, but couldn't tell how high they were, so occasionally kicked one, sending pain up my leg. The continuing problem was that I couldn't see gray or dark rocks causing me to stumble and stagger like a drunken sailor.

At times clouds would obscure the Moon and finding the trail became much more problematic. I had a mini light, but used it sparingly, mostly under trees. Besides being exhausted now I developed a headache. Quick, Scotty beam me up! My original goal in this area was to climb Kings Peak (the highest in Utah) however at this point I was convinced that my body could not recover in time to do it this year.

Now I could barely hike 30 minutes before I had to lie down, where I'd curl up in the dirt until after 15 minutes (when I cooled off again) I'd began to shiver. Time was now slowed to a crawl and it was taking forever to hike the last 3 miles. I'd see a bright place ahead and hope it was the parking lot, but time after time only discover another meadow. Finally I came to the bridge over the creek and thought it was about ½ mile to Tonja. However slowly plodded on for what seemed to be hours before getting to the trailhead, where I was surprised to find the time was only 12:30 PM.

Next day I stayed in bed until 10:00 AM, then began getting ready for Janice's arrival. While she visited we: experienced the Mountain Man Rendezvous in Ft Bridger; traveled the Lake Mirror Scenic Drive; in the Wasatch Forest where we picked up a hitchhiker who had found Jesus, sold everything and was hiking 15,000 miles around the country for charity; explored the North Slope back to Henrys Fork and on Labor Day hiked a couple miles up the trail toward Kings Peak.

KINGS PEAK

Another goal from my bucket list

The day after Janice left and shortly after 7am I again reentered the High Unitas Wilderness, at 9400 feet. Hiked from where I camped on Henrys Fork a mile or so to where Janice and I had hiked the day before and stopped to rest, since I remained tired from my hike to Red Castle Falls. My plan was to hike for 1 hour, then stop to read my book for 20 minutes. After about 6 miles I came to Elkhorn crossing; crossed the wooden bridge, then continued up along Henry's Fork. The creeks in this area aren't called so and so creek, but so and so Fork. The trail became rocky, but not nearly as much as the trail to Red Castle Mountain. There were a few ups and downs, but generally the trail was just a steady climb. I thought about how these meadows should have herds of Elk and Deer, unfortunately as long as hunting is permitted near this wilderness, there will be few large wild animals.

After 8 miles I neared Henry's Lake and could see a tent, so far the first sign of other humans. I thought about camping there, but decided to go further (or is it, farther) up toward Gunsight Pass, so the distance to Kings Peak would be shorter. After hiking over a rise I began to worry that no water would be available above my elevation, since all the streams had been dry and on my map I didn't see any ponds indicated. About half a mile down from the pass I found a single level spot next to the trail; decided to camp here although I'd have to walk down a mile or so for water. At this point I'd hiked up about 1600 vertical feet.

After setting up my tent I walked around and to my delight discovered a spring just below my camp, so pumped some water thru my filter, then prepared dinner. In my backpack I found there were two freeze dried dinners so tonight would be Mac Chili and Beef. Now I was above the treeline (which is around 11,500 feet) and since fires were not allowed around the lakes I'd carried up some sticks from the forest, fortunately on the way up I had also removed bits of sap from some trees as fire starter. Due to the wind in this open area I had a hell of a time keeping a fire going just to boil water. The meal was intended for two, so I was really stuffed.

A guy from Maryland came by, the only person I saw all day and told me that the shortcut to Kings Peak was **at** the carne (at Gunsight Pass) and that the trail was very rocky. Well he was correct about rocks, but unfortunately not clear about the trailhead.

During most of the afternoon I had worn my shorts, however as soon as the Sun dipped below Mt Powell the temperature dropped precipitously. Just after dusk I crawled into my sleeping bag, but had trouble getting to sleep. Several times in the nite I'd awake, read and near daylight was somewhat chilled. At that elevation the temperature dropped into the 20's.

I was awake before first light; stayed in bed until a little before 7 am; stuffed a bagel in my pocket and headed out. Got to Gunsight Pass at 7:40, thinking: '***Wow, this is going to be a quick trip to Kings Peak***'. Wrong, very wrong, extremely wrong!

At the large, rock carne at the pass I looked to the right and all I could see was a cliff that would be impossible to climb. The instructions (for the correct trail) said that some hiking books describe going 'slightly uphill' and 'pick out the natural route above and through the first cliffs'.

Not realizing that this was not the correct trail I climbed 'slightly uphill'. Well there were cliffs to the right and left and certainly no 'natural route'. Around to my right was a steep slope that seemed to be an easier route. [On my return I learned the actual beginning of the correct trail began about 200 feet past and downhill from the carne at the pass.]

I begin climbing diagonally along the north face of an un-named mountain, still assuming this was the correct way to go. The higher I climbed the larger the rocks became and now I was in an area where the VW size rocks were precipitously balanced above my route. I thought of the worst case scenario where a rock tipped and I'd be trapped until I died, since no one knew I was up here, I didn't even have a knife to cut off my arm. [While visited Moab Utah I heard of a guy trapped by a rock for several days and ended up hacking off his arm with a dull knife.] One place along the trail there was a huge rock barely perched on another rock and it appeared that a gust of wind could send it down on me. After about an hour I came to a sheer cliff and finally realized this trip was not going to be a 'piece of cake'.

Some people tell me that I take risks to get an adrenaline rush, although I've never really noticed such a rush, but I'd prefer that to anxiety I was now feeling. On the way around I hadn't noticed that I was on an almost vertical cliff of loose rocks and one slip or slide would have been the end of Barry. With extreme apprehension I slowly backtracked across this cliff and started back down.

This is where I re-injured the ankle I had twisted while hiking in Silverton. At first I thought this would terminate my adventure, however after a short time the pain subsided a bit, so I continued.

I had read something about the trail passing between openings in cliffs; didn't want to lose the elevation I had gained, so decided to head back up and through an opening in the cliffs here. It didn't appear to be that far to the summit and then I would be able to see just where I would need to go. Had begun to scramble up the loose rock and when I got to where I had a better view I realized the summit was several times higher than I saw from the below. So, in this scree slope I scrambled further, on all fours, occasionally slipping downhill where a mistake that could have been fatal. Now I could see that I had much further to go, so moving down was not an option. Matter of fact again I was in a perilous situation, then, as loose rock tumbled around me, what I'll call extreme anxiety overtook me. Carefully I scrambled on, beginning to tire, but making progress. However, now I had to skirt far to the left to climb along the face of an almost vertical cliff, so began crabbing to the left. Finally I was out of that slide zone in terrain not as steep.

For a while I was slowly heading up then decided there was no way the route to Kings Peak could be at this elevation, so began to slowly work my way around this mountain. Finally I could see Kings Peak and it appeared so far away.

Now I was around 12,500 feet, then it took forever to work my way down the south side of that unnamed mountain. Looking toward Kings Peak I could see what seemed to be miles of rocks, no visible ground, just rocks. This became my first exposure to hopping over fields of rocks that were from a foot across to several feet.

After 4 ½ hours I arrived at the trail up to Anderson Pass, where I intended to rest for a while before attempting Kings Peak. However a guy showed up shortly after my arrival and he waited for some time for his friend Jeff, coming up from the west side of the pass. They were from LA and had a goal of climbing most of the highest peaks in America; they had just finished Mt Borah, the highest peak in Idaho. He said that was a brutal climb; with a few switchbacks and even though the distance is only 3 miles it took them 10 hours. I was at the mountain a couple of times, intending to climb it, however it was always too snowy.

Since I really wanted someone to take my photograph atop Kings Peak I tagged along with them rather than resting. This is a badly eroded mountain with sheer cliffs to the west and jumbles of huge rocks on the east face; I don't mean rocks generally a foot across, but a solid expanse of huge rocks up to 8 feet wide. There wasn't a trail, you just scrambled from rock to rock and hoped they didn't tumble down with you on it. They were going much too fast; I wanted to keep up, so trudged up at an angle of about 45°, across the boulder field. We reached a peak, but their altimeter indicated it was not the highest peak. Finally we found the peak, however were discouraged to see a peak to the south that appeared to be even higher. We did not want to go any further, so considered this to be Kings Peak. Later I found that the other peak is called South Kings Peak and its 16 feet shorter than Kings Peak, which is at 13,528 feet.

We took photos although the mid-day clouds had rolled in, then ate lunch. While walking around to get a panorama video I stepped onto a flat rock about 6 feet in diameter that tipped me down to the ground. To catch myself I thrust out my hand and violently smacked the video camera on a rock. I lost some of the panorama video, but the camera continued to work. Here's is a photo of Barry on top of Kings Peak with Henrys Basin behind.

Barry on King's Peak, highest in Utah

After an hour or so I began my descent. Hiking downhill is always more difficult, especially on loose rock. When climbing up the difficulty is lugging your weight, however going down (with every step) you must brace your legs, producing a shock to your knees and for many years my knees have been abused. This is especially difficult here because you never know if the somewhat flattened rocks you step on will be stable or tip you down into other rocks. Evidently my balance is still pretty good because I see most people occasionally stumble and fall, although frequently I had to do some 'dancing'. After a ways I saw no need to cross directly down to Anderson Pass, so I just staggered diagonally down to the start of the trail. I'm amazed that my knees took the punishment; I never fell, although my ankle was in pain. I was so weary of crawling over rocks, yet before me lay a mile of rocks, before reaching a grassy area.

After a very tiring crossing I reached the cliffs above Painter Basin; switchbacked down to the trail, then back to my tent where I prepared Beef Stew for dinner. I wasn't nearly as exhausted as the Red Castle hike, I guess my body must be adapting. Now I see that I saved 3 miles hiking by camping where I did.

I slept better than the nite before and in the morning was surprised that I didn't have any major pains, just my big toe and ankle. First I hiked down to the spring for water, where I talked with some guys camping nearby, then packed and departed about 7:30. I wanted to visit Dollar Lake so went off-trail, then back down and the last mile seemed to take forever.

Arriving back at Maybellene I was tired, but not thoroughly exhausted. So within a week I hiked 50 miles in the mountains, not bad for a 68 year old fart from Florida.

SACRAMENTO CALIFORNIA

In 1961 I was scuba diving across the channel at Bodega Bay California, where **The Birds** had been filmed. I had a cold; could not clear my ears, so planned to stay in shallow water. On my return, crossing the channel I heard a boat; then surfaced to see a huge fishing boat barreling down on me. My only option was to dive to the silty bottom, so couldn't see the boat, but could hear the thrashing propeller and feel the prop wash as the boat passed directly above; an ear drum was perforated and became infected. An extremely painful episode!

When Judy and I began dating I had a 1934 Ford with a bored and stroked Chevy engine. Along the sides I installed 3 inch diameter, stainless steel exhaust pipes from a B-52 bomber. This made a rather loud noise that sounded like a stock, flathead Ford. That fact got me into a number of drag races.

In those days girls didn't go off for a weekend with a boy without being chaperoned. At Mather Air Force Base (near Sacramento California) I was a member of the scuba diving club that also had a few civilian members. One of those, Mrs. Johnson, agreed to watch over Judy on our Abalone diving weekend to Van Damme, north of San Francisco.

Driving up, Judy was shifting gears for me, missed a shift and knocked out a couple of gears. Later we cruised up Hiway 1 along the coast and thru the small town of Mendocino. I was "getting into" the curvy road, but was concerned for what I thought was a whine from the damaged transmission. Well that wasn't the issue. A policeman had been chasing us from the last town and the noise was his siren. He believed me when I insisted I wasn't trying to escape, but did give me a ticket for loud mufflers.

At the campground we unloaded Judy's stuff, including her sleeping bag. Later we drove on up the coast and became stuck on a sandy beach at the mouth of Russian Gulch and were forced to spend the night. This sounds similar to the *"**Oh, we've runs out of gas.**"* ploy, however we really were stuck in the soft sand. I did the chivalrous thing and gave Judy my sleeping bag and intended to sleep in the seat of my car. Unlike Florida beaches, Pacific beaches get really cold at nite. We ended up in the same mummy bag, back to back, still intending to 'behave'. Well that didn't last all nite.

After a month of 'seeing' each other almost every nite, we moved in together at her sister Nellie's, at Sloughouse. In those days living together was also forbidden, also we thought Judy was pregnant, so after a while we decided to get married. Her uncle, a compulsive gambler, was going up to Carson City Nevada to gamble, so we impulsively said we'll go to avoid the waiting period in California. We were married, at nite, in a wedding chapel, by a woman in a nite gown, to the sounds of the wedding march on a phonograph. [People this day probably haven't even heard of a phonograph.] We spent our honeymoon in the back seat of his car, while her uncle lost most of his money. Although this was far from a typical beginning we remained married almost 19 years and experienced some great adventures.

Another experience with that Ford (before we married) was, after parking next to Folsom Lake (sans Johnny Cash and the song, *Folsom Prison*). The battery had completely died and when we turned the headlights 'on' the engine would die. I pushed her down a hill to get started. So here we were driving back to Judy's home through the town of Folsom, with no headlights, occasionally using a flashlight to maneuver. The car was black with a white convertible top. Then, flashing red lights from behind, we were busted; the cop said he was beside the road and was at first baffled when he saw a white top pass by; it was very late and sparse traffic so, to our amazement, he let us go. We made it back to Elk Grove using the flashlight.

On another date we were parking along the Sacramento River and again the car wouldn't start. Judy's eyesight never was good, but I put her in the driver's seat while I tried to push start the car; just as I got her (the car) up to starting speed the bumper shot up and the car lurched down the river bank, ripping out the bottom from my pants; then the car careened down the bank onto the river bed. I don't recall how we got out, but we spent another nite together in that mummy bag.

After we were married and before I was released from the AF I sold the car and put the engine in a '55 Chevy. (The engine was a 352 CI, built from a 283 CI block, before 327's were introduced). We towed the car back to Florida with the intention of getting my father interested in drag racing. He was interested, but didn't want to do it as seriously as me.

I've made some remarkable marriage proposals, however the success of the marriage is the inverse of the effort. Judy and I just talked about getting married and lasted 19 years. I proposed to Linda anchored in my sailboat off-shore from Shell Point; after a nice dinner and wine. Our marriage lasted 12 years. My proposal to Connie was quite elaborate; involved climbing to one of my favorite places, Babel Tower in the Linville Wilderness of North Carolina; presented beside a roaring fire; a bottle of wine and mushy words. That marriage came apart within months and I mostly block it out of my mind.

While in the Air Force I was teaching a scuba diving course at the pool on base. One of the students, a blond woman, was a real knockout. Problem was that she was married; however her husband was currently in Thule Greenland. 'Reluctantly' I said I'd give her advanced lessons in Folsom Lake and teach her a few things. We took my speargun, I guided her toward a fish that she shot and then began crying, underwater. Well it was obvious she needed more training, so we planned another trip. Being a good Catholic she brought her nephew, apparently she was having concerns over self-control. I proposed a plan by which we would swim underwater; along shore and come up behind some rocks, away from her nephew. All was going well, we were among the rocks making out and (from the top of some nearby rocks) this little brat calls out "*I see you!*" Well that ended future 'lessons'.

Another adventure in California was my first ski trip. There were 2 other inexperienced guys from Florida, bad planning. I dressed in 3 pair of socks, 2 pair of jeans and 3 or 4 shirts. Obviously playing in snow was not something I grew up doing. We knew nothing about the difficulty of slopes, but picked one near Strawberry. It seemed a little steep, had rocks and boulders, but what did we know. After we finished some trial runs on level ground we removed most of our unnecessary clothes, then hopped aboard the lift, which dumped all of us onto the snow, not on our skis. Now the slope looked impossibly steep. There was no way we could go straight down so would ski from side to side and fall down each time we turned. After a while we became separated. The lucky guy was Jim who broke a collar bone and was carried down, I also wanted down, but at my pace it might take 2 days. Another lesson was what happens when the sun drops below the trees. I was absolutely soaked and when the warming sun abandoned me I was freezing! Figuring I must get down before dark I tried a vertical attack and ended up, more than once, head over heels. But I made it down without breaking anything.

TONJA AND SAMMIE

Some people could justifiably say that I abuse my vehicles, however the way I see it is that a vehicle is there to get me where I want to go. As I've previously stated, if I set a goal I really have a problem turning around. I have suffered reaching many of my goals, so I don't see that it's unfair that my vehicle would also suffer.

Most of these photos are from 2005 forward, we've had many more such adventures:

Flooded road near Quartzsite Arizona:

Sammie tumped, on Hole in the Rock trail in Utah.

On 'Fins and Things' trail near Moab Utah with Janice.

Mining road near Yuma Arizona

Poison Spider near Moab Utah.

Metal Masher trail, Moab Utah

Lola road in Idaho.

The Wall near Silverton Colorado.

THE WALL AT POUGHKEEPSIE

Imogene road near Ouray Colorado.

rough spot along Imogene Road

Tonja now has several scars from her exploits: a bent tailgate from when I was on a one-lane mining road (near Silverton) when we came to snow blocking the narrow road. So we had to turn around on a road barely the width of Tonja, bashing against an unseen rock. Another time I was exploring a deep canyon in Utah; again had to turn around and on a rock bruised her behind and broke a tail light. While in Arizona Chris and I were on a narrow road (across the Colorado River, into California) and slid sideways into a rock, denting Tonja's door. I repeated this sideways slide in the mountains of Montana, adding to the dents. Several times we've been 'high centered' on rocks, resulting in minor damage. In various places we collided with rocks, completely destroying the skidplate under her engine. I also broke a shock-strut; bent the drive shaft; twice knocked off the front bumper; replaced a universal joint; replaced the ball joints in the front suspension and broke the transmission mount in two places. Tonja has obviously suffered, but she has always gotten me home, after all she is a Toyota.

INTERNET DATING

While camping on a beach in Baja I had contacted a woman on the Internet thru the Science Connect site; she was from New Jersey; to my surprised she flew all the way to Baja, well, after she asked if I was an axe murderer;

we made several hikes in nearby canyon; visited Agua Verde; took **Rose Bud** out to see the Whales and camped on the island where I had found the human body. That nite the wind blew so hard that in the morning we were covered in black sand. However in the nite I got up to check on **Rose Bud** and found a baby Sea Lion snuggled up next to the rubber boat. I guess it had lost its Mother and **Rose Bud** seemed to be a temporary substitute.

The point I want to make is that Terry said this was the best vacation she'd ever had and caused me to think of my years traveling North America in my motor home. I've had many, many what I call exciting adventures in some of the most beautiful locations in the world, however I've mostly traveled alone. There has to be thousands of adventurous women who would consider just a few of the experiences as high points in their lives. It's just unfortunate that I couldn't find a woman who met my idealistic criteria.

DEATH VALLEY NATIONAL PARK

While visiting Death Valley I heard about the hot springs in Saline Valley, so decided I needed a warm dip. First, over a very rough road, I traveled to The Racetrack.

Obviously this is not a typical race track with cars going around in circles but rocks 'racing' across a dry lake. This was once an active lake 2.8 miles long and the bed is extremely level, with an elevation difference of only 1.5 inches. Incredibly there are rocks on the surface that mysteriously move around leaving tracks across the dry mud; some tracks intersecting other and some stopping and turning another direction. No one has ever seen the rocks move and unfortunately too many whacky people believe the rocks have spiritual characteristics so steal the rocks from this National Park. I have a theory: after a light rain the raised cracks in the mud become slippery and after freezing, rocks move before a strong wind.

Anyway, it was Halloween; I camped at the south end of the lake; a group of Mensa Club members (from Las Vegas) camped next to me; they espoused some strange beliefs such as human babies swim because we evolved from Dolphins; for these strangers I was placed in charge of cooking potatoes, in aluminum foil, but the most interesting thing we did was with a 5 gallon glass jug. First they placed rubbing alcohol in the jug; blew into it, then lit the fumes and it produced some color. So we put vodka into the jug; heated it in the fire; lit it and it produced a fascinating, pulsating, colorful plasma, that exited the opening with repeated 'whooshes'.

Next morning I began driving over the mountains toward the warm springs; the first sign said '4-wheel drive recommended' and the second sign said '4-wheel vehicle required'. My Toyota pickup was not 4 wheel drive, so figured I'd drive up a ways for a look see; then I was on a shelf 'road' were I was unable to turn around; so banged and crashed over huge rock; thru deep gullies then steeply down into rocky canyons. I was determined to get across those mountains, even after impaling on some rocks and using my jack to extract Tonja I.

Merged Pumice along Warm Spring road

Finally I arrived in Saline Valley, however once on level ground I became stuck in the pumice rock. Pumice is a light volcanic rock and tires just sink into it. [This rock also floats on water and I took some (not from the Park) back to the grandkids.] I had to walk a ways; find flat rocks; return and build a road; became stuck at the end of the 'road', move the rocks forward and start over.

At this point I realized two problems: going over that mountain the top of the battery had come off and acid was all under the hood and my gas gauge was on zero. I was hoping it was a short ways to the springs, well so much for optimism.

I was told that you turn at a huge rock; continued way down the valley; ran into some hippies in a VW bus who said someone had stolen that rock and I had to go back several miles to a road with a bat hanging from a pole.

Finally I found the springs and was astonished to see naked people walking across the road, in a National Park. [In California, if something is over 50 years old it becomes historic. This had been a clothing optional springs for ages.] I also spied an outhouse with only 3 walls, later I discovered that the west wall is missing so they can watch the sunset while doing your business.

I walked around to a spring and jumped in; then began thinking, 'why is no one else here', so walked to another spring with a few folks soaking and asked about the rules here. They said: "***There are only two rules here, don't go into the head spring and don't piss anybody off.***" Well, I'd attempt to not upset anyone, but I had already been into the head spring.

That evening I soaked with a few folks in a communal pool decorated with crystals, where they told me the wild Burros were a problem and a sign in the library says to put the cover back over the books, so the Burros won't eat them.

library at Warm Springs

Next day, at higher elevation it snowed making it difficult to get out the South Pass. Now gas was critical and it was several miles to the hiway, however when I get there I was drawn to Darwin Spring in a directing opposite the gas station, because it sounded really interesting. Finally I found the spring and figured I'd drive on down the canyon back to the hiway. After a few miles the canyon ended, now my gas needle was well below the empty mark. I backtracked; saw a road out of the canyon that I assumed would to a short cut, but wasn't. I was relieved to find the hiway; drove a ways; found the gas station and it was closed! This was not a well-traveled road and the likelihood of running out of gas imminent. I passed thru Panamint Valley and speeded across the next mountains with the idea that I could coast down the other side. Going down I shut off the engine; coasted up to 80 mph to a gas station near a sign indicating I was below sea level.

STORM OF THE CENTURY

In was March of 1993 when Linda and I drove to Boone in the original Sammie, the Suzuki. Unknown to us, an intense low developed over The Gulf of Mexico and struck the panhandle of Florida with tornados; high winds and torrential rain.

We arrived at the Appalachian ski area a little late and wanting to get in a full day of skiing so Linda asked, ***"Do you ever close the slopes early?" "Never."*** They said. We began to ski as the wind picked up and turned colder; I took a break and was looking at barograph; beside the instrument was a scale indicating if the barometric pressure was 30" plus it would be fair skies and below 29", stormy weather, well, the needle was off-scale on the low pressure side! The wind was already gusting to 40 mph plus and the temperature near freezing. I don't recall what the wind chill factor was, but it was certainly more than chilly. A short time later they announced that all skiers had to immediately get off the slopes and everyone in the county must be inside by 6 pm.

I looked for Linda, but there was a whiteout on the slopes. I waited and waited, as more and skiers returned, and everyone commented on the deterioration conditions. After a while I became worried, 'where was she?' You could barely see out the windows and the wind screamed at gale force. Seems like Linda was one of the last people down, not realizing there was a curfew.

We tried to open the door from the lodge, but it was temporarily blocked by snow. When we got to **Sammie** snow had piled up on one side; across the hood and top and had blown under the convertible top and covered our bags inside.

We got out of the parking lot and began inching our way down the mountain, concentrating on the road just a few feet in front; the wipers were globs of ice compounded the problem of seeing thru the blowing snow. Of course we were quite concerned whether we could find a motel. Just before Boone we stopped at one motel, but there were no vacancies. Luckily we found a motel in town and were relieved that the power was still on. Watching TV, the full gravity of this storm was made evident from the damage all up the east coast and into Washington DC. Power lines were downed; snow stranded travelers; tornados destroyed buildings; (unusual for a snow storm) there was thunder and people were dying.

Don't recall the highest winds, but it was howling and every few minutes there was a complete whiteout. I was invigorated and went outside, but could barely stand against the gusts. The wind blew so violently that it came in thru the roof vent and covered the bathroom wall. We were justifiably concerned about having power and heat thru the nite, however they remained on. Seems like Linda brought some rum and coke: surprise!

When we awakened the snow was up covering most of the back window and when we tried to get out the front door it was blocked by snow. I finally worked it back and forth; got out to see Boone almost covered in snow and the **Sammie** had become a mogul of snow.

The prudent thing to do was wait here another day, but Linda was to begin a new job that Monday. She insisted that we get back to Tallahassee and since we had a 4-wheel drive vehicle we figured it was doable, incorrectly figuring that when we got down (out of the mountains) into Ashville, going south would be 'a piece of cake': wrong!

Of course there was no one else on the streets of Boone, but the snowplows had cleared the main hiway, although in places not all the way to the asphalt. Just outside Boone (around Grandfather Mountain) the hiway goes steeply up and compounding the problem was ice on the 'road'. This was not a situation familiar to a Florida boy. Many times we had to drive off the road to get around trees and now we were driving on deep snow and assumed we were traveling over the hiway.

We mistakenly thought once on interstate 40 traveling would improve, wrong again! After a short distance, as we approached Black Mountain, before us was a 'truck parking lot', trucks and cars were stopped all over the Interstate, some having spent the nite. The snow was too thick to get thru, although we tried anyway. As luck would have it a snow plow came by, so we followed.

After some hours we arrived in Asheville to discover that they didn't have enough snow removal equipment and the town was gridlocked. We called Linda's uncle who gave us directions out of town and we headed on south. If only we could just make it to I-85 we assumed we'd be able to pick up speed. Further south, there were snow free sections, but under the overpasses were ice humps, some cars were hitting the ice and spinning out; on closer to Atlanta the snow had melted, but (later in the day) as we came into Atlanta that water froze and there were cars along the interstate that had spun out. What traffic there was in Atlanta was moving at 10-20 mph over icy bridges. South of Atlanta I-75 was free of ice and snow, so after 14 hours (totally exhausted) we arrived back in Tallahassee. Mark up another noteworthy adventure.

RETIREMENT

Of course retirement is different for every person. In my travels I've found that the vast majority of Americans consider retirement as a time to become inactive; attend flea markets; fatten up at restaurants; sleep late and procrastinate about what they should have done in the past or will do in the future. I just can't relate.

To me, retirement is a release from restrictions on life that prevented me from being able to savor life to its fullest. I'm always up before daybreak to experience the exhilaration of sunrise; the nocturnal animals still scurrying about and usually on the road or path to discovery. On the day before I've planned an exploit and am now prepared for a full day of adventure.

I could have retired with more toys and be financially secure, however I've always being optimistic and reckoned that if I retired at 57 I'd catch up on lost time and somehow (maybe too idealistically) hardships would be overcome. My most prominent regret was not sharing these adventures with a compatible woman. For a short time I thought my wife would be a permanent soul mate, but that would not be so. Unfortunately I've never discovered a woman who seeks adventure with the same intensity and risk. That idealistic woman would have greatly enhanced my adventures over the past 15 years; however I need not dwell on 'what if'.

In those 15 years I've had wonderful experiences at a physical level few similarly aged humans are capable. While exploring the American west I've been in areas that few locals have visited. For example I've seen much more of Arizona than 99% of the residents. I've also visited areas to have locals who grew up in that area being astonished at the surrounding places they had never visited and I've explored.

I recall years ago a friend telling me that if you want to retire early you must reduce you expenses and that's what I've done. At first I had some savings, but that gradually drained away. So I've been living on Social Security and a small pension from the state of Florida by living in a motor home and mostly staying on public land in the west. I really don't like to stay in RV camps; all I need is a place to park, because I'm out exploring every day.

Other than the opportunity to experience the beauty of North America I sincerely enjoy meeting people from all over the world. With 300 million Americans I was surprised to find a disproportionately large number of Europeans in the areas I visited, especially National Parks. Another advantage of meeting these friendly people is their description of infrequently visited places I could explore.

THE RIVER SHANTY

In 2011 I was in Maybellene staying in an RV park along the St Johns River, near East Palatka. Damijan and I had been taking trips on the rivers across North Florida and were now on the Withlacoochee River, having launched in Dunnellon. This was a drought year in Florida and the rivers were extremely low. Without difficulty we motored several miles upstream; passed Stump Knockers restaurant where rock shoals began. To pass thru shoals we had a swerved from side to side avoiding the larger rocks; stopped at the Blue Hole spring; I went off the rope swing; moving on upstream we came to a really shallow shoal where the engine banged on rocks; reached a point at which **The River Shanty** could go no further; got out into the dinghy; continued upstream a few more miles, even crossing a dam on an airboat ramp.

Back in **The Shanty**, on our way downstream we were drifting thru that shallowest shoal and collided with rock. We motored on down to Rainbow Run; went upstream a ways and pulled in an open area that had been excavated for phosphate mining; in this area were posts sticking from the water; as I walked around in **The Shanty** I could hear water flowing back and forth in one of the pontoons, not good; however water wasn't coming

289

in too rapidly and my desire to not abandon the existing plan kept us there. During the nite something didn't feel right; I got up and discovered that we were impaled on one of the posts. Now, even with a minor leak, by morning we would be permanently skewered on this post so I attempted to drive us off; then pull from another post and even tried cussing. Finally I gave the engine full throttle and we broke free, what a relief! This could easily have become another Barry Experience.

HAVASUPAI, A WONDER OF THIS WORLD

A paradox: Americans travel to Europe to see old buildings and Europeans travel here to see the stunning natural beauty. Few Americans realize that such wondrous beauty is right here in America.

HISTORY OF THE SETTLING OF HAVASU RIVER.

The first evidence of native Americans in this area was more than five thousand years ago, evidently the Havasupai arrived around 800 years ago and in 1880 the reservation was set aside for this small band of Indians, the Havasupai (havsum' baaja) who call themselves 'people of the blue green water'. Much of their traditional lands are now part of the Grand Canyon National Park.

Not only is the Havasu River noted for its magnificent, turquoise waterfalls, but the heavily mineralize water also forms attractive terraces along the river.

In August of 2008 there occurred a 100 year flood that wiped out most of the terraces; redirected the river; eliminating some waterfalls and caused extensive damage in the Supai village. The area was closed until May of 2009 and the rehabilitation cost was $2.5 million.

Then in 2010 there was another damaging flood. Fortunately I visited Havasupai in 2000 when the travertine terraces were at their peak.

BACKPACK TRIP TO HAVASUPAI IN OCTOBER OF 2012

From my past trip I knew the rigors of hiking into the canyon, especially the brutal hike back up to the Hualapai hilltop. I felt that to take the helicopter was somehow cheating; however this time did consider having my backpack taken down on horseback.

This time I had my own plan, I would hike part way on Monday and on Tuesday get an early start to the campground. In Flagstaff the low temps have been in the 30's and highs in the 70's and I had anticipated the same here, wrong again. When I arrived at the parking lot the temperature was in the 90's!

Looking down into the Hualapai Canyon I had forgotten just how far down it was, it looked like the Grand Canyon. The elevation here is 5200 feet and the Supai village is at 3000 feet and the first drop from the parking area is over 1500 feet! Around 2 pm I started hiking down as the red rocks radiated a temperature more than 100 degrees. As they passed, horse packtrains covered me in red dust; I had to be careful where I stepped and had to begin ignoring the odor from the horse discharges. Finally I arrived in the wash and began looking for any shade enough to provide some relief from the heat. Around 4 pm the sun would occasionally drop behind the cliff walls and the instant coolness was welcomed.

Soon after 5pm I found a sandy spot behind a huge rock spire; laid out my ground pad; ate some nuts and berries then rested. At just about dark I could see the silhouette of something that was soundlessly dashing along the limbs in the bushes just above. I was hoping it was birds, but soon discovered it was mice that scurried all around my camp and after dark one darted across my sleeping bag.

I awakened at 4am; ate a bagel; packed and headed on down toward the village of Supai. The moon was bright, so, much of the way I experienced the exhilaration of hiking under moonlight. Soon I was on a shelf trail high above a dark gash that looked bottomless. As morning broke I was down on relatively level ground, among Cottonwood trees and now could hear water that flowed in from Cataract Canyon. From the millions of boots and hooves the trail was a deep powder that easily formed clouds of dust with occasional areas of beach like sand. Nearing the village I was pleased to pass a young couple of Indians who greeted me with: "**Welcome to Supai**." At 6:30 I entered the check-in building where I paid my $81 for two nites of camping. Actually camping was $17 per nite, a $35 entrance fee and a $5 environmental fee, whatever that is.

The village was as I remembered it from 11 years ago; barely adequate houses and lots of horses and dogs, although not as many dogs as I recall. Also, all along the trail, ample amounts of horse poop. Among the subsistence houses were giant Cottonwood trees with trunks 6 feet in diameter. Above the village are two rock pinnacles, the <u>King and Queen</u> or '<u>The Watchers</u>', and the fable is that as long as they stand above the village the people will prosper.

Just outside the village I came to little Navajo Falls. In the big flood the river had changed course eliminating Navajo Falls and uncovering what they now call Little Navajo.

Now the dusty trail began to steeply descend and I finally came to the beautiful Havasu Falls. In many ads for the Grand Canyon they use a photo of these falls although they are not actually in the Grand Canyon. In my past visit the falls were more scenic, flowing over the cliff in several places and now (after the two big floods) they fall 100 feet from only one point.

I hiked on down to the campground, thus ending a 10 mile hike wearing a backpack that had gained weight every few feet.

After setting up my tent without the rain fly (there was no chance of rain) I returned to Havasu Falls, however the sun was too low for the photos I wanted. So I waited for 3 ½ hours for the sun, a very long wait for me. Then (to my distress) discovered that this time of year the sun will not shine on the pool below the falls. Now I need to return in July to get the photo I want.

I returned to camp; ate the pb and j sandwich I had brought, then hiked down to Mooney Falls. This falls is also spectacular, falling 190 feet over great sheets of travertine, frozen in time.

MOONEY FALLS FROM TRAIL DOWN

By the time I returned to camp, darkness was approaching so I crashed early to rest up for the next day's long, arduous day hiking down to the Grand Canyon. Around 4am a strong wind blew dust into my tent so I had to get up and lay the rain fly over the tent.

On Tuesday I left camp at 6:30 am and began my hike, first traversing the vertical wall beside Mooney Falls. I think the falls was named for a guy who attempted a descent, falling to his death. Fortunately this trail prevents most visitors from going any further down the canyon.

First you meander down jagged travertine (calcium carbonate) rocks, then come to a tunnel; some steps are hewn from the rock and descend almost vertically; from the exit you get a magnificent view of the falls, before entering another tunnel. Popping out of this tunnel all you see is sky and a 120 foot vertical drop. The locals have put chains along this route and left the rock 'steps', el natural. You must hang onto the chains or you will slip only to follow Mr. Mooney's fatal plunge. After a ways you come to a short, homemade ladder and below this the rocks are wet from spray and quite slippery made even so by the smoothing foot traffic across them. Near the bottom you find an aluminum ladder that at first seems safer than the one (made of some local tree parts) I recall from my first visit. However some of the rungs on this ladder have been repaired with sticks and bailing wire.

I got off the trail and began hiking along the river where I saw some interesting falls and disappointed that the travertine terraces had been destroyed by floods. Soon I came to the first river crossing, so stopped, removed my boots and socks and waded the thigh deep water. The next crossing was even deeper. I ran into a guy, Andrew, who was apprehensive about going all the way to the Colorado River alone. I told him not to fear and that I was also going alone and had previously made this trip. Turned out that we were the only two people going all the way to the Colorado.

RIVER CROSSING

After 2 miles I came to a Palm Tree that I remember from my past visit. Brenda and I had come to this spot; where there is a vertical rock wall beside a Palm Tree so we 'assumed' the route remained along the river, double wrong. After wading across waist deep water and jumping some rivulets we came to the impassable Beaver Falls.; backtracking we could see a lone rope hanging down behind the tree; there didn't seem to be any other way down river so we rock climbed up and up that wall until we came to a ledge a couple hundred feet above the river.

Well now there is still a rope, however a series of rickety ladders have been added. This still remains a harrowing climb. Next is a wide ledge festooned with cactus and an occasional ocotillo.

SHEEP TRAIL

After a ways I could look down on Beaver Falls and could see Andrew at an overlook.

After a short distance you enter Grand Canyon National Park and the ledge becomes narrow, quite narrow! I recall Brenda and I calling this a 'Big Horn Sheep trail' and evidently they still use this route since there was scat everywhere. After a ways you come to an equally daunting climb down, however there are no chains, or ladders or chipped out steps, you descent steeply back down to the river by finding a rock here and there to place your shoe.

The next river crossing turned out to be deeper and the water swifter than the previous and getting across barefoot was painful and nerve wracking. I wasn't worried about me getting wet, but I'd had enough wet cameras for a lifetime.

The next crossing was a surprise, where the trail ended at a rock wall the river was too swift to cross, so I scrambled upstream and found a place that was only crotch deep. After this I ran into a group who were rafting the Grand Canyon and hiking up to Beaver Falls. They told me there were only 2 more river crossings. At this point I was tired of taking off my boots, so began just wading the river without stopping to remove my boots. From my first visit I didn't recall so many river crossings. Later ran into an older (a relative term) couple who said there was a Big Horn Sheep grazing just below; I got some photos and pressed on. Then came to a rock wall with no obvious passage and the river was not crossable. The only choice was to rock climb up the steep wall. After a short distance, above the very narrow canyon, I could see the greenish waters of the Colorado River. There was a stark contrast between the blue waters of the Havasu mingling with the Colorado.

In the mouth of Havasu River were an amazing number of rafts and some kayaks. Since it had taken 5 ½ hours and the time was noon I quickly took some photos and started back upstream. Soon I met a group of rafters from Durango Colorado, including a beautiful young woman who previously lived in Silverton. She loved the winters because she was obsessed with skiing and snowshoeing. Later I ran into a couple of Ewe Sheep, one on the trail and later met people who saw a Ram just upstream. I slowly hiked ahead looking for the Ram, but saw nary.

Just below Beaver Falls I came to the rock climb up to the 'sheep trail'. I'm certain that not a few rafters get to this point and say "***I am not going up that rock wall!***" There is no doubt that the climb is dangerous or rather the sudden stop if you fall. Got back into tribal land and hiked down to an overlook of Beaver Falls and rested.

BEAVER FALLS

Let me briefly describe this 'trail' to the Colorado. A normal trail 8 miles long is not a rigorous feat, however this trail is more like an obstacle course with mountain climbing thrown in. At every waterfall the trail climbs steeply, sometimes almost vertically; there are passages thru dense fields of vines where the vines hang almost across the trail; natural and manmade tunnels and the rickety ladders that looked as if they would collapse at any moment. Wading thru the swift river numerous times is not in a normal hike, then you have rock climbs without any support and narrow, frightening ledges. And to complicate the ordeal you must contend with cactus and flood debris. Add to this the apprehension of climbing up and down Mooney Falls. All in all hiking this 8 mile trail is more like hiking twice the distance and is incredibly tiring.

By the time I arrived back at Mooney Falls I was exhausted, to a point that I looked up at the travertine wall thinking, *"**Am I really in the right place, could I have gotten off trail, there is no way to climb that wall.**"* Anyway I did make it up and slogged into camp at dark and straight into my tent. I was totally exhausted and wondered if I would be physically be able to hike back down Mooney Falls in the morning. At 71 years, exhaustion sneaks up on an active person.

The air is so dry that during the nite my boots, socks and underwear dried. Also the wind returned around 4am only to stop an hour or so later. I was again up at 5am and observed the interesting sight of strings of flashlights snaking throughout the campground; this was gaggles of people leaving early for the hike out so as to avoid the heat of the day. The previous morning the campground was almost packed with tents, now it looked like a ghost town. In the morning I wasn't as sore as expected, but wouldn't know how tired until I began to hike. At a little before 7am I slowly hiked back to Mooney Falls, not relishing the idea of climbing back up.

However I'm delighted that I did it. Down below, first I hiked up a narrow, steep walled canyon just covered in Maiden Hair fern, my favorite. Then to an overlook where I could see three waterfalls, including Mooney. At that point a Ranger asked if I had paid, since I didn't have a red tag on my pack. I explained that I was not given a tag and showed him my paper work. He hikes to Beaver falls 5 days a week and has seen Big Horn Sheep almost every day, including two Rams. This year they intend to charge rafters if they hike outside the National Park, although none of the rafting companies know about this. I think it's ridiculous to charge people $40 to pass 100 feet into tribal land to see Beaver Falls. Almost every year the fees here increase and at some point will reach a saturation point. I think many of the villagers feel that getting as much money from the white man is admirable. I saw some graffiti in the village that read: **get money**.

After that I hiked down to an absolutely lovely falls, with pools below and caves festooned with Maiden Hair Ferns.

A short distance was another waterfall with a growing stalactite and drapery travertine covered in fern. I'm so delighted that I took this side trip. Reluctantly I climbed back up Mooney and by the time I arrived at camp was awfully tired.

I was going to rest for a while, but only stopped for 15 minutes; packed; got water and headed up toward the village. This trail is dusty and very steep and at 10am, hot! At Little Navajo falls I hiked around to the beautiful cascading falls. I mean these falls were magnificent, reminiscent of Victoria Falls in Africa.

Then I returned to the trail to the village. For two days I had been thinking about a juicy hamburger, I knew it would be pricy, but just had to have one. For almost $20 I bought a burger; a huge coke and the largest plate of fries I've ever seen. Although I had felt starved I couldn't eat all those fries. For a while I hung around in the café in the AC; drank more icy coke; then watched the helicopter travel back and forth and talked with some folks. To copter out costs $85 each way and many people who hike down decide they'd pay whatever not to have to hike back up to the parking area.

As I recall from my first trip the size of the residents varies from fat to obese, including the kids. I had also fantasized about having an ice cream, but was too full to go for it.

After an hour or so it was time to go with plan 2, find the head spring. I asked about the spring at the permit office and she said there were actually multiple springs. By the time I hiked to the other side of the village I felt that I just couldn't pass the store (in the back of a house) and not have an ice cream bar.

Now it was after 1pm and at least 90 degrees, however I knew I'd soon be back under the shade of the Cottonwood trees.

Left my backpack under a tree and headed into Cataract Canyon searching for the springs. Later I discovered that visitors are not supposed to hike into that canyon. After a ways I came to a 'trail' marked by red tape and incorrectly assumed it lead to the springs. After hiking way up into the canyon I was not seeing water so crossed the canyon and found it dry, so headed back down. The closer I got to some trees the denser the undergrowth and more numerous the Cactus. Soon I was bleeding in several places (from the Acacia trees) and had not a few cactus spines in my legs. After hiking back and forth among the trees I came to some small springs bubbling from the ground, I had expected springs from the canyon wall. Still I had not found the main spring, so headed back up-canyon. Finally I realized that there wasn't a main spring, but many small springs, frequently with a sand boil less than a foot across.

Back at my pack I lay down among some rocks and rested for half an hour, then got back on the trail out.

On my way down, the trail didn't seem to follow much of a decline, however getting out involved hiking up <u>all</u> the way. Whereas it's 10 miles down to the campground it seems like 20 miles back up. I was going to hike until dark, but at 5pm I was spent. I found a level, sandy spot; dug a place for my hips and shoulders and inflated my ground pad. It was too hot for a sleeping bag so I just laid out and rested. Around sunset I watched some very unusual clouds float by that changed color to strawberry.

Then, just after dark, I had a momentary fright. I was mesmerized by the thousands of stars and observing the Milky Way when suddenly a 'huge' animal appeared over me. Since I was laying on the ground the 'beast' looked gigantic and for a second (seeming like minutes) didn't know if it had criminal intent. I had been thinking whether Mountain Lions were in this area, having just heard all about them at a lecture at the Festival of Science, in Flagstaff. Anyway I soon realized it was a large dog that had jumped over me.

While lying there I recalled a 'joke': Sherlock Holmes and Watson were camping in a tent. During the nite Holmes asked Watson, "***What do you make of the stars and the Milky Way***?" Watson went on and on about the beauty of the stars, thoughts on space travel; origin of meteorites etc. Holmes interrupted and said that his observation was that someone had stolen our tent.

I have always been sensitive to caffeine and normally had no more than one coke per day and always before 10am, whereas today, around noon, I had two giant cups of delicious coke. I knew this could be a problem, but rationalized that I'd work off its effects in my hike, no! <u>I was buzzed, I could not get to sleep</u>. I continued to watch the stars; noted the beauty; thought of the millions of people stuck in polluted cities who have never seen the Milky Way; me exploring 'where no man has been before' and just the enlightening beauty of the view.

Now it was 11:30 and sleep just would not come. It was too hot to fully get into the sleeping bag; some bugs (that sounded like dental drills) continued to buzz around my ears and my tossing and turning had gotten sand into my sleeping bag, so I packed up and began to hike toward the Hualapai Hilltop, about 5 miles up. My body said I was exhausted, however my mind concentrated on how wonderful it was to experience the primitive state of hiking under just the light of the Moon. I hiked 'til a rest stop for what seemed like most of an hour, but turned out to be only 20 minutes. When I'd be in the shadow of the Moon I'd have to turn on my little LED light to watch out for rocks and horse poop.

Now it was time to really start up The Wall, at a time that my body was saying, 'time for a nap'. In this area there were trails all over and I wasn't certain I was on the correct trail. However, around 2am, I did see a string of lights coming down the side of the mountain so knew I was in the right area.

This is a photo of the wall, not taken at 3am.

Now I was barely moving up, one foot a short distance before the other. It seemed forever up until I reached the especially steep portion of the trail. Every time I'd think I was near the summit I'd come around a switchback and see more climbing trail. It was 3 am before I struggled back into the parking lot.

So I had backpacked 20 miles and hiked 19 miles, for a total of 39 miles, more than a jaunt for a 71 years old geezer.

I had considered beginning my drive back, but was completely exhausted. Now the air here was downright cold. I had experience this phenomenon when previously hiking into the Grand Canyon, the temperature on the rim could be in the 30's and a mile down, at the river, hover in the 90's.

I inflated my air mattress and got into the back of my truck, Tonja. As I snuggled into my sleeping bag I began to shiver uncontrollably. This first occurred a few years ago on an almost fatal backpacking trip in the Rockys. I had completely exhausted my body; it was shutting down and was attempting to warm my core by shivering. Fortunately now I was so tired that I soon fell asleep and remained so until almost 6am. Got up; ate some M&M's and began to drive back to flagstaff.

So this ends just a few of my many adventures. I'm now 73 years old; will continue to seek adventures and exploration, however probably not to the extreme degree as some of my past experiences.